MODERN SLAVERY
AND THE FIGHT FOR FREEDOM

The Plan of The Money Manipulators
To Enslave The World!

LARRY BALLARD

ISBN: 978-0-9844733-1-1

Published by

BRIDGER HOUSE PUBLISHERS, INC.

P.O. Box 2208, Carson City, NV 89702, 1-800-729-4131

Larry Ballard

www.GeopoliticalAffairs.net

email: larryballard1@yahoo.com

Printed in the United States of America

Layout / Typesetting:
Julie Melton, The Right Type Graphics USA

10 9 8 7 6 5 4 3 2 1

Table of Contents

Introduction

Communism is at the Door:

*We Must Take Back Our Government
Before It's Too Late!*

People all across America and the World are scratching their heads saying what happened? How did we get in such a mess? What does the future hold in store? Quite simply we allowed our complacency to lull us to sleep! We trusted our leaders even when they demonstrated that they didn't have our best interest at heart! We allowed a group of self serving financial elite and their political pawns to hijack our monetary and political systems! We stood idly by while they took over our schools, the news media and entertainment industry turning them into little more than a propaganda machine and in the name of fairness and tolerance we are allowing religious and political freedom to be systematically suppressed. Socialism comes in the guise of fairness and equality but it is the harbinger of oppression and bondage and the forerunner of Communism. It preaches redistribution of wealth and in the process causes social strife by pitting the lower and middle classes against one another. It calls itself Progressive and Liberal but in reality it is oppressive and creates disincentives to honest labor!

> **VITALLY IMPORTANT:** Those in power tax us into poverty and steel what little wealth we have by purposely causing boom bust cycles which allow them to buy our assets for pennies on the dollar! They would have us believe that Capitalism is evil and inherently oppressive. It is a lie! The truth is that *The Money Manipulators* and *Power Mongers* have corrupted the system and pitted us against each other.

This book will expose their deception. Armed with the truth and a spirit of mutual trust and true equality we can forge a better tomorrow! But I tell you this! The time for action is now! We don't have a second to waste!

"It is difficult for common good to prevail against the intense concentration of those who have special interest, especially if the discussions are made behind closed doors." – President Jimmy Carter

"In this present crisis, government is not the solution to the problem, government is the problem." – President Ronald Reagan

PAY CLOSE ATTENTION! What America needs is a good spring cleaning, or perhaps I should say a good house cleaning. We need to sweep Washington clean of all the special interest and all those who would run our government from behind closed doors! That means come the election we need to vote out virtually all incumbents, both Republicans and Democrats! We need to return the reins of government to the people and in the process restore the Constitution, reinstate the critically important balance of power between the Executive, Legislative and Judicial branches of government and take from the Federal Government those powers which our founding fathers never intended them to have and return them to the States and Local Governments where they were intended to reside.

Wake Up! Wake Up! The Enemy Is At The Gate!

The Hour is late! The Enemy is at the gate! The enemy is from within not from without! The enemy has lulled us to sleep and transformed us while we slept! They dismantled us brick by brick and sold us bit by bit! They have stolen our wealth and left us a shadow of our former self! Wake Up! Wake Up! For God's sake wake up! The Enemy is at the Gate! Wake up before it is too late!

There is a saying *"knowledge is power."* This book discloses exactly how and why our Federal Government is manipulating our economy and what their ultimate goal is. I promise you that by the time you finish this book you will be able to make sense of the decisions coming out of Washington and other governments around the world. Most impotently this book will empower you to stand up and join the ever growing ranks of concerned citizens who are committed to making America once again: *"The land of the free and the home of the brave."*

Please read the following quote by Founding Father Samuel Adams and honestly ask yourself if virtually every safeguard to our freedom and liberty which he describes has not been subverted, diluted, and stripped away rendering America morally destitute and vulnerable to loss of our National Sovereignty?

"And that the said Constitution be never construed to authorize Congress to infringe in the just liberty of the press, or the rights of conscience; or to prevent the people of the United States, who are peaceable citizens, from keeping their arms; or to raise standing armies, unless necessary for the defense of the United States, or of some one or more of them; or to prevent the people from petitioning, in a peaceable and orderly manner, the federal legislature, for a redress of grievances; or to subject the people to unreasonable search and seizure of their persons or possessions."

Never in its history has America or the world stood in greater peril; not in WWI nor WWII, because in both of those epic wars we knew who our enemy was and we stood united against what we all understood to be an evil that must be subdued at any cost. Today that evil is once again at our door, but this time it has come in sheep's clothing. It is intent on destroying us from within by eroding our values and by pitting us against one another. It has crept into our government, our corporations, our banking institutions, our schools, our churches, and the press and has skillfully and systematically twisted the truth and turned it against us. It is as Linen the father of Communism said: *"A lie told often enough becomes the truth."*

So who is this mysterious enemy that comes in sheep's clothing, that hides in the shadows and exerts it power from behind closed doors through those it has carefully placed in positions of power to control us from cradle to grave, to deceive us and to ultimately enslave us?

You may be surprised when I tell you, and initially you may call me a conspiracy theorist, but I assure you that by the time you finish this book if you are even the least bit open minded you will agree with me because the evidence is simply overwhelming. As the Bible tells us; the darkness gives away to the light, so the objective of this book is to cast light on the evil that threatens us and in so doing put a name to the enemy so we can cast it out.

The common enemy that all the sovereign nations of the world face is a group of self appointed Financial Elite **[international bankers]** who seek to enslave us all by forming a tyrannical One World Government!

The First Step in Their Plan is To:

<u>**Control The Monetary System of Governments All Over The World:**</u> through creation of a network of privately owned central banks with the World Bank and International Monetary Fund at the apex of their banking cartel. Through their control of both the money supply and interest rates they are able to initiate a variety of ponzi financial schemes designed to create a world wide debt crisis making the sovereign nations of the world **[Most importantly the U.S. which is their key strategic target]** pliable to their plan to implement a One World Government. Consider the following quotes.

"Give me control of a nations money supply and I care not who makes the laws."
  – Baron Mayer Rothschild, founder of Rothschild Banking Dynasty

Carol Quigley, Georgetown Professor, Member Trilateral Commission and Mentor to Bill Clinton wrote that the goals of the financial elite who control central banks around the world are: *"Nothing less than to create a world system of financial control in private hands able to dominate the political system of each country and economy of the world as a whole...controlled in a feudalist fashion by central banks of the world acting in concert by secret agreements arrived at in private meetings and conferences."*

Step Two is:

The Hijacking of The Legitimate Governments of The World: through secret organizations such as the Bilderberg Group, The Trilateral Commission, and in the U.S. The Council on Foreign Relations [CFR] whose members include Royalty, governmental and corporate presidents as well as influential individuals from the military, news media, and academia. Through this network they not only control the economies of nations all over the world, but in this information age they also control our access to information which gives them the most efficient propaganda machine the world has ever known. They not only have plausible deniability, but they can feed us totally false information thus limiting our ability to recognize what is being done. There are those in positions of power who have over the years warned us. Consider the following quotes.

"The case for government by elites is irrefutable."
– William Fulbright, U.S. Senator

"The real rulers in Washington are invisible and exercise power from behind the scenes."
– President Franklin D. Roosevelt [1933]

"The dirty little secret is that both houses of congress are irrelevant. America's domestic policy is now being run by Alan Greenspan [Chairman of the FED] and the Federal Reserve. America's foreign policy is now being run by the International Monetary Fund."
– U.S. Senator Barry Goldwater

The Third and Final Step is To:

Create Various Types of Global Crisis: such as economic instability, orchestrated famine, energy shortages, wars and or terrorist events which create crisis of sufficient magnitude to get free people to give up freedoms and liberties which they would otherwise never relinquish.

This lays the groundwork for creation of a police state, domestic at first and ultimately a global police state headed by the United Nations which is a pawn of the World Banking System. I bet you didn't know that the CFR was instrumental in the founding of the U.N. CFR members Nelson Rockefeller, John Foster Dulles, John McCloy and others were part of the delegation which drafted the charter of the U.N. and the U.N. sets on land donated by none other than banking mogul Nelson Rockefeller. Consider the following quotes:

"And before us the opportunity to forge – for ourselves and for future generations a new world order... When we are successful and we will be. We have a real chance at this new world order. An order in which a credible United Nations can use its peace keeping role to fulfill the promises and vision of the U.N.'S Founders."
– George H.W. Bush, President and Member Council Foreign Relations

So just what exactly was the vision of the U.N.'s founders? Not everyone believes it was humanitarianism. J. Smith, <u>America On The Eve of Destruction</u> (P.32-33) says that, *"... it is sheer ignorance to consider the U.N.'s intentions to be anything other than world political and military power."*

"He (Obama) can give a new impetus to American foreign policy because the perception of him is so extraordinary. His task will be to develop an overall strategy for America in this period when really a New World Order can be created. It is a great opportunity given such a crisis."
– Henry Kissinger Former Secretary of State and Member Council on Foreign Relations June 2006 Ottawa Canada

And what is to become of those individuals and nations that don't want to join the New World Order? It is clear from the following quotes that if necessary they are prepared to force our participation!

"The New World Order will be built...an end run on national sovereignty, eroding it piece by piece will accomplish much more than the old fashioned frontal assault."
– Council on Foreign Relations Journal 1974, P558

"We shall have world government whether or not you like it. The only question is whether World Government will be by conquest or consent."
   – James P. Warburg [Representing Rothschild Banking Concern] While speaking before the United States Senate [Feb. 17, 1950]

I want to make one thing absolutely clear! What we are talking about here is not Capitalism or Socialism. It is Communism! Their political propaganda machine [The Progressive Movement] promises to create social justice through redistribution of wealth, but in reality what it strives to do is limit competition and create a system of modern slavery where we their slave labors are controlled through control of wages and the depreciating value of money.

The truth of this statement was first demonstrated when, disgruntled over the creation of the Greenback by Abraham Lincoln; American and British Banking interest circulated an internal memo stating that:

"...Slavery is but the owning of labor and carries with it the care of labors, while the European plan...is that capital shall control labor by controlling wages. It will not do to allow the Greenback...as we cannot control that."
   – *Hazard Circular,* July 1862

By the late 19th century their current strategy began to take form. Anthony Sutton, research fellow Hoover Institute For War, Revolution, and Peace at Stanford University put it this way: *"While monopoly control of industries was once the objective of J.P. Morgan and J.D. Rockefeller, by the late nineteenth century the inner sanctums of Wall Street understood the most efficient way to gain an unchallenged monopoly was to 'go political' and make society go to work for the monopolies—under the name of public good and the public interest."*

PAY CLOSE ATTENTION! The current strategy of Global Domination emerged as corporations went international and national monopolies could no longer control their competitive strangle hold. The answer was to create a one world economic and political system controlled secretly from within the various governments of the world. It is vitally important that we understand that in order for their plan to work the **U.S. must fall** and the best way to accomplish that is through control of key politicians including most U.S. Presidents since the time of Wilson and especially since Carter. More on this later.

Having explained the economic and political game plan for achieving a One World Government we can get to the really important topic which is the Social Deception; which they are using to pit lower class and middle class Americans against each other through the Progressive Promise of Redistribution of Wealth. They promise massive social entitlement programs which they use to elicit support from the disenfranchised lower class particularly illegal aliens and those on welfare or at or near poverty level. The reality is that they have no intention of keeping their promises long term. <u>It is a bate and switch strategy designed to economically collapse the U.S. economy and when that happens there will be no money for any social welfare programs</u>. If you want proof that Socialist entitlement programs are unsustainable and lead to ruination just look at the economic crisis in Europe. When they have successfully collapsed the economic system we will be forced to accept massive cuts in spending which will seriously <u>curtail even essential community services</u>. When this happens there will be massive unemployment and the middle class will merge into the lower class creating a two class society—the poor and their oppressors the elite banking interest and their puppets in the government which brought this misery on us all.

As bad as this sounds the worst is yet to come. There is a second driving force behind their agenda. <u>In addition to controlling us economically they are convinced that **over population** is a serious problem and they have a simple solution. They will kill off several billion of us reducing the population to somewhere between 1 ½ - 2 billion people which is construed to be a sustainable level.</u> How will they do it: With War, Healthcare Reform, Cap and Trade, Land Management and Utilization Policies and Artificially Engineered Food Shortages in addition to Mass Executions. I can hear the refrain of voices saying no way! This is insane! No not insane. It is Communism and that is what Communist regimes do. It is estimated that during the 20th century between Stalin and Mao approximately 100 million people lost their lives, victims of starvation, and ethnic, political and intellectual cleansing. Dissidents and those deemed undesirable for what ever reason were interned in labor camps and or executed. This is historical fact!

I want to close with the reminder that the elite who are determined to bring about a One World Government have gone political working through our political and military leaders, particularly through the highest office in the land. I won't belabor the point, but anyone who has paid attention to the news over the last year or so knows that President Obama has surrounded himself with an entourage of Marxist/ Socialist/Communist. I could quote Van Jones amongst several others in the Obama Administration but I will limit myself to the two quotes I find most offensive and frightening.

"Mao Tse Tung [Mass Murder] and Mother Teresa, [Catholic Nun] not often coupled with each other, but the two people that I turn to most."
— White House Communication Director, Anita Dunn

"We know that the free market is nonsense. We kind of agree with Mao that political power comes largely from the barrel of a gun."
— Manufacturing Czar, Ron Bloom

So Bloom is supposed to advise the President on Manufacturing and he says that *"The Free Market is nonsense."* Kind of makes me think that the collapse of the U.S. economy was no accident. And then both Dunn and Bloom seem to espouse violence as a political tool. It would certainly seem that the American people are being told *"you will cooperate with our Socialist agenda or suffer the consequences."*

PAY CLOSE ATTENTION! A word of caution to those who support the administrations Socialist/Communist agenda of Redistribution of Wealth; you have no idea the kind of danger you are in! You see the very lower socioeconomic groups which they are appealing to in order to usher in their One World Government will be amongst the first to be purged because you are viewed as dead weight. Simply put anyone who cannot produce more than he consumes is expendable! That means the entire lower socio-economic class is expendable.

Consider what Nobel Prize Winner and Fabian Socialist and Prominent Soviet Supporter George Bernard Shaw had to say along these lines: *"I don't want to punish anybody but there are an extraordinary number of people whom I want to kill. I think it would be a good thing to make everybody come before a properly appointed board just as* *he might come before the income tax commissioners. And say every five years or every seven years..., just put them there and say, sir or madam will you be kind enough to justify your existence. If your not producing as much as you consume or perhaps a little more then clearly we cannot use the big organization of society for the purpose of keeping you alive because <u>your life does not benefit us</u> and it can't be of much use to yourself."*

I want to leave you with hope. For a brief moment in time there was an economic system which strove to elevate the condition of people all around the world. That System was called **The American System of Economics** and it was the key to America's meteoric rise to Global Economic Superstardom. It was systematically dismantled by those intent on bringing America down. The good news is that it, along with surrender to God, holds the key to saving America and perhaps the world from the grips of a One World Government. It holds our greatest hope for a better tomorrow, a tomorrow where men around the world learn to live in peace and harmony. Here is what Henry C. Carey, economics adviser to Abraham Lincoln had to say about the American System:

"Two systems are before the world.... One is the English system; [the self appointed banking elite we have been discussing] *the other we may be proud to call the American system ... the only one ever devised the tendency of which was that of <u>elevating while equalizing the condition of man throughout the world.</u>"*

Quoting Carey again I want to give you an idea of the fate that awaits America if we don't wake up and take back our economy and our government. *"It [the British System] is the most gigantic system of slavery the world has yet seen, and therefore it is that freedom gradually disappears from every country over which England [the Moneyed Elite] is enabled to obtain control."*

PAY CLOSE ATTENTION! The Good News is that the American System of Economics can supply us a blueprint for how to restore America to its former greatness. We don't have to start over and grope in the dark for answers. All we have to do is go back to what worked before and tweak it slightly to adjust for time lapse.

Before you finish this book you will know exactly what the American System is and why it represents our best chance to save America from economic and social collapse. I will identify exactly who our enemies are so you can put names and faces to them and make sure we get them out of power. Equally important I will outline a political platform entitled the American Reformation Platform structured around the precepts of the American System. These are easy to understand proven principles which we can use to chart our course to recovery and restoration. Lest we forget about the seriousness of the threat we are facing I want to leave you with two quotes from my modern day hero JFK.

"Communism has never come to power in a country that was not disrupted by war or corrupted, or both."

– John F. Kennedy

At the present time in America we face both of these realities!

"In the long history of the world, only a few generations have been granted the role of defending freedom in its hour of maximum danger. I do not shrink from this responsibility I welcome it."

– John F. Kennedy

I ask each and every American:

Do you have the courage, like JFK, to stand up and be counted? The future of the world depends on your answer!

Consider the words of Thomas Jefferson: *"The spirit of resistance to government is so valuable that I wish it to be always kept alive... Whenever any form of government becomes destructive of these ends— life, liberty, and the pursuit of happiness—it is the right of the people to alter or abolish it, and to institute new government..."*

By the time you finish this book you will know what our leaders have done to destroy America and you will be empowered by having a step by step plan for how to restore our freedoms! We must join in peaceful revolt and take back our political system, our monetary system and our liberty before they are taken away for ever!

Chapter 1

The Seven Spheres of Influence:

That Control the Seat of Power

Please if you have not read the introduction do so before going any further. It lays the foundation for the entire book and contains information not presented elsewhere. I assure you it is important. Please read it before you proceed.

The government understands something that most Americans do not. They understand how to control what we think, how we act and ultimately what we believe! They are masters of <u>mind control</u> and they understand that in order to effectively control us they must control virtually every aspect of our lives.

In order for the government to control us they must brainwash us which means they must control the:

The Seven Spheres of Influence
That Control the Seat of Power!

1. **<u>The Political Process:</u>** In order to make sense of what is happening in Americana and elsewhere we need to understand that our current political and economic crisis is not a matter of Democrats

VS Republicans. Both houses of Congress and the President are irrelevant, controlled by a shadow government who put who they want into the White House [as their puppet leaders] and when it is politically expedient they simply change from one side of the isle to the other. Political party is irrelevant because the real power resides elsewhere protected from the volatility of their actions by a cloak of anonymity which this book will unveil. As the following quotes demonstrate it is incumbent on the public to learn the truth and then to act on it.

"If a nation expects to be ignorant and free, in a state of civilization, it expects what never was and never will be."

– Thomas Jefferson

"Liberty cannot be preserved without general knowledge among the people."

– President John Adams

In 2010 the American people need to vote out anyone regardless of party who has failed to listen to the voice of the people. Governments around the world need to do the same thing because they are controlled by the same shadow government that controls America. We need to rebuild our economy and reestablish our Republic. That does not mean more billions to Wall Street. It means loans to the small business owners who provide the majority of new jobs in this country. It means ending the Free Trade Agreements which have caused America's manufacturing base to be eroded resulting in devastating trade deficits which have systematically siphoned off the wealth of what was once the richest nation in the world! It means that as a nation and as individuals we must learn to be financially responsible and learn to live within our means and learn to be self-reliant rather than depending on a big corrupt government to take care of us. I urge you to reflect on these words and take this warning to heed!

"Remember that a government big enough to give you everything you want is also big enough to take away everything you have."

– Senator Barry Goldwater

It is time we woke up and realized that the endless stream of entitlement programs coming our of Washington are designed to make us dependent on big government, to make us relinquish our rights to that government and to eventually bankrupt us at which point the government will impose emergency measures which will effectively take away our liberty and make us slaves of the state. It means protecting our Constitutional Rights which include freedom of speech and the right to bare arms, both of which are being assailed. President Obama wants a million man domestic army to supposedly provide homeland security, yet at the same time he is doing everything he can to take away our right to bare arms so we can protect ourselves. His every action indicates he is establishing a police state. Consider these words from Thomas Jefferson: *"No free man shall ever be debarred the use of arms. The strongest reason for the people to retain their right to keep and bear arms is a last resort to protect themselves against tyranny in government."*

By the time you have finished this book you will understand that the policies coming out of Washington are not about creating economic stability or homeland security, but about collapsing the economy, stripping us of our National Sovereignty, and one way or the other forcing us to accept a One World Government. In the name of globalization this strategy is being imposed on sovereign nations around the world.

I will close this section with a quote which I do not expect you to believe as yet, but before you finish this book I assure you that you will not only believe it but you will cringe at the implications of what it means to America and the world!

"The dirty little secret is that <u>both houses of congress are irrelevant</u>. America's domestic policy is now being run by Alan Greenspan [now Ben Bernanke] and the Federal Reserve. America's foreign policy is now being run by the International Monetary Fund."
        – Robert Reich, Member President Clinton's Cabinet
                                                    Jan. 7th USA Today

This statement is true of governments around the world whose political and financial systems have like America's been compromised by the same global elite which have hijacked the American financial and political system. Their Central Banks and the private cartels which run them are the real power behind all the governments of the world.

When you realize the validity of the above statement you will have some decisions to make Do you stand by and do nothing or do you join in the fight to save America from the oppression that is on the horizon? Read on.

2. **Our Religious Freedom:** Let us not forget that The U.S. Constitution is based on Christian morality. If the government can weaken our religious beliefs then they have appreciably greater latitude as to what they can pawn off on us as radical social policy because our moral barometer is damaged! That is why for example pornography is legal yet our children cannot pray in school and a man was recently arrested for holding church in his home. The government knows that devoutly religious/spiritual people are willing to die for their beliefs. That makes them dangerous to a government that is intent on radical change. We must oppose any legislation which in any way challenges our freedom of speech and our religious freedom. As we shall see later, the government is assailing the internet, our last bastion of truly free speech, as well as talk radio and programs like Glen Beck who challenge their socialist agendas. With regard to the importance of our religious beliefs consider what James Madison the father of the U.S. Constitution had to say:

"We have staked the whole future of American civilization, not upon the power of government, far from it. We have staked the future of all our political institutions upon the capacity of mankind for self-government; upon the capability of each and all of us to govern ourselves, to control ourselves, to sustain ourselves according to The Ten Commandments of God."

God does not abide a slacker. He rewards a man according to the fruits of his labor, but what we are seeing transpire under the Obama administration is a massive redistribution of wealth that takes from the most productive portion of society to give to the least productive in the name of social justice. As the following quote demonstrates our founding fathers realized that this tactic of seizure of assets invariably leads to ruination.

"The Democracy will cease to exist when you take away from those who are willing to work and give to those who will not."
                                                                    – Thomas Jefferson

By the time you finish this book you will understand that Obama's Socialist Communist policy of Redistribution of Wealth is not intended to help the poor; far from it. There are much better ways to help the poor than by destroying their dignity by making them dependent on hand outs from the government. No this strategy is to make people dependent on the government and therefore compliant to their will, even if it means loss of freedom and self determination. Reflect on these quotes in light of Obama's policies of redistribution of wealth:

"You cannot help men permanently by doing for them what they could and should do for themselves." – Rev. William J. H. Boetcker

Couple this with Senator Barry Goldwater's quote from a couple of pages back. *"Remember that a government big enough to give you everything you want is also big enough to take away everything you have."*

And one of the things they want to take away is Religious Freedom, because they view a moral, self sufficient society as a society which will stand up and resist their tyranny!

3. **The Educational System:** The government controls our educational system and stilts the curriculum to foster the social and political beliefs they want. That is why our children graduate high school knowing virtually nothing about personal finances, the principles upon which our Republic was founded or the salient facts of U.S. and world history which would allow them to engage in critical thinking about political and social issues. The goal is less to educate our children than to control the way they think and what they believe. Parent's rights are secondary to the wishes of the state. For example the state has determined that children do not have to tell their parents when using contraceptives distributed by the school, or when seeing a school nurse and not even when scheduling an abortion. Similarly that is why prayer is no longer allowed in schools and why our educational system fails to engender critical thinking. They don't want moral conviction or critical thinking because it might cause the children to challenge what they are taught in school. They want placid compliant robots. To give you an idea of just how deep this indoctrination goes consider this; at one point the California Appellate court ruled that

parents do not have a Constitutional right under California law to home school, a decision that was later overturned. Their justification was that: *"A primary purpose of the education system is to train school children in good citizenship, patriotism, and loyalty to the State and the Nation as a means of protecting public welfare."* If that isn't brainwashing then what is? We have an obligation to become informed and involved and to see to it that our children are armed with the truth and that they have the tools necessary for critical thinking. Consider the following quotes and then ask yourself if you can conclude other than our government run schools have intentionally failed to equip our children for life and citizenship?

"The goal of education is the advancement of knowledge and the dissemination of truth." – President John F. Kennedy

"Education is dangerous. Every educated person is a future enemy." – Herman Goering [Hitler's designated successor]

I contend that our government run schools have not only not engendered creativity and critical thinking, which are the basis of knowledge and enlightenment, but they have intentionally stifled them because in the future they envision an educated populous as dangerous. If this isn't true then why did Mao, Stalin and Hitler make it a point to take control of the schools and imprison or kill the intellectuals?

Oh, by the way! Do you know that 2,000 page healthcare bill that none of our legislators read, the bill that was passed despite overwhelming opposition by the American people. Not only did it hijack our healthcare it also hijacked our educational system. Slipped into the body of the bill was a totally unrelated provision for the Federal Government to take over the Student Loan Business. Ask too many questions, show too much inquisitiveness, oppose the wrong political agendas and you will have about as much likelihood of getting a school loan for college as a *"snowball in hell."* Welcome to the Brave New World of the Thought Police!

4. **Our Family Values:** The Bible says there will come a time when children will not respect their parents. Madison Avenue advertisers have sold us on materialism to the degree that we largely

believe that who we are is more defined by what we have and how we look than by what we stand for. We were brainwashed into believing that it is more important to give our children "The Good Life" *[Things]* than it is to be home where we can influence their values. Filmmaker Aaron Russo says the Women's Lib movement received financial support from David Rockefeller and his fellow Progressives because they wanted to get moms in the work place so they could tax them and so they could get access to the minds of our children at an earlier more pliable age. Is it any wonder our children do not respect us. They are more a product of the system than they are of the family structure. We need to rebuild the family structure, censor our children's exposure to unhealthy entertainment vehicles and take back control of our children's minds and hearts. The following quotes punctuate just how important this is.

"The family is the nucleus of civilization." – Ariel & Will Durant

"To put the world in order, we must first put the nation in order; to put the nation in order, we must put the family in order; to put the family in order, we must cultivate our personal life; and to cultivate our personal life, we must first set our hearts right."

– Confucius

5. **The Entertainment Industry:** In our pursuit of materialism we have largely abandoned our children to the sex and violence propagated by the music industry, TV, the movies and the anti-social behavior fostered by video games and computers. Add in the influence of the state run educational system and the brainwashing is nearly complete. Is it any wonder the divorce rate has topped 50% and our value system is being progressively diluted? As parents we need to control what our children watch and what activities they participate in. We can no longer afford to let TV and Video Games be our children's baby-sitters. This is going to require a willingness to turn our backs on the brain washing of Madison Avenue and live *simpler less materialistic lives* so we can spend less time pursuing materialism and more time raising our children to be the people we want them to be. Make no mistake entertainment is used to distract us, dumb us down, influence what we think and how we act:

"The entertainment industry is encouraging young people to defy and deceive their parents." – Mike DeWine

6. **The News Media:** The largely corporate owned news media has become primarily a propaganda machine of the White House and the Corporations, and the purpose of the news is less to report the news than to direct public opinion. For example shortly after Obama aids approached the National Endowment For The Arts [NEA] asking them to support the president's agendas we coincidently had a slue of TV programs taunting the merits of Obama's volunteer program. And then there is GE owned NBC who is supporting Obama's Green Movement. Never mind that GE stands to make a financial killing on the smart grid. They are not biased, no not much! The powers to be, know that if they can define what is perceived as the facts they can control what we think and they can largely control opposition and dissension. That is why they are so aggressively assaulting the internet and our 1st amendment right of free speech. We must oppose any legislation which further degrades our freedom of speech and we must protect the internet and talk radio at all costs. If they can stifle free speech they have won. Pure and simple. Consider the words of George Washington: *"The freedom of speech may be taken, and dumb and silent we may be led, like sheep to the slaughter."*

Now consider these quotes by contrast and ask yourself if our freedom might not be in jeopardy!

"The Central Intelligence Agency owns everyone of any significance in the major media."   – William Colby, Former CIA Director

"The enormous gap between what U.S. leaders do in the world and what Americans think their leaders are doing is one of the great propaganda accomplishments of the dominate political mythology."
                        – Michael Parenti, Author and Historian

7. **Our Financial System:** It should not come as a surprise to anyone that the banks in concert with the government have orchestrated the current financial crisis in order to facilitate the largest transfer of wealth in history. This crisis and Obama's response to it could have come directly out of 1960's strategy of Columbia

University Marxist professors Cloward and Piven who espouse a radical agenda based on bringing the Capitalist System down by bankrupting it through social welfare entitlement programs designed to redistribute wealth according to Socialist ideology. As we will discuss later, President Obama can be tied directly to this strategy through his community organizing activities with the scandal ridden ACORN group. In short the American people have been robbed in an effort to transition America into a Socialist Communist Government. Once you have full details on this subject you will be able to see that rather than trying to save the U.S. financial system, Obama's every move was calculated to drive us into unmanageable debt and bankruptcy. Compare the words of Thomas Jefferson and the actions of Obama and you will begin to see just how much danger our country is in.

"A wise and frugal government, which shall leave men free to regulate their own pursuits of industry and improvement, and shall not take from the mouth of labor the bread it has earned – this is the sum of good government." – Thomas Jefferson

We cannot let our legislators pass any more bills that increase our already catastrophic debt burden and we must force our legislators to become financially responsible and give us a balanced budget! The following quote from John Adams, second U.S. President points out just how vitally important this is. *"There are two ways to conquer and enslave a nation. One is by the sword. The other is by debt."*

Up till now the government has controlled the SEAT of POWER by controlling **The Seven Spheres of Influence** and most Americans have been oblivious to the fact that they were being manipulated and controlled. President Obama's recent actions are so blatant that there can be little doubt that he is building a; Propaganda Machine to Push His Socialist Agenda. For example he recently defiled the concept of separation of church and state by pandering to pastors to get their support for his healthcare plan. He undermined the family structure by taking his agenda to our children in the government run public schools where he distributed lesson plans calling for children to make posters and write papers supportive of his agenda. He solicited The National Endowment for the Arts [NEA] asking them to create art to subliminally influence us. *"By the way his attempt to solicit aid from a Federally Funded NEA is illegal."* He has inundated millions of Americans with unwanted e-mails. In an effort to influence the elderly he has used the influence of the AARP and he is using tax payer money to launch a multimillion dollar add/propaganda campaign.

What Obama Meant By:
The Fundamental Transformation of America!

Obama allowed the Corrupt Community Organizing Group Acorn to help write the Stimulus Plan and in the process they give themselves $8.5 billion of tax payer money so they could put a literal army of bodies on the street to further his plans to Redistribute The Wealth of America and Transition the Country into a Socialist/Marxist State Run Government! Lastly, and most offensive of all he has employed Chicago Style Machine Politics to slander, malign, and intimidate what he derogatorily referred to as the *"Tea Partiers"* for daring to stand up for the principles upon which this nation was founded.

The following quote from Michelle Obama sheds a lot of light on Obama's actions.

"Barack is not a politician first and foremost. He's a community activist exploring the viability of politics to make change."
                          – Michelle Obama, The New Republic, 2007

So, at his wife's admission Obama has a hidden agenda. *"The Fundamental Transformation of America,"* which he spoke about was not what Americans naively thought it was. His intention was to redistribute the wealth in the name of what he calls **social justice**. As sited earlier, this is the very action which Thomas Jefferson assured us would cause Democracy to cease.

"The Democracy will cease to exist when you take away from those who are willing to work and give to those who will not."
                          – Thomas Jefferson

Obama and Jefferson stand polarized. One standing for self-reliance and the other stands for Government Handouts! Gee I wonder which approach built this great nation—Self-reliance of Handouts? Seems to me it was self-reliance! We are headed down a slippery slope!

The President's True Agenda

President Obama's agenda is to grab power and use it to transition the U.S. into a Socialist/Communist country that in no way resembles the nation generations of Americans have fought and died to protect! He then plans to transition a bankrupt and pliable U.S. into the infamous One World Government which our politicians are now openly touting. This plan has been long in the making and Obama is just the latest in a long list of puppets to work toward its realization. Consider this warning from Congressman John R. Rarick:

"The Council on Foreign Relations [CFR] is dedicated to one-world government, financed by a number of the largest tax exempt foundations [i.e. Rockefeller], and wielding such power and influence over our lives in the areas of finance, business, labor, military, education, and mass communication media, that it should be familiar to every American concerned with good government and with preserving and defending the US Constitution and our free-enterprise system. Yet, the nation's right-to-know machinery, the news media; usually so aggressive in exposures to inform our people, remain silent when it comes to the CFR, its members and their activities. The CFR is the establishment. Not only does it have influence and power in key decision-making positions at the highest levels of government to apply pressure from above, but it also finances and uses individuals and groups to bring pressure from below, to justify the high level decisions for converting the U.S. from a sovereign Republic into a servile member of a one-world dictatorship."

Subsequent chapters will show that Obama's agenda when fully implemented will transition this country into a Communist Slave State:

His Spending Policies: will likely result in hyperinflation and bankruptcy.

His Healthcare Program: will give the government control over who lives and who dies and despite claims to the contrary it will drive us into unsustainable levels of debt which are intended to hasten our financial demise. All other arguments aside we simply cannot afford another massive entitlement program when we can't fund the ones we already have. We must fight to repeal Obama Care!

His Cap and Trade System: will impose the highest tax increase in the history of our nation and given that it includes no technology solutions it will have little impact on CO2 emissions. Additionally by controlling the cost of virtually all consumer goods he will be in a position to systematically force consumption patterns and cause price driven shortages including food shortages. This happened in the Great Depression when farmers dumped Milk in the streets in protest, slaughtered Cattle and let Apples rot on the trees, Meanwhile Americans virtually starved. We should heed the warning of **President Ronald Reagan:** *"Approximately 80% of our air pollution stems from hydrocarbon released by vegetation, so let's not go overboard in setting and enforcing tough emission standards from man made sources."*

There is an entire chapter dedicated to this subject.

His Green Policy: will give him control over food and energy costs and their availability.

His Restrictions on Freedom of Speech and Our Right to Bare Arms: will usher in a Police State designed to effectively crush any opposition to his policies.

Obama's agenda literally takes all control from the individual and places it in the hands of the state. Or put another way we lose our individual freedoms and become the slaves of the state.

By the time you finish this book you will have the *facts* required to make you an Informed Citizen of the United States of America and the Republic for which it stands. As such you will be empowered to participate in the greatest political system on the planet. If we are to protect and preserve the values and freedoms upon which our nation was founded we need to end our apathy and get involved, we need to put aside our differences and party biases and stand for what has made this the greatest nation in the world. Lastly, we have to remove the money vultures and their puppets from the seat of power and return to the principles which our government was founded upon. This book will show you exactly how we can accomplish these goals!

The Brave New Totalitarian World!

I can't close this chapter without heralding an alarm! Paul Reviser shouted from horseback that *"the British are coming, the British are coming."* **Today I shout a warning that *"Tyranny is at the door."* What is about to be imposed on the U.S. and the world is a *"Totalitarian Hybrid Capitalist Communist Regime."*** I know I have not yet developed the case to prove this statement, but before you finish this book you will have your proof. And when I do provide the proof and you realize the truth, then the warning I am about to give will resonate in your soul!

Pay Attention This May Save Your Life!

As I touched on it in the introduction: If we look back at the Communist regimes of Hitler, Mao and Stalin; in order for them to rise to power and control the people certain groups of individuals had to be imprisoned or killed. This group included: **[The devoutly religious, dissidents, intellectuals, and entrepreneurs].** The devoutly religious, dissidents and the intellectuals had to be imprisoned or killed because they were deemed dangerous! It is dangerous to think and question! Additionally the entrepreneurs were purged because they challenged the state run economic system! This time around the major corporations will be allowed because they are in cahoots with the government, but what we now consider the free enterprise system will not be tolerated. They will finally be in a position to implement their decades old plan for population control which is based on *"Hitler's Genocidal Eugenic Programs."* Eugenics for those of you, who may not be familiar with the term, is the effort to produce a master race by weeding out of the gene pool all those with perceived negative attributes such as physical defects or low IQ's etc. This can be done by selective breeding or mass murder of the elderly, handicapped and mentally impaired. As we will discuss they view over population as a serious problem and they have a solution which is Eugenics and mass extermination! As I touched on in the introduction the largest group to be targeted will be the poor because they are viewed as excess baggage who can't carry their own weight! How ironic the very people who put the Socialist into power will be among the first to die! There is a saying that unfortunately applies here: "they eat their young don't they?"

With this in mind we can expect a virtual genocide of the Elderly, the Hispanics, [especially illegal aliens] and the African Americans because they are vied as dead weight and their existence does not benefit their slave masters! They will not tolerate anyone who is a threat or who cannot contribute to society!

By the way I am a senior citizen and a dissident so I am in the boat with you! In case you think I exaggerate remember that during the 20th century Communism killed approximately 100,000,000 people. There were Hitler's death camps and the mass starvations caused by the collectivizing of farm land by Mao and Stalin. And if you doubt what I say about Eugenics consider these chilling words from Nobel Prize Winning Fabian Socialist and staunch Soviet supporter George Bernard Shaw: *"If you're not producing as much as you consume or perhaps a little more then clearly we cannot use the big organization of society for the purpose of keeping you alive because your life does not benefit us...."*

In another chilling quote Shaw said: *"I appeal to the chemist to discover a humane gas that will kill instantly and painlessly; in short a gentlemanly gas deadly by all means but humane not cruel."*

Then there were the reports of some 600 reported Internment Camps in the U.S. which at first I dismissed as so much bunk till I came across two ads on government websites advertising positions for Internment Guards. At first I saw they were calling them Resettlement Camps and I wasn't too disturbed. My initial reaction was that these camps were for victims of natural disasters like Hurricane Katrina or say a major earthquake. Then I read on and my heart almost stopped when they referred to the detainees in the Resettlement Camps as **Prisoners**! All of the sudden I envisioned the Communist Work Camps/Concentration Camps and realized that, that was what these camps were. Concentration/Death Camps where Dissidents who resisted the New World Order and Non-productive/non-useful People would be interned. This was a place you were sent for *"Rehabilitation or Extermination."*

All of the sudden I was a believer. I finally believed the words of James P. Warburg, Representing Rothschild Banking Concern, while speaking before the United States Senate, Feb. 17, 1950. *"We shall have world government whether or not you like it. The only question is whether World Government will be by conquest or consent."*

There can be no question about it. The enemy is at the gate and he is more evil than we can possibly imagine!

We can expect the most ruthless totalitarian government in history, because it is as the say: *"Power corrupts and absolute power corrupts absolutely."*

United We Stand Divided We Fall!

The one world government which is emerging will be the closest thing to absolute power and absolute evil the world has ever seen or could ever imagine! Either we rise up and stop it before it takes hold or we will suffer under its oppression till Christ returns to set us free! This is not a time when humanity can afford to be divided. There is no room for old hatreds or prejudices. This is not about Black VS Whites – not about U.S. Citizens VS non-citizens – not about Muslims VS Christians – not about the well to do VS the less well to do – not about liberals VS conservatives – not about Republicans VS Democrats. This is about those who would be free in a free society VS those elite few who believe it is their right to enslave us and make us subject to their tyrannical rule! This is a time when we need to once and for all learn what the "Brotherhood of Man" actually means! This is a time when we must unite against evil or succumb to it!

During the course of this book I will lay out a Complete Action Plan outlining step by step exactly what we need to do to resist this evil regime, but the first and most important step is to put aside our differences and Unite Under the Banner of Freedom! For as never before it will be true that, *"United we stand and divided we fall!"* As this story unfolds I will prove what I am about to say, but for now I ask you to accept it at face value. <u>In order for the one world government to accomplish its take over America must fall and submit to their rule.</u> Then American forces combined with those of the UN will comprise a military force so powerful that most if not all of the world will be forced into submission. My fellow Americans we are the last bastion of hope for a free society. But <u>one of the things that is going to have to</u>

happen in order for us to fight back is that we are going to have to take off the blinders and: **See America For The Imperialist World Power Which It Has Become**. I have an entire chapter dedicated to this subject, and I think it will surprise and shock you to truly understand what the shadow government which rules America has done to us and other countries around the world.

The last thing I want to say before bringing this chapter to a close is that at least one thing they have told us is true and that is that there is real inequity between the middle class and lower class in America and even more inequity in underdeveloped countries. They tell us that the answer to this social injustice is to take away from those who are willing to work and give to those who will not, which is the basis of their supposed Redistribution of Wealth which is nothing more than a strategy to pit the middle class and lower classes against each other. This is a strategy which has been employed by every Communist regime in history with the same outcome every time. And that outcome is not a Socialist Utopian Society! The outcome has always been and will always be the destruction of the middle class resulting in a two class society of a perpetually poor enslaved lower class and a ruling elite upper class. In this scenario both the lower class and middle class are enslaved and end up far worse off than they were. The only winners are the Elite Ruling class who pitted us against each other while they set back and laughed at our naiveté! I contend there is another choice.

How to Avoid Slavery and Preserve Our Liberty!

We the people can rise up, but not against each other, but against the Financial Elite who control upwards of 90 percent of the world's wealth and redistribute that wealth, the true wealth of the world! To do this we will have to put an end to the illegal Federal Reserve and Income Tax, cut our military expenditures by putting an end to Wars for Profit and Imperial Empire Building [again the subject of an entire chapter], rebuild our infrastructure including our manufacturing base, and withdraw from all Free Trade Agreements which impose intentionally losing trade policies on the American people [again the subject of an entire chapter].

This is just a small part of the comprehensive American Restoration Plan which I will lay out in the pages of this book, but that is premature. Before we can know what to do to fix America we must understand what has been done to destroy it. Then we will realize that we do not have to be a rocket scientist to fix it. All we have to do is put back in place what was systematically dismantled. You see there was a reason we became the wealthiest nation in the world. **All we have to do is put back in place that which originally made us great,** but to know how to do that requires an in-depth knowledge of our history, because our past holds the key to our future. The caution I want to throw out is that what needs to be done must be done in a very careful systematic step by step fashion and even then there will be financial hardships because we have waited too long to address the problems to avoid the hardships. But I promise you any hardships we face will be far better than the alternative which is slavery and oppression under an oppressive one world government. We are in for the fight of a lifetime, but it is a fight we can and must win no matter what the cost!

What Can We Do To Unite The Nation?

I have been periodically asked what we can do to unite the American people, to bring together the Republicans and Democrats, the Progressives and Conservatives, the Blacks and Whites, the Citizens and Noncitizens, the financially well off and less well off, and the Muslims and Christians and any other divergent groups.

My answer to that question is that the key to our cooperation lies in our understanding that we have a common enemy namely the Moneyed Elite that would rule us all! Share this book with not only those who share your views, but even more importantly share it with those who do not share your views. It is imperative that we all understand that the only hope we have is in not allowing ourselves to be pitted against each other, but in standing together in unity.

After we win the fight it is incumbent on each of us to build a society that more equitably distributes wealth, a society which rather than exploiting people elevates the condition of all mankind!

As you read this book you will learn that surprisingly, that very precept is what made America the greatest, wealthiest, most powerful nation in the history of the world and it holds the key to saving us from ruination! Either we allow our greed and prejudices to destroy us from within or we come together and form a Brotherhood of Man which elevates us all and saves civilization from tyranny. If we will come together in unity we can take what man meant for evil and with God's help we can turn it into good and in the process we can learn God's true plan for mankind; which is to prosper us, not to harm us! The choice is ours and the future of mankind rest in the balance. But if we are to be victorious in this battle we must turn away from Mammon [Materialism] and turn to God. We must surrender to God's will and once and for all set aside our differences and focus on the two greatest commandments which instruct us to love thy God with all our hearts and to love our neighbor as our self. If we do this then there is no telling the marvelous future which could await us all! May God bless us all and bring us through the battle that awaits us.

Chapter 2
A Glimpse Into The Future:
America in 2030

This chapter is based on facts as they existed at the time of the writing of this book projected into the future in order to give you an idea of what our future holds if we don't wake up and face the truth about what is happening in the U.S. and the rest of the world.

The date is June 24, 2030 and Erick Jefferson is spending his 21st birthday with his grandfather Ephraim, a retired history professor.

Gramps: Erick, today you enter manhood and to commemorate the occasion I have two special books for you. The first book is the Holy Bible. As you know it has been outlawed so you can't let anyone know you have it. You are always asking me how God could abandon us. God didn't abandon us, we abandoned him. Erick my son, you need to know what God's word says and the promises he has made us. He has not forgotten us.

The second book is an unpublished manuscript which I wrote before you were born. As a history professor I saw what was happening to America, where things were headed and I wanted to warn people, but unfortunately I waited too long. By the time I finished the book the government was censoring free speech and no publisher would touch my book for fear of retaliation from the government. I kept this manuscript for you till you were old enough to understand it. You are always asking me and your Dad what happened to America. Hopefully my manuscript will answer some of your questions. Erick, here is the manuscript. It is entitled **MODERN SLAVERY: And the Fight For Freedom!**

Without Vigilance Freedom Cannot Prevail!

Erick: Thank you Gramps. I can't wait to read it, but as long as we are spending the day together could you tell me in your own words what happened to America? That way I can ask questions. All my life Mom and Dad have told me how great a nation America used to be and how we were the envy of the world, but all I can remember is struggling to survive. Dad talks incessantly about how America used to be known as *"The land of the free and the home of the brave,"* but all I know is that's not the America I grew up in. I watch old movies and I see how beautiful everything was. Now everything is rundown and in decay. It's depressing! All I have ever known is the oppression of a tyrannical Communist Government that taxes us to death and affords us virtually no human rights. Dad says people used to be able to choose what they wanted to do for a living. Now the government controls virtually every aspect of our lives, who goes to college and who doesn't, where we work, where we live, who gets health care and who doesn't, who lives and who dies! We have no freedom. I can't imagine the America Dad cries over. If America was so great and if the people had a voice in the government how could they ever let it be taken away from them?

The Story of The Fall of The U.S.

Gramps: They didn't just give it away. Our fall came on us slowly, so slowly most people didn't know anything was wrong till it was too late. Our Founding Fathers had lived under tyranny, like what we have in America now, so they knew that money and power corrupts and they tried to warn us, but we were too busy living the good life to pay attention. They warned us that: *"A nation could be conquered by **debt** as surely as it could by the sword"* and they cautioned us to *"never allow **private bankers** to get control of our currency or they would manipulate it and eventually enslave us all."* Unfortunately we didn't pay any attention to their warnings and in 1913 we allowed the

Federal Reserve Bank to be established. <u>From that point on our currency was controlled by **private bankers** who printed our currency and **charged us interest** on it, effectively driving us deeper into debt with every dollar that was printed. We didn't understand that controlling debt was the key to controlling the country.</u> The bankers manipulated interest rates to create a series of speculative economic booms which were always followed by devastating financial collapses. What we didn't realize was that every time this happened the banks got richer and we got poorer. They bought our homes, our corporations and our nation's infrastructure for pennies on the dollar while driving the average man deeper and deeper into debt till we reached the point where we Drowned In Both Personal And National Debt.

It's a shame we didn't heed the warning of Thomas Jefferson: *"I place economy among the first and most important virtues, and **public debt as the greatest of dangers**. To preserve our independence, we must not let our rulers load us with perpetual debt."*

Debt Is But The Illusion of Freedom!

Erick: Surely there had to be more to it than just charging interest on our currency.

Gramps: Yes there was a lot more to it. By the 1890's America had developed the first intercontinental railway system and had emerged as a major super power. Then in 1945 at the end of WWII America emerged from the war with its manufacturing intact and with the allied nations owing America massive war debts. From all indications America was at the apex of the economic pinnacle, but most Americans were unaware that since 1913 when the Federal Reserve [private banking cartel] had gotten control of the currency they had been systematically manipulating the economy in an effort to bankrupt the nation and they had no idea the damage they had already caused.

The U.S. Allegedly Declared Bankruptcy in 1933!

Then in 1993 Congressman James Traficant made a speech before

Congress that at the time could only be described as provocative and conspiratorial. In his speech he charged that; On March 9, 1933 in the depths of The Great Depression the U.S. Government had been declared bankrupt and had been declared to exist in name only. Its Republican form of government having been dissolved and replaced by a Democratic, Socialist/Communist Order. He alleged that the office of Secretary of the Treasury had been transferred to the international Monetary Fund and the Federal Reserve and that the World Bank and the International Monetary Fund were the receivers of the Bankruptcy. He further stipulated that unknown to most Americans, our gold, property and future labor had been pledged as collateral to the receivers of the bankruptcy.

Erick, I cover this in detail in my manuscript. I leave it up to you to decide if the information that James Traficant disclosed in his speech before Congress was true or not. I leave it to each individual to decide if he was a whistle blower and a patriot or a self serving conspiracy theorist and criminal. It cannot be denied that he was a maverick, but the question is was that because he was out of touch with reality or because he told things as he saw them regardless of the consequences. He wasn't the only one making such allegations he was just the most outspoken and most controversial. For example during the Great Depression President Franklin Roosevelt warned us saying: *"The real truth of the matter is that a financial element in the large centers has owned the government since the days of Andrew Jackson."*

And then there is this quote from the Clinton era:

"The dirty little secret is that both houses of congress are irrelevant. America's domestic policy is now being run by Alan Greenspan (Chairman of the FED) and the Federal Reserve. America's foreign policy is now being run by the International Monetary Fund."
                    – Robert Reich, Member President Clinton's Cabinet
                                                    Jan. 7, USA Today

Erick, I will say this much. With the passage of time Traficant's statements seemed to line up with political events as they unfolded. As you read my manuscript you will see that the facts support the thesis that America was intentionally bankrupt by banking interest and the way it was done pretty much coincides with Mr. Traficant's charges that the American political system had been hijacked by a socialist/communist shadow government headed by international banking concerns, but you read the manuscript and decide for yourself.

If Traficant's allegations are correct the U.S. declared bankruptcy in 1933 and has been a Communist State since that time. Based on events unfolding in the late 1990's I predicted that we could expect a second bankruptcy somewhere between 2010 and 2016 and this time the goal would be to force the U.S. into a Global Communist State which would mean the end of the U.S. as a Sovereign Nation State. I also predicted that the collapse of the U.S. would bring about a cascade of events which would collapse the world economy leading to realization of the Money Manipulators plan to establish a One World Government headed by them the Moneyed Elite. The collapse of the U.S. was the lynch pen in their plan for world dominance.

The Gilded Cage of Material Greed!

Erick: Gramps how did they pull it off without the public catching on?

Gramps: It is complicated so I will just give you the highlights here and you can read about the details later. It started in 1913 when the Fed got control of our currency and the government imposed an illegal Income Tax in order to raise the money to pay the Fed their interest charges for printing our currency. This immediately drove up the National Debt, because every dollar that was printed was effectively a loan issued at interest. This was exactly why our Forefathers had declared their Independence from England, but most Americans didn't know their history so the significance of what had been done went by largely unnoticed. Then in 1933 when we declared Bankruptcy we were forced to turn our gold in and the government issued a new currency backed by **the pledge of our gold, our property and our future labor,** but again the public was for the most part kept in the dark. The public was of course aware of having to turn the gold in, but as to the pledge of our property and future labor they were for the most part oblivious. A property tax was imposed and Social Security was established. This was the means by which the wealth was transferred.

It is too involved to cover in detail now so you will have to read about it later.

Additionally they wanted to drive us into personal debt. The banks and corporations started by brainwashing us into believing that our happiness was in some way linked to our material possessions. We became an overindulgent society whose motto was *"I want that and I want it now."* Our entire society became addicted to the good life, which meant we had an insatiable appetite for big houses, expensive cars, and lavish vacations. You name it, we wanted it and the banks and corporations were more than willing to accommodate us. They offered us cheap credit and when we were addicted they got their cronies in the government to allow them to charge **usury rates** and set up **predatory lending practices** which drove millions of people into unmanageable levels of debt. As bad as that was that was just the beginning. Not only did they want to drive us into debt they wanted to siphon off all our wealth and systematically drive down our salaries to the point of subsistence. Then they stepped in and promised to take care of us. They would give us retirement benefits, subsidize our education and our prescription drugs, provide our health care and literally take care of us from cradle to grave, which we were to dumb to realize meant control us from cradle to grave.

This tactic is what I call Modern Slavery and is where the name of my manuscript originates. The concept was that conventional slavery was messy. It required that you care for and control the slaves. Modern Slavery was based on the illusion of personal freedom while all the while the government insidiously enslaved the population little by little by debasing the currency and by gradually increasing the taxes and imposing more and more government controls till finally the people were enslaved and yet they didn't realize it. Erick, it is similar to the way they catch monkeys. It is what I call the snare of greed. You take a gourd and cut a hole in it large enough for the monkey to get his hand through. You tether the gourd to a post and bate the trap by placing food inside the gourd. The monkey puts his hand in and grabs the food, but the hole is too small for him to get his closed fist out. All he has to do is let go and he is free. But he doesn't and he is caught and his freedom is taken away. Likewise all people needed to do was stop being suckered into buying things they couldn't afford on credit and they could have escaped the snare, but like the monkey they were blinded by their greed and were enslaved. The only difference between the monkey and the American people is the monkey was caught immediately while the American people slipped into slavery little by little over decades. It is like John Adams said: *"I believe there are more instances of the abridgement of freedom of people by gradual and silent encroachment than by violent and sudden usurpation."*

That was the whole idea. If you spring the trap too quickly the people will figure out what is up and revolt, but if it is done slowly enough they never know what hit them.

It is like Henry Ford said: *"It is well enough that the People of the nation do not understand our banking and monetary system for if they did, I believe there would be a revolution before tomorrow morning."*

The Global Agenda of Imperialism!

Erick: So Gramps if I understand you correctly you are saying that the government helped the banks and corporations prey on the American people and drive them into debt and poverty. Okay I get that, but why would they want to take it to the point of actually collapsing the government like they did?

Gramps: You can't understand that by focusing exclusively on the U.S. This was a global phenomenon. Do you remember that I said earlier, that the End Game was to establish a One World Government? The Money Manipulators are nothing if not patient and visionary. They saw that given the rate of population explosion and the rate of technological advancement, particularly medical advancement, there would come a time when the planet would be taxed by overpopulation. When that time came they wanted to be in a position to control the resources of the planet and thereby control global events. So while they were busy bankrupting the U.S. they were likewise doing the same thing to countries all over the world. Remember this was a world wide banking cartel that was pulling the strings, so they had a global reach. Their strategies differed slightly from country to country, but it always came down to controlling them through debt. They were focused on controlling resource rich third world countries and in particular countries rich in oil. The strategy was to make massive loans to resource rich countries to supposedly develop infrastructure so they could join the industrialized world, but the real strategy was to drive them into bankruptcy just like they had done to the U.S., then they would loan them still more money but this time they had to pledge their natural resources as collateral much as the U.S. had pledged the property and the labor of our citizens. There is a chapter in the manuscript dedicated exclusively to explaining what they did, but for now I hope you get the gist of it.

Erick: Okay I get the big picture, but Gramps I still don't understand how they brought the richest nation in the world down and I am still fussy as to exactly why it was necessary.

PAY CLOSE ATTENTION! Gramps: As I said we had entered the era of Globalization. They didn't care so much what happened to America per say. What they were really focused on was global domination and they knew that a financially and militarily strong U.S. could threaten their plans of global domination, so the U.S. had to be made compliant which meant we had to be bankrupted a second time and driven into accepting a world government. The other aspect of their strategy was that once they had the U.S. firmly in their grips they could use the military might of the U.S. to leverage other countries into submission.

Erick: Now I understand why they had to bring the U.S. down, but you still haven't explained how they did it the second time around.

The Intentional Dismantling and Pillaging of America!

Gutting America's Manufacturing Sector: Gramps: America was the only major industrialized nation in the world that didn't have a Value-Added Tax to protect their trade balance. I won't go into how it worked just now, but suffice it to say that other nations had a significant tax advantage [in the neighborhood of 30%] over America when it came to international trade. By not imposing a Value-Added Tax like other countries the U.S. government was in fact encouraging and

enabling U.S. corporations to have their products produced abroad
and then imported back into the U.S. This allowed the corporations to
make obscene profits. They could seek out the cheapest labor on the
planet [china and India] avoid EPA standards, health benefits, and pensions and as importers into the U.S. they could even take advantage of
the Value-Added Tax. **This policy gutted America's Manufacturing
base and the ongoing trade deficit siphoned off our wealth,** but that
alone wasn't enough to collapse the U.S. Economy.

Controlling America's Transportation Costs and Trade Balance:
In order to further gut our manufacturing base the globalist needed to
control transportation cost so that imports could be sure of being able to
undercut U.S. domestic goods. And once again the U.S. Federal Government was there to accommodate their needs. A number of government initiatives were required. Containers from China were allowed to
enter the U.S. by way of Mexico. Mexican Truck Drivers were allowed
to bring containers from China into the U.S. and on the way back they
were allowed to pick up loads bound for Mexico. As much as this cut
cost it wasn't enough for the globalist, so the Federal Government
further accommodated them by establishing the **Trusted Trader Program** which allowed Mexican truck drivers to cross our border **without
manual inspection** by using an electronic device similar to the I-Pas
devices used on U.S. toll roads. Lastly, containers were tracked within
the U.S. by an electronic tracking system developed by a company with
ties to Communist China. In order to serve the interest of the globalist
the U.S. Federal Government exposed our borders to drug smuggling,
illegal aliens and terrorist threats and undercut the Teamsters and Long-
shoremen's Unions putting further downward pressure on U.S. wages.
Additionally the **Open Borders Policies** caused an influx of Mexican
illegals which cut deeply into the unskilled labor market. Construction workers who were once well paid were forced to compete with
illegals for jobs at wages which simply couldn't sustain their families.
Even America's one remaining enclave, high-tech, was eventually penetrated. It started with the loss of computer support jobs and computer
programming and spread to pharmaceutical research and law research
and moved into electronics and computers. By the time they were done
America's wealth was siphoned off, our manufacturing was gutted, our
unions were irreparably damaged and wages for both unskilled and
high-tech jobs had been pushed to subsistence levels.

Even that wasn't enough to collapse the economy. Let's go to the year 2008. That was a tipping point for the U.S. economy. Driven by low interest rates and predatory lending practices facilitated by then President George W. Bush the U.S. was experiencing a catastrophic collapse of the housing market which weakened the dollar to such as extent that the entire world realized that America was on the brink of financial collapse. We were by then the world's number one debtor nation and we also had the dubious distinction of running the world's largest trade deficit. The handwriting was as they say was on the wall. America was in economic freefall.

Intentional Bankruptcy of America and Imposition of A Police State: All that remained was to trigger the final collapse. That distinction fell to President Barack Obama who started his Presidency as arguably the most idolized President in American history and ended it as arguably the most reviled President in American History. He forced massive budget deficits on the people and forced unpopular healthcare and energy reform down the throats of a resistant population and even more than his predecessor George Bush he systematically stripped the American people of their Civil Liberties, flagrantly ignoring the constitution as he methodically put in place the structure for our present police state. He finally collapsed the dollar by driving it into hyperinflation leading to its abandonment by other nations of the world. With its credit exhausted, its dollar ruined, its people impoverished, the U.S. finally gasped its final sigh and collapsed in economic ruin. One by one the dominos fell as nation after nation collapsed and fell to Communist rule. The once wealthiest nation in the world reduced to the status of a third world country. From there it was easy to force the nations of the world into the One World Government that rules us to this day.

Destroy A Notions Infrastructure and You Destroy Its Wealth!

Erick: All I can say is what a shame. Gramps, this may be somewhat out of the sequence of events but Dad tells me there was a time when American's infrastructure was public property, built and paid for with taxpayer money. As long as I can remember our infrastructure has been owned by international corporations. On the other hand Dad told me that the banks which are now pretty much government owned used to be privately owned. What happened and what did it mean to America?

Gramps: This is actually another component of how the U.S. was brought down. I guess I skipped over this part. Let's start with the banks. In 2008 the banking system imploded. There were those who argued that the speculative predatory lending practices of the banks had resulted in their insolvency and the banks should be declared bankrupt. The government took another position. They told us that we needed to bail the banks out in order to provide the necessary credit to keep the economy afloat. As it turned out when the government gave the money to the banks they supposedly forgot to tell them that they had to use the money to **stimulate credit,** so they paid dividends to investors, paid executives multimillion dollar bonuses and did just about everything with the money except use it to help the American people. On the other hand when the government gave the roughly $800 billion stimulus to the banks they remembered to put in the necessary clauses to **allow the government to acquire ownership interest in the banks.** Then after allowing the banks to pay out millions in bonuses to executives they claimed to be outraged and put caps on the incomes of top bank executives. What should have been done was to pass legislation to prevent usury lending rates which would have helped the American people and at the same time put an end to the predatory lending practices which got us in the mess in the first place, but that wasn't what the government wanted. What the government wanted was to use the outrage of the American people in order to be able to control salaries. Once they got control of salaries in the banking industry the precedent was set and they gradually established wage controls on most of the private sector.

By that point we were well on our way to economic slavery. We were running multi-trillion dollar per year budget deficits as the government bailed out the banks, the auto industry, AIG Insurance Company and others. What was happening was that the government was using tax payer money to buy our homes and businesses while leaving us with a staggering tax bill. By 2009 the National debt was approximately $12 trillion dollars which was roughly $185,000 for every man, woman and child in the country. We had been buried in a sea of debt and in the process the government had taken over key industries using our money. What all this meant was that taxes went up and salaries went down. The middle class that had been the backbone of America was wiped out and all that was left was the very rich and the poor.

As bad as things were they still weren't done with us. You asked about our infrastructure. Of the original $800 billion dollar bail out package only 9% or $72 Billion was allocated for infrastructure projects. This was despite the fact that most of our infrastructure was in danger-ously bad condition. The American Society of Civil Engineers gave our infrastructure a "D" rating and estimated that it would take $2.2 trillion just to bring our infrastructure to acceptable standards. To give you an idea of just how bad it was there were an estimated 160,000 structurally deficient or functionally obsolete bridges, 177 levees at risk of failure and some 4,000 unsafe dams and our interstates were woe-fully under capacity leaving our highways in gridlock and commerce at a standstill. Even worse millions of American families were at risk of becoming the next New Orleans when one of those unmaintained levies broke. – *Crumbling of America,* History Channel 6/22/09

PAY CLOSE ATTENTION! The government doesn't seem to care about our crumbling infrastructure. Why? They had other plans. <u>The government was quietly implementing executive orders and passing laws to</u> **allow private corporations to exercise emanate domain to evict Americans from their homes** <u>for projects that benefited pri-vate corporations and international investors</u>. At the same time the government was busy setting up websites telling states how to sell or lease public infrastructure projects and investment bankers were holding seminars attracting international investors eager to learn how to funnel potentially trillions of dollars into Public Private Partner-ships [PPP's] in order to acquire U.S. infrastructure projects. Our once publicly owned highways, water departments, schools, prisons, sea-ports and airports were for sale to the highest bidder. In addition to oppressive taxes we were now forced to pay international investors to use our infrastructure, not to mention the threat to national security that was posed by turning over control of our highways, water treat-ment plants, sea ports and airports to foreign entities. As bad as all this sounds there was an even more sinister reason for selling off our infrastructure. <u>If international companies owned our infrastructure,</u>

particularly our sea ports, airports and highways they could make sure they were **designed to facilitate international Free Trade,** the very free trade system which destroyed our economy in the first place, but it wasn't about protecting the U.S. economy. It was about globalization and Free Trade.

When Security is More Valuable Than Freedom — Freedom is Lost!

Erick: Gramps, given what you have told me I can see how they destroyed our economy and made us indentured servants but, how did they take away our freedom?

Gramps: In much the same way that they took away our economic freedom a little at a time till we were buried in debt. If you put a frog in hot water he will immediately jump out, but if you put the same frog in cold water and gradually turn up the heat he will stay in that pot till he dies. It is no different with people. It is called **Incrementalism** and the concept is that if you impose change on a society slowly over time allowing the people time to acclimate they will never realize what is being done to them and you can get away with almost anything.

Again our forefathers warned us but we didn't listen. James Madison the fourth U.S. President warned us that: *"If Tyranny and Oppression come to this land it will be in the guise of fighting a foreign war."* Erick, the 9/11 Terrorist Attack was a crucially important strategic event, because without such a shocking and horrifying event the American people would never have allowed the Patriot Act and other such legislation to have been passed. They would never have allowed their Constitutional Rights to be stripped away from them for any reason other than **Homeland Security.** Representatives of the government were on record saying *"it is a shame to **not** take advantage of a **crisis** when it presents itself."* And take advantage they did. They used both 9/11 and the 2008 sub-prime collapse to reshape the American political landscape. My manuscript details exactly how our civil liberties were stripped away one by one till finally our Democracy was replaced by our current tyrannical Socialist Government.

A Nation Without God Shall Succumb to its Enemies!

Gramps: Erick there is one question I am surprised you haven't ask me.

Erick: What is that Gramps?

Gramps: Why did they come against Christianity?

Erick: So why did they?

Gramps: <u>They knew that America's greatness rested on a foundation of Christian principles, so if they wanted to usurp our laws they had to first undermine our Christian foundation.</u> James Madison the father of the U.S. Constitution said: *"We have staked the whole future of American civilization, not upon the power of government, far from it. We have staked the future of all our political institutions upon the capacity of mankind for self-government; upon the capability of each and all of us to govern ourselves, to control ourselves, to sustain ourselves according to The Ten Commandments of God."* These are the words of a free people with faith and conviction, the words of a people with the will to stand for what they believe in.

As with everything else at first the changes were slow. Immorality crept into TV and the movies. They used the First Amendment to allow pornography. Abortion was legalized along with same sex marriage. They undermined our educational system stripping out the information we would need in order to be responsible citizens of a Republic. Erick, we were by the way a Republic, not a Democracy, and most people don't even know the difference and it is a very important difference. I cover this in detail in the manuscript. They took prayer out of our schools and undermined our entire moral structure. They addicted us to materialism and cheap consumer goods from china and in so doing made us self indulgent and even worse they made us party to the Chinese slave labor that was used to produce the consumer goods which we were addicted to. We should have realized that if the Globalist would use Chinese slave labor they would have no compulsion enslaving us. They didn't imprison us like the Chinese, but we are none-the-less slaves, victims of a system of Modern Slavery that enslaves us through a system of debt and taxation. A morally bankrupt society is much easier to control than a society which has a unified set of convictions which they are prepared to fight to uphold. That is why Christianity had to go. Unfortunately the American people like the ancient Jews forgot about their covenant with God. They stopped praising God for their blessings and he removed his hand of protection and you can see the outcome.

Erick I have a dream, it is that you and other young men like you will regain the moral fiber we have lost, that you will learn what it takes to be a responsible member of a Republic and that you will take back this nation and restore it to its former greatness.

If we repent and turn to God he will empower us, and through him all things are possible.

Gramps: Erick I have one last thought for you. Benjamin Franklin said: *"The Man who trades freedom for security does not deserve nor will he ever receive either."*

Corruption Must Go Before Liberty Can Be Restored!

There is an important lesson to be learned from this story, one that may yet save our great nation. America has fallen victim to *"incrementalism"* as the government slowly usurped our civil liberties and drove us into bankruptcy transforming our government from a Republic into a Socialist/Communist State.

If we hope to regain control of our Government we have to come to grips with the reality that:

- **We Cannot Blindly Follow Our Governmental Leaders:** Both political parties have proven themselves to be complicit in attempting to hijack the U.S. Constitution and the freedoms which it guarantees.

- **The Intent of Our Founding Fathers Was A Small Decentralized Government:** not a large centralized Federal Government that controls virtually everything.

- **America Was Established As A Republic Not A Democracy:** All Democracies have been short lived and inherently unstable because rather than being based on Law; <u>The Constitution</u> they are based on <u>Majority Rule</u> which invariably leads to <u>mob rule.</u> The inherent flaw of Democracy is expressed in the following quote.

"A government policy to rob Peter to pay Paul can be assured of the support of Paul." – George Bernard Shaw

This is exactly the problem Thomas Jefferson was referring to when he said: *"The Democracy will cease to exist when you take away from those who are willing to work and give to those who will not."*

Our leaders would have us believe that America is a Democracy and that is dangerous because Democracy invariably leads to Socialism and Communism, because it leads to out of control spending on Entitlement Programs funded at the expense or Peter [the most productive segment of society] to pay Paul [the least productive segment of society]. This type of governance invariably leads to unmanageable debt. This mentality explains the government's immigration policies. Obama wants to count illegal aliens in the next census because he knows they will support legislation to rob from Peter to give to Paul further driving America into bankruptcy and transitioning it into a Socialist/Communist State.

<u>As members of a Republic:</u> <u>we are expected to be an informed citizenry which forces our legislators to pass **moral laws** which protect the citizenry as a whole rather than vested interest groups who would bankrupt us by wanting something for nothing.</u> Americans have become apathetic and largely disengaged from a political system that we have increasingly lost faith in. It is time to wake up, get informed and involved and drive the future of our nation.

By the time you finish this book you will understand exactly how our political system has been derailed, how vulnerable that makes us and exactly what we have to do to save our Republic.

They always say that if you want to find the truth of a matter follow the money trail, so I want to close this chapter by doing exactly that. Once you realize who owns the majority of the U.S. Debt obligation you will begin to understand that the President of the United States is just a puppet. The Federal Government of the United States is controlled by the Chairman of the Federal Reserve who is in turn controlled by the IMF and World Bank or what I refer to as the Money Manipulators.

As we look at our debt holders I am reminded of this quote:

"The borrower is slave to the lender and the debtor to the creditor."
    – Benjamin Franklin, *The Way to Wealth*, 1785

Holders of U.S. Treasury Bills / U.S. Debt

(Ranked From Least to Most)

15. **Russia:** .... $128.1 Billion
14. **Depository Institutions (Banks)** .... 154.4 Billion
13. **Hong Kong** .... 146.2 Billion
12. **Brazil** .... 157.1 Billion
11. **Insurance Companies (i.e. AIG)** .... 162.2 Billion
10. **Caribbean Banking Concerns** .... 174.8 Billion
9. **Oil Exporting Countries (i.e. Arab Oil Cartel)** .... 187.7 Billion
8. **United Kingdom** .... 277.5 Billion
7. **Pension Funds / Private and Govt.** .... 490.2 Billion
6. **State and Local Government** .... 528.3 Billion
5. **Mutual Funds** .... 694.5 Billion
4. **Japan** .... 757.3 Billion
3. **China** .... 789.6 Billion
2. **Other Investors & Savings Bonds (General Public)** .. 1.114 Trillion
1. **Federal Reserve & Intergovernmental Holdings** ... 5.127 Trillion

So what can we conclude from these figures. Basically it is as Benjamin Franklin said *"The borrower is slave to the lender."* By looking at these figures we start to understand a lot of the government's policy decisions. Let's see: we bailed out the banks, the mutual funds, the insurance companies and the unions. Was it because they were too big to fail or was it because we owed them so much money? In terms of international affairs do you think it is possible that our policy decisions are influenced by our debt obligations to China, Russia, The United Kingdom, Brazil and the Arab Oil Producing Nations? Likewise do you think there is any chance that recent policy decisions in regard to Israel might in any way be influenced by our debt obligations, and likewise do you think our trade deficits might have anything to do with unfavorable trade agreements forced on us by our debtors? Similarly do you think that owing massive amounts of money to foreign governments who are ideologically opposed to America might in any way be a threat to National Security? As the economic crisis deepens both domestically and globally do you think it is possible that failing governments might liquidate U.S. Treasury Bills in order to pay their debts, and if that were to happen do you think it could bankrupt the U.S.? It is worth noting that every day the U.S. needs to borrow approximately 20% of the world's available currency to cover our National Debt. This brings us to the Federal Reserve. Did you know that as I write this in 2010 the international market is not buying enough T Bills to cover our debt so the Federal Reserve is buying up the shortfall with worthless money which they print with absolutely nothing tangible to give it value?

In closing it is fair to say that the banks, unions, insurance companies, and foreign countries unduly influence U.S. policy to the detriment of the general public and that our national security and our economic security are jeopardized. As important as it is for the American Public to realize the outside influences that negatively affect our government's policy decisions it is imperative that we realize that our entire political system has been hijacked by the Federal Reserve, IMF and World Bank otherwise known as The Money Manipulators or International Monetary System.

If you understand that the Fed Chairman and not the President of the United States calls the shots it becomes a lot easier to understand the policies that are coming out of the White House. As this book will prove it is the goal of the Money Manipulators to drive the U.S. into economic collapse and transition it into a Communist State where we have no inalienable rights and where the Constitution is a worthless piece of paper. We cannot allow that to happen. We must rise up in peaceful protest and launch a revolution to take back America and put it back in the hands of the people where our founders intended it to be!

God Bless America!

Chapter 3

America In History: [The Colonial Era]

The Key To Understanding Our Past and Charting Our Future!

As the chapter opens it's one week later and Erick and Gramps are continuing their discussion about how America fell to Communist oppression.

Erick: What are we going to talk about today Gramps?

Gramps: I thought we might talk about U.S. History.

Erick: History is boring! Isn't there something else we could talk about instead?

Gramps: Erick, in order to understand what happened to America you need to understand the forces that forged the nation as well as the forces that eventually lead to her downfall?

"Those who don't know history are destined to repeat it."
        –Edmund Burke Statesman and Philosopher 1729-1797

Erick: OK history it is. Where do we start?

Gramps: Erick do you remember when you were little and we played Monopoly?

Erick: Sure, but what does that have to do with history?

Gramps: More than you think. Remember the time you landed on Park Place the first time around the board? You bought Park Place and then on your very next move you landed on the Community Chest which directed you to advance to Boardwalk which you also bought. You immediately put hotels on both properties. You got out ahead of the rest of the players and eventually you ended up with most of the money and real estate and won the game by a landslide. In a matter of speaking that is what happened when the Colonial Empire was founded. France, Portugal, Spain, Holland and England were all maritime nations whose wealth came from colonizing foreign lands and exploiting cheap labor and natural resources in order to develop vast fortunes. The most successful of the colonizing nations was England. At its peak around 1922 The British Empire encompassed the globe and ruled over a population of approximately 458 million people or roughly one-quarter of the world's population [at the time] and covered an expanse of over 13 million square miles or roughly one-quarter of the earth's total land mass. They used to say the sun never sets on the British Empire. http://en.wikipedia.org/wiki/British

Naval Power:
The Key To Wealth and Empire!

PAY CLOSE ATTENTION! The key to the wealth and power of the Colonial Empire and most especially the British Empire rested in its control of the sea lanes and what it called *"Choke Points"* which are key ports and water ways which if controlled allow control of the shipping lanes which translates into control of trade and literally control of the wealth of the world! Having few natural resources of their own the British pillaged the natural resources from its colonies, while holding down wages and denying the colonies the means to develop manufacturing capability or infrastructure thus assuring their perpetual dependency on the British. In effect the Colonies were the indentured servants [slaves] of the British Empire. They existed to enrich a group of ultra rich and powerful men who saw them as nothing more than forced laborers. When it came to commerce the British had no moral conviction, for example they transported more slaves than all other European powers combined and were heavily involved in drug trafficking, trading opium for tea. They developed what became known as The British Free Trade System.

The British Free Trade System: An Empire of Oppression!

Erick: Gramps I don't see what all this has to do with America's downfall.

Gramps: Erick, stay with me a little while longer and it will make perfect sense.

PAY CLOSE ATTENTION! Understanding The Free Trade System Is The Key To Understanding Both Communism and The Fall of The U.S. Free Trade relies on *"low tariffs and cheap natural resources."* The British were able to flood world markets with *"cheap consumer goods"* manufactured by English interest, with cheap resources from their colonies. Nations which fell pray to The *Free Trade System* invariably found that in an effort to compete their wages were lowered, manufacturing declined, trade deficits occurred, and the standard of living was reduced. This is exactly what happened to the U.S. and I will shortly show you exactly how it came about, but first you need a little more background. Erick, it is important to understand that Britain was a Monarchy, which is to say it had a King, but more accurately it was an **Oligarchical form of government,** which means it exerted the rights of an elite ruling class over the working class who exist to serve them. **Though you may not realize it this is Communism in disguise.**

Erick: How so Gramps?

Gramps: Under Communism what happens is that the lower class and middle class are pitted against each other and the limited wealth of the middle class is redistributed to the lower class eventually resulting in a two class society, the poor working class and the elite ruling class. That is Communism, but it is no different from the Oligarchical System of the British Free Trade System with its Elite Ruling Class.

Erick: Gramps, what does any of this have to do with America?

Gramps: More than you can imagine. Bear with me Erick. This is the key to understanding what eventually lead America and most of the world to fall to the oppression of Communism! It's like your Monopoly game when you owned both Boardwalk and Park Place and dominated the game. The Colonial Empire and most especially the British Empire with its [Free Trade System] became the wealthiest entities on the planet. There is a saying *"money is power"* and you will soon understand just how true that statement is. The Colonial Empires were the super powers of their era but as the world transitioned from a maritime dominated world to an industrial based society the prominence of the Colonial Empires faded from the spotlight and countries like the U.S. Germany, Russia, Japan and eventually China and India emerged to take prominence on the world stage. It appeared that the Colonial Empire had simply faded away into the sunset, but it hadn't. It simply faded into the background where it continued in power just not as a recognized Sovereign Nation. The Oligarchy that comprised the Colonial Empire, that group of super rich and powerful men who comprised the Elite Ruling Class who felt it was their destiny to rule over the working class who existed to serve them continued in power. The only thing that changed was they now operated from the shadows. Erick it is worth noting that I am not speaking of the English people, or for that matter the Europeans per say. They were as oppressed by the Oligarchy as the rest of the world. After all it was that oppression that caused English and European Citizens to come to America in the first place. Again I say we are not dealing with a Sovereign Nation. **We are dealing with a shadow government, what I call the Money Manipulators.**

Erick: Gramps I am sorry but you lost me. I just don't get it.

The Rich Rule Over The Poor!

Gramps: Erick there is a saying that punctuates the situation. *"The rich rule over the poor."*

The ultra rich ruing elite of the Colonial Empire <u>never</u> lost their power or their control over world politics. They simply became the power behind the legitimate recognized governments of the world.

They financed the industrial revolution and increased their wealth even more. Through their banking interest they controlled most of the major corporations and governments of the world. They put people into power and took people out of power. They controlled the fate of Corporations, Nations and the World by pulling the strings of those who they placed in power. Their goal was nothing short of world dominance. They started wars for profit and tilted the balance of power in favor of those they wanted to win. Through their **control of** the banking industry these *"Money Manipulators"* patiently infiltrated governments and corporations around the word. They placed their people in power and incrementally, step by tiny step steered us away from a world made up of Individual Sovereign Nations toward a globally integrated economy and eventually toward their goal of a One World Government headed by them the Elite Money Manipulators of the original Colonial Oligarchy.

Erick: I guess I can see how the Money Manipulators as you call them pulled the strings from behind the scenes, but I still don't understand how they got control of the U.S. and turned it into an oppressive Communist Government.

The Real Reason America Declared Its Independence From England!

Gramps: Okay Erick, let me ask you a question. Why do you think the Colonies declared independence from England and fought the Revolutionary War?

Erick: That's easy. The colonists were upset about the issue of *"no taxation without representation."*

PAY CLOSE ATTENTION! Gramps: That is correct as far as it goes, but there was more to it. <u>The King of England was trying to force the Colonies to submit to the Central Bank of England</u>. What this meant was that the colonies would be prohibited from issuing their own currency. Their currency would be issued **at interest** by the Central Bank of England. They knew that this would drive them into debt and allow the Central Bank to control the value of their currency and manipulate economic events in order to keep them subservient to the king. This was unacceptable and was instrumental to their decision to declare their independence.

Erick, the weapon of choice to exact the fall of the U.S. was in fact <u>debt</u>. America won the Revolutionary War and became an Independent Nation and eventually became the preeminent super power of the world, but the Money Manipulators never abandoned their plan of achieving a One World Government headed by them as the Elite Ruling Class. And in order to achieve their goals the U.S. had to be collapsed economically.

It is important that we remember that our forefathers originally came to America to escape the economic and religious tyranny of the British Oligarchy. They were painfully aware of what happens when massive wealth and power are concentrated in the hands of an elite ruling class. They knew first hand what happens when a Central Bank is allowed to manipulate the currency of a nation. They knew exactly what it was like to live under a system of government which oppressed the masses and placed sanctions on freedom of speech so when they set up the government of the United States they built in safeguards to protect future generations of Americans so they would retain their freedoms and not fall prey to the old tyrannies.

In the words of Henry C. Carey, economic advisor to Abraham Lincoln: *"It [the British System] is the most gigantic system of slavery the world has yet seen, and therefore it is that freedom gradually disappears from every country over which England is enabled to obtain control."*

Gramps: Erick we have discussed the British Free Trade System, but did they ever teach you about the "American System" in school?

Erick: No. I never heard of it.

Emergence of The Progressive Movement!

Gramps: I am not surprised. We will discuss it in a minute, but first we need to discuss why you never heard of the American System. It was only the basis of Americas rise to the status of Economic Super Power and it wasn't taught in school. By the time you were in school the school curriculum was controlled by the government which also controlled the entertainment industry and the news media. It was one big propaganda machine. The Money Manipulators had infiltrated virtually every aspect of society, including both the Republican and Democratic Parties. In the name of social justice and fairness they popularized what came to be known as the *"Progressive Movement."* The Progressive Movement; doesn't that have a nice ring to it? Instead of the Progressive Movement it should have been called the *"Destructive Movement"* because it was effectively the vehicle for transitioning the country from the small government of our founding fathers, a government where most of the power was vested in state and local government into a large Federal Government which increasingly controlled every aspect of our lives. The Progressives championed massive *"Entitlement Programs"* as a means to *"redistribute the wealth"* to those they deemed less fortunate. In reality they didn't care about the less fortunate. All they cared about was driving the nation into *"unmanageable debt"* so they could transition it into a Communist Government ruled by them the Elite Ruling Class. They were using the play book of a pair of Columbia University Marxist professors Cloward and Piven who espoused a radical agenda based on intentionally overwhelming the U.S. Capitalist System and collapsing it under the burden of unmanageable debt.

It was exactly what John Adams our second U.S. President warned us about: *"There are two ways to conquer and enslave a nation. One is by the sword. The other is by debt."*

Gramps: Erick, I know I promised to tell you about the American System but before I do that I need to jump ahead to 2008. That is when the U.S. economy really got in trouble and people started to realize that the end was near. The Money Manipulators in collaboration with their banking cartel and their pawns in the U.S. Government supported Predatory Lending Practices which resulted in a massive housing bubble which drove the economic system into near collapse. Republican President George W. Bush was leaving office as arguably the most despised President in U.S. history. Then Democratic candidate Barack Obama was elected based on his promise of honesty and transparency in government and the promise that in his administration there was no place for special interest groups and lob-byist. He promised to *"Fundamentally Transform America"* and based on his campaign promises the American people naively thought that he was going to restore their confidence in the political system. Unfor-tunately the 2008 election was merely a diversionary tactic. Sentiment had turned against Bush and the Republicans so the power brokers just changed candidates and political parties and continued unim-peded with their agenda to bankrupt the economy. **What the Ameri-can people failed to understand was that both the Republican and Democratic parties were corrupted.** The Money Manipulators now operating in the open under the guise of *"Progressivism"* had infil-trated both parties and corrupted them. President Obama turned out to be even worse than President Bush. He quickly showed his true colors as he pursued a Marxist/Communist agenda of redistribution of wealth that drove the American economy into a death spiral of debt.

The following quote explains what the end game of the Progres-sives really was: *"The New World Order will be built...an end run on national sovereignty, eroding it piece by piece will accomplish much more than the old fashioned frontal assault."*

– Council on Foreign Relations Journal 1974, P558

Erick, remember the Progressives were really nothing more than the front men for the Oligarchy of the Colonial Empire which is in turn just another name for Communism. Remember under Communism what happens is that the lower class and middle class are pitted against each other and the limited wealth of the middle class is redistributed to the lower class eventually resulting in a two class society, the poor working class and the elite ruling class.

In reality Communism and the British Free Trade System are one in the same and the result is an elite ruling class that views the masses as nothing more than their slave labors!

Gramps: Erick, it's getting late so let's adjourn for tonight and tomor-row we can finally discuss The American System. As I said earlier it holds the key to what made America the greatest economic Super Power the world has ever known as well as the key to what we have to do in order to restore our economy and take back control from the Money Manipulators.

Chapter 4

The Fight For Freedom Continues: [Post Civil War ERA]

The American Economic System VS
The Free Trade System!

Gramps: Erick at last it is time to discuss The American System which means the history lesson isn't quite over, but please stay with me a little longer. It is crucial that you know about The American System. As I said before it holds the key to restoring American freedom and prosperity.

Erick: It's OK Gramps. I realize how important it is, so please go on.

Gramps: Erick this may well be the most important conversation we ever have so if there is anything you don't understand please stop me and ask me to explain. If you want to see America restored to her former greatness then you need to know what made her the World's number one Economic Super Power and what brought her down.

Erick: Gramps how will that help restore America to her former greatness?

Gramps: The politicians would have us believe that economics and politics are too complicated for us to understand. That is bunk. It is as easy as 1, 2, 3.

The Key To Restoring America To Greatness!

<u>**Step 1**</u>: Find out what our Founding Fathers put in place that resulted in America becoming the land of opportunity that the world looked to with envy.

<u>**Step 2**</u>: Find out how the Money Manipulators and their corrupt politician puppets destroyed our system of government and took away our liberty.

<u>**Step 3**</u>: Put back in place that which was proven to work.

What could be simpler? No rocket science required. No need to be an economist or an egg head. **Just take what our founding Fathers put in place that worked and restore it!** The only hard part is that it requires that the American people need the courage to face up to the truth and have the will and determination to demand that control of their government be given back. Erick, this is a serious undertaking. Those in power will not relinquish it unless forced to. It is as Patrick Henry said: *"Is life so dear, or peace so sweet, as to be purchased at the price of chains or slavery? Forbid it, Almighty God! I know not what course others may take but for me; give me liberty or give me death."*

Erick: Gramps, I want liberty more than anything and I for one am willing to do what ever it takes to restore it.

Gramps: Then let's get to it. You are going to need to know what The American System was and how it differed from its nemesis the Free Trade System. The American System was based on the principal that *"all men are created equal with the right to life, liberty and the pursuit of Happiness."* <u>It was based on the belief that the **single most important resource is human creativity** which it sought to encourage as the basis of technological advancements.</u> It was seen as using technology to elevate the standard of living for all.

As we discussed by contrast The Free Trade System depended on cheap labor and resources from its Colonies which they oppressed by denying them the ability to develop their own infrastructure and monetary system because that would have allowed them to develop economic independence. <u>Remember, the system was based on an Oligarchical form of rule which **exerted the rights of an elite ruling class over**</u>

the working class which were seen as existing to serve them. This is just another name for Communism. They had an economic strangle hold on the world which originated from their control of the sea ways and virtual monopoly on global trade. This in turn gave them enormous wealth which they used to leverage political events in America and around the world. Remember, we fought the American Revolution in the first place because the ruling Oligarchy of Europe tried to force the Colonies to submit to the **Central Bank of England.** Our founding fathers knew that would lead to economic enslavement.

Their tactics haven't changed, control the monetary system and the politicians and you can enslave the populous.

Erick: Gramps I get the theory behind The American System, but how did it actually work?

Basis of The American System: Gramps: The economic structure for the American System was established by Alexander Hamilton the Nations First Secretary of The Treasury. He set up a National Bank that issued U.S. currency and was committed to reducing usury and facilitating the growth of industry and agriculture through the provision of credit and through protective tariffs.

ACTION STEPS: When these things were eventually stripped away is when America fell, so if we want to restore America we have to: **1) Replace The Federal Reserve Banking System with a National Bank** effectively putting the issuance of currency and control of the Monetary System back in the hands of the government where our Founders intended it. **2) End Usury** which is another word for predatory lending **3) Impose Tariffs** to protect the balance of trade **4) Extend Low Credit Rates To Businesses** to facilitate economic growth and jobs and for development of **infrastructure projects** including our crumbling bridges, dams, levies etc, but most importantly we have to **rebuild our manufacturing capacity.** We will discuss exactly how to do these things a little later.

Erick: I thought America had a Central Bank, The Federal Reserve and it issued the money not the Treasury.

The Federal Reserve:
The Power Behind the Throne!

Gramps: Erick you are right, but it wasn't always that way. This is an important question so I am going to answer it in some detail then we will get back to our discussion of the American System. The Story of the Federal Reserve is what I call the Trail of Blood which is the story of the efforts of the Money Manipulators to gain control of the U.S. Banking system in order to systematically bankrupt America and take over the government. They knew if they could control the money supply it didn't really matter who made the laws. The politicians could always be bought. They tried to impose a Central Bank during Andrew Jackson's time. Matter of fact when asked what the greatest achievement of his Presidency was he said, *"I killed the Bank,"* referring to the attempt to form the central bank of the United States. He also said: *"The bold effort the present bank has made to control the present governments are but premonitions of the fate that awaits the American people should they be deluded into perpetuation of this institution, or the establishment of any other like it."*

Gramps: I might add that it just so happens that the last time the National Debt was completely paid off was in 1835 after president Andrew Jackson shut down the central bank that preceded the current Federal Reserve Bank which was established in 1913.

Why The British Assassinated Abraham Lincoln!

During the Civil War The Bank of England once again tried to usurp the right of The American Government to print its own currency, a right which Abraham Lincoln understood and was prepared to fight for. He said: *"The government should create, issue, and circulate all currency. Creating and issuing money is a supreme prerogative of government and its greatest creative opportunity Adopting these principles will save the taxpayers immense sums of interest and money will cease to be the master and become the servant of humanity."*

Faced with financing the cost of the Civil War Lincoln refused funding from the Central Bank of England because he understood full well that it would open the door to the opportunity to control and manipulate our economy. He decided instead to do what our founding fathers had, which was to create a debt free, interest free currency which he called the Greenback. Disgruntled over the creation of the Greenback, American and British Banking interest circulated an internal memo stating that:

"...Slavery is but the owning of labor and carries with it the care of labors, while the European plan...is that <u>capital shall control labor by controlling wages</u>. It will not do to allow the Greenback...as we cannot control that." – Hazard Circular, July 1862

Could they have made their intentions any clearer? In this quote you have the **definition of Modern Slavery** from which my manuscript derives its name; *"That Capital shall control labor by controlling wages"* and I might add it also *"controls the value of the money* **[Inflation/Devaluation]** *used to pay those wages."*

So as they said the Green Back could not be allowed. Something had to be done. That something came in the form of Lincoln's assassination as part of a British backed Coup attempt orchestrated to keep Lincoln from further challenging the power of the British Central Bank by implementing his plans for the industrialization of the world through The American System, which the British saw as a serious threat to The British Free Trade System. Between the Green Back and the American System Lincoln posed a world wide threat to Britain's corrupt monetary system and he had to die.

The Federal Reserve Bank and Woodrow Wilson's Betrayal of America!

Finally in Woodrow Wilson they found a President who was willing to be bought. In 1913, Woodrow Wilson [contrary to his campaign promise], but loyal to banking interest that had contributed heavily to his election campaign instituted a Central Bank under the innocent sounding name *"The Federal Reserve."* Wilson later expressed regret at having been the person who imposed the corrupt Federal Reserve

Bank on the American people. He said: *"Our great industrial nation is now controlled by its system of credit. We are no longer a government by free opinion, no longer a government by conviction and the vote of the majority, but a government by the opinion and duress of a small group of dominant men...Our great industrial nation is controlled by its system of credit. Our system of credit is privately centered. The growth of the nation, therefore, and all our activities are in the hands of a few men...Who necessarily by very reason of their own limitations chill and check and destroy genuine economic freedom. We have become one of the worst ruled, one of the most completely controlled and dominated governments in the civilized world."*

Erick: Gramps it seems like I heard somewhere that the Federal Reserve Act was actually illegal!

The Federal Reserve: An Illegal Institution!

Gramps: Erick you are right on the money. There was subterfuge from the onset. According to G. Edward Griffin author of <u>Creature from Jekyll Island</u> a Secret Meeting was held in 1910, off the coast of Georgia, on Jekyll Island owned by J.P. Morgan: The meeting resulted in *"The Central Banking Bill"* called *"The Federal Reserve Act."* <u>It was written by bankers not legislators</u> and then it was snuck through Congress over the Christmas break when most Congressmen were at home with their families. The bill was pushed through Congress by their front man Senator Nelson Aldrich who shortly after married into the Rockefeller family. <u>Even worse it was illegally passed without the required Constitutional Amendment.</u>

<u>Incidentally the public was sold a bill of goods about how *"The Federal Reserve Act"* would create economic stability, and prevent inflation and how a financial crisis like that of 1907 could never happen again.</u> But that wasn't the case at all. There was another banking crisis in 1920 in which 5,400 Non-Federal Reserve Banks closed, and then came the 1929 crash which saw 1,600 more Non-Federal Reserve Banks close, further consolidating the monopoly of the international banking cartel. Then in 2008 the residential real estate market collapsed driving the economy into near collapse. Again Presidential

tampering was uncovered when it was realized that President George W. Bush had refused request by all 50 Governors to pass legislation to curtail predatory lending practices which they believed would have averted the crisis. Then in 2009 President Obama pushed the now infamous Stimulus Bill on the American people. Like the Federal Reserve Act it was not written by members of Congress. It turned out that the Stimulus Bill had been written by the scandal ridden Acorn Community Organizing group which had been instrumental in getting Obama elected. <u>Acorn helped write the Stimulus package and in the process gave themselves a whopping $8.5 billion dollars.</u> How is that for conflict of interest? As if that wasn't bad enough the government hand picked the banks they wanted to bail out and <u>as a result of the bail out the Government got a **stakeholder position** in the largest banks in the country and effectively became partners with the Predatory Lending Money Manipulators. So much for any hope that the legislators would represent the best interest of the American people!</u> They were as they say, *"Sleeping With The Enemy!"*

<u>Erick in short indications are that, Presidents Wilson, Roosevelt, Bush and Obama were bought and paid for by the Money Manipulators</u> as were most of the Presidents from Wilson's time on. These puppet leaders took their orders not from the people who elected them, but from the Fed Chairman who in turn took his orders from the private banking cartel who controlled the [IMF] International Monetary Fund. <u>In this fashion America and the rest of the world were ruled by a Shadow Government who used Central Banks all over the world to manipulate interest rates and orchestrate boom bust cycles and with every bust cycle they bought the hard earned assets of the common man for pennies on the dollar.</u> This process went on for decades till they finally culminated in the One World Government that dominates us all. This is exactly why Lobbying and Influence Peddling are so dangerous and why they have so insidiously corrupted our political system.

ACTION STEPS: If you want to return the seat of political power to the people and restore the Republic then it will be necessary to **5) Ban Lobbyist:** to get control back from special interest groups. **6) Implement Election Reform:** which imposes **term limits and bans gerrymandering and limits contributions etc!** Nothing short of this will free the political system from control by special interest groups such as the Banks, Unions, Community Organizing Groups, Pharmaceutical Companies, Insurance Companies, Energy Companies and Munitions companies. More on this later.

Erick: Gramps I am sorry I keep getting you off track, but since we are talking about the Federal Reserve right now I wonder if you could comment on something else. I heard they caused the Great Depression. Is their any truth to that?

Charges That the Federal Reserve Intentionally Caused The Great Depression!

Gramps: What do you want to know?

Erick: According to what I learned in school the official account of the 1929 stock market crash, which lead to the Great Depression, was that it was caused by speculation by greedy investors, so in essence the American people brought the depression on themselves? Well Erick as usual they gave you a half truth! It was caused in part by speculation, but the real question is what caused the speculation and more importantly what brought the house of cards down?

What Caused The Speculation: There were a lot of marvelous new inventions like for example radio and people were excited about investing in them which is in and of itself healthy for the economy. But the Money Manipulators manipulated the situation to their advantage and in the process intentionally bankrupt the country and hijacked Wall Street. Here is what actually happened.

Between 1923 and 1929 the Fed expanded the money supply by 62%. At the same time the government [controlled by the Money Manipulators] made it possible for people to buy stocks [on margin] with as little as 10% down. Minus these two events the speculation in the stock market would not have occurred and therefore neither would the 1929 crash or the Depression which followed.

What Caused The Crash: Since the Fed were the ones who created the money and issued the credit all they had to do was dry up the credit and they could cause the crash. According to the book <u>None Dare Call</u>

It Conspiracy: in March of 1929 Paul Warburg tipped off the insiders that the crash was on. They discretely pulled their money out and a short time later massive margin calls resulted when the money supply mysteriously dried up.

How They Hijacked Wall Street: After the crash the Money Manipulators who had their money parked safely out of the country came back into the market and made a literal killing buying stocks for pennies on the dollar. They literally fleeced America!

Subsequently in 1933 Congressman Louis McFadden, Chairman of the United States House Committee on Banking and Currency made a 25 minute speech before the House of Representatives in which he introduced *"House Resolution No. 158, Articles of Impeachment"* for the Secretary of Treasury, two Assistant Secretaries of the Treasury, The Board of Governors of the Federal Reserve, and the officers and directors of the twelve regional banks.

McFadden said of the crash and depression: *"It was a carefully contrived occurrence. International bankers sought to bring about a condition of despair, so that they might emerge the rulers of us all."*

Then some time later, in the book FDR My Exploited Father-In-Law Curtis Dall said: *"It was the calculated 'shearing' of the public by the World-Money powers triggered by the planned sudden shortage of call money in the New York Market."*

And going back to an earlier era when President Andrew Jackson came into office he said of the international bankers: *"You are a den of vipers and thieves. I intend to rout you out, and by the Eternal Gods, I will rout you out."*

And he did. He got rid of the Central bank which was in place when he took office, but thanks to President Wilson we got it imposed on us again in 1913. Will we never learn?

Erick, let me get back to Congressman McFadden and his fight against the Fed. He died a short time after issuing the Articles of Impeachment. There had been an unsuccessful assassination attempt and then while at a State Dinner he became ill and later died of what was believed to be poisoning. He was a true American hero because without his heroism the American people might never have known what was done to them.

Erick I want you to get a sense of just how sinister an organization like the Federal Reserve is so if you don't mind I would like to read you some excerpts from Congressman McFadden's speech before Congress in 1934.

"Mr. Chairman, we have in this Country one of the most corrupt institutions the world has ever known. I refer to the Federal Reserve Board and the Federal Reserve Banks, here after called the Fed. The Fed has cheated the Government of these United States and the people of the United States out of enough money to pay the Nation's debt... several times over."

"This evil institution has impoverished and ruined the people of these United States, has bankrupted itself, and has practically bankrupted our Government. It has done this through the defects of the law under which it operates, through the maladministration of that law by the Fed and through the corrupt practices of the moneyed vultures who control it."

"Some people think that the Federal Reserve Banks are United States Government institutions. They are private monopolies which prey upon the people of these United States for the benefit of themselves and their foreign customers; foreign and domestic speculators and swindlers; and rich and predatory money lenders. In that dark crew of financial pirates there are those who would cut a man's throat to get a dollar out of his pocket; there are those who send money into states to buy votes to control our legislatures; there are those who maintain international propaganda for the purpose of deceiving us into granting of new concessions which will permit them to cover up their past misdeeds and set again in motion their gigantic train of crime."

"These twelve private credit monopolies were deceitfully and disloyally foisted upon this Country by the bankers who came here from Europe and repaid us our hospitality by undermining our American institutions. Those bankers took money out of this Country to finance Japan in a war against Russia. They created a reign of terror in Russia with our money in order to help that war along. They instigated the separate

peace between Germany and Russia, and thus drove a wedge between the allies in World War I. They financed Trotsky's passage from New York to Russia so that he might assist in the destruction of the Russian Empire. They fermented and instigated the Russian Revolution, and placed a large fund of American dollars at Trotsky's disposal in one of their branch banks in Sweden so that through him Russian homes might be thoroughly broken up and Russian children flung far and wide from their natural protectors. They have since begun breaking up of American homes and the dispersal of American children. "Mr. Chairman, there should be no partisanship in matters concerning banking and currency affairs in this Country, and I do not speak with any."

"In 1912 the National Monetary Association, under the chairmanship of the late Senator Nelson W. Aldrich, made a report and presented a vicious bill called the National Reserve Association bill. This bill is usually spoken of as the Aldrich bill. Senator Aldrich did not write the Aldrich bill. He was the tool, if not the accomplice, of the European bankers who for nearly twenty years had been scheming to set up a central bank in this Country and who in 1912 had spent and were continuing to spend vast sums of money to accomplish their purpose."

"We were opposed to the Aldrich plan for a central bank. The men who rule the Democratic Party then promised the people that if they were returned to power there would be no central bank established here while they held the reigns of government. Thirteen months later that promise was broken, and the Wilson administration, under the tutelage of those sinister Wall Street figures who stood behind Colonel House, established here in our free Country the worm-eaten monarchical institution of the "King's Bank" to control us from the top downward, and from the cradle to the grave.

"The Federal Reserve Bank destroyed our old and characteristic way of doing business. It discriminated against our 1-name commercial paper, the finest in the world, and it set up the antiquated 2-name paper, which is the present curse of this Country and which wrecked every country which has ever given it scope; it fastened down upon the Country the very tyranny from which the framers of the Constitution sought to save us."

"The danger that the Country was warned against came upon us and

is shown in the long train of horrors attendant upon the affairs of the traitorous and dishonest Fed. Look around you when you leave this Chamber and you will see evidences of it in all sides. This is an era of misery and for the conditions that caused that misery, the Fed is fully liable. This is an era of financed crime and in the financing of crime the Fed does not play the part of a disinterested spectator."

Gramps: Erick, less you have any doubt just how sinister the Money Manipulators are I want to read you this quote from Mayer Rothschild, founder of Rothschild Banking Dynasty: *"Give me control of a nations money supply and I care not who makes the laws."*

No wonder the bankers fought so hard to install the (privately owned) Federal Reserve Bank. They knew it was the key to our economic enslavement and political overthrow!

The Federal Reserve and John F. Kennedy's Assassination!

Gramps: Erick, there was one last assassination which was the direct result of opposition to the Federal Reserve and the Money Manipulators. Appearing before Congress President John F. Kennedy referred to the Federal Reserve as: *"This establishment that virtually controls the monetary system; That is subject to no one; That no Congressional Committee can oversee; and that not only issues the currency, but loans it to the Government at interest."*

Shortly after this address, on June 4, 1963 President John F. Kennedy signed Executive Order #11110: which started the process to strip the [Privately Owned] Federal Reserve of the power to loan money at Interest to the Federal Government of the United States of America. With the stroke of a pen President Kennedy had taken the bold move to take it upon himself, for the sake of the American People, to put the Federal Reserve out of business and return control of the Nation's Money Supply to the duly elected Government of the U.S. Unfortunately the order never went into effect because just after that like McFadden, Lincoln and McKinley before him President Kennedy was assassinated. He was my American hero. I only hope there will be such a man as John Kennedy or Martin Luther King who will rise to lead us out of bondage.

Gramps: Here is another of the things the American people must do if they want to restore America to her former greatness.

ACTION STEPS: As stated before The Federal Reserve must go and the issuance of currency must be put back in the hands of the duly elected government! This also means that **7) The Federal Income Tax Must Be Repealed and Replaced With A Flat Tax:** that the Government cannot use, as it does the *"Progressive Income Tax"* to reward supporters, punish adversaries and impoverish the working class. More on this later.

Erick: It sounds well and good to say the Fed has to go, but the question is how do you do it?

Gramps: Erick that is an excellent question and I promises we will discuss that in detail, but it is too involved to discuss right now. For right now let's get back to proving the case that the Fed must go.

Erick: OK Gramps. So what else do you want to tell me?

Gramps: I just want to make sure that I give you enough information to absolutely convince you, because to get rid of the Fed will take courage and convection. History is full of statements from men in a position to know and they always point to private banking interest as being the power behind the scenes. For example John F. Hylan, Mayor of N.Y. (1918-1925) said: *"The real menace of our republic is the invisible government which like a giant octopus sprawl its slimy length over city state and nation. Like the octopus of real life it operates under cover of a self created screen. At the head of the octopus are the Rockefeller Standard Oil interest and a small group of powerful banking houses generally referred to as international bankers. The little coterie of powerful international bankers virtually run the United States government for their own selfish purposes. They practically control both political parties."*

Erick I love it when the bad guy opens his mouth and puts his foot in it and convicts himself for you. Alan Greenspan said when appearing on PBS' *The Lehrer Report* when asked: *"What is the proper relationship between the Chairman of The Federal Reserve and the President of the United States?"*

Greenspan: *"Well first of all the Federal Reserve is an <u>independent</u> <u>agency</u> and that means basically that, uh, **there is no other agency of government which can overrule actions that we take.** As so long as that is in place there is no evidence that the administration or the Congress or anybody else is requesting that we do other than what we think is the appropriate thing than **what that relationships is, uh, don't frankly matter.** "*

So according to Greenspan the relationship between the government and the Fed doesn't matter and there is no agency of government which can overrule their actions. So the only conclusion you can make based on Greenspan's statement is that **the real power is with the Fed and The Congress and the President are just puppets.**

Even worse Ben Bernanke, the Fed Chairman during the Obama Presidency said in a speech 2002 at the University of Chicago honoring Milton Freedman's [economist] birthday said: *"You're right we did it. [Referring to the cause of the Great Depression] We're very sorry. But thanks to you we won't do it again."*

Gramps: That too was a lie because they did it to us again when they triggered the real estate collapse of 2008.

PERSONAL NOTE: I am going to break character for a second and speak to you directly. I am writing this in early 2010 and what happened in 1929 is being repeated. The only difference is that in 1929 the trigger was speculative investing in the stock market facilitated by cheap money and stocks sold on margin. This time it was cheap money coupled with predatory lending practices in the real estate market which allowed the creation of the Collateralized Debt Obligations [CDO's] which figured so prominently in the sub-prime collapse. As you will recall a CDO is a bundle of loans that are put together, rated by a rating company and then sold on the stock market to buyers all over the world. A bundle of CDO's typically contained some Conventional Loans, but it also contained a large number of high risk Sub-prime Toxic Loans. It was these CDO's which toppled the housing market.

Just look at what our government in concert with the banks is doing. First they crashed the housing market and destabilized the economy, then nationalized the losses of their friends. It is amazing how things always seem to work out in their favor and to the detriment of the public. <u>The bankers are quick to Privatize their profits, but **losses are the public's responsibility**</u> so they have to be Nationalized/Socialized i.e. there is AIG Insurance - Nationalized, Fannie & Fredie - Nationalized [along with 50% of U.S. real estate] and then there is the $700 Billion Dollar Bail Out of the banks which has now grown to at least $9 Trillion. Paulson and Bernanke are acting like receivers in a bankruptcy controlling receivership of a bankrupt country. This sounds eerily reminiscent of what former Senator James Traficant [driven out of office] said about the 1929 crash:

PAY CLOSE ATTENTION! *"...It is an established fact that the United States Federal Government has been dissolved by the Emergency Banking Act, March 9, 1933, 48 Stat. 1, Public Law 89-719; declared by President Roosevelt, being bankrupt and insolvent. H.J.R.192; 73rd Congress in session June 5,1933 ..."* All United States Offices, Officials, and Departments are now operating within a de facto status in name only under Emergency War Powers. With the Constitutional Republican form of Government now dissolved, *the receivers of the Bankruptcy have adopted a new form of government for the United States. This new form of government is known as a <u>Democracy</u>, being an established <u>Socialist Communist Order</u> under a <u>new governor for America.</u>"* – Senator James Traficant

PAY CLOSE ATTENTION! We haven't discussed the Trilateral Commission [TC] yet, but they are part of the shadow government. We will discuss them in detail later but for now suffice it to say they were founded in 1973 with the stated purpose of *"creating a new international economic order."* What is important here is that Obama is their puppet. <u>We have TC member Timothy Geitner as Secretary of the Treasury and Paul Vocker The Fed Chairman during the Carter Administration appointed to the position of</u> **Chairman of The Economic Recovery Committee.** <u>This a repeat of what Congressman McFadden exposed in 1933.</u> The Fox is in the Hen House and he is feasting on the hard earned money of the American people. We need to be vigilant and we need to get the crooks out. More on this later.

Gramps: Erick I want to get back to our conversation about the American System but there are just a couple of more things we need to cover on this subject first.

PAY CLOSE ATTENTION! Shortly after the crash Franklin D. Roosevelt [a pawn of the Money Manipulators] took the country off the gold standard which opened the flood gates for the unconstrained printing of money. This was crucially important because Roosevelt's cornerstone program THE NEW DEAL which was heralded as the way to economic recovery had to be financed through heavy borrowing and who do you suppose the Government borrowed the money from The Fed of course. So the Fed [private banking cartel] caused the Depression, then they turned around and loaned the American public money at interest driving up the National Debt and as if that wasn't bad enough they put one of their own in charge of the recovery, or should I say robbery! This was done through the National Recovery Act [NRA] banking interest headed by Hugh Johnson a member of the Council on Foreign Relations. They were given the power to regulate wages, prices, and working conditions. It was as Herbert Hoover said: in his memoirs: *"...pure fascism...merely a remaking of Mussolini's corporate state..."* The NRA was eventually ruled to be unconstitutional by the Supreme Court.

PAY CLOSE ATTENTION! Then they did the same thing to us again in 2008. As I mentioned a second ago Paul Vocker The Fed Chairman during the Carter Administration was appointed to the position of Chairman of The Economic Recovery Committee so once again the Fed crashes the economy, real estate, and banking losses are nationalized, the Fed loans the U.S. money at interest to stimulate the recovery and then puts their man in place to make sure the recovery was obstructed at every opportunity. Meanwhile the National Debt skyrockets.

NOTE: Stepping out of character again. As of 2010 everything mentioned above has happened except the regulation of wages, prices and working conditions which I fully expect to occur. Obama has already started by messing with the salaries of top banking executives which is a Trojan Horse for wage controls down the road.

The Real Cause of The Civil War and Why Lincoln Was Assassinated!

Gramps: Finally let's get back to our discussion of the American

System. Let's pick things up at the Civil War. This was the period in which the American System first emerged and the Money Manipulators of the British Oligarchy tried to kill it while still in the womb. That attempt was known as the Civil War. Erick let me ask you a question. What in your mind was the single most important cause of the Civil War [1861-1865 Civil War]?

Erick: From what I learned in school The Civil War was fought because the North wanted to abolish slavery and the economy of the South depended on it in order to operate their cotton and tobacco plantations.

Gramps: Erick your answer certainly represents general opinion and there is some truth to it, but it was actually an ideological war. The south favored the British Free Trade System while the North favored the newly emerging American System and the two sides were destined to clash on the battlefield. The following quote from Abraham Lincoln's First Inaugural Address clearly states that prior to the war Lincoln had no intention of banning slavery so it was not the cause of the Civil War: *"I have no purpose, directly or indirectly, to interfere with the institution of slavery in the States where it exists. I believe I have no lawful right to do so, and I have no inclination to do so."*

Slavery didn't become the central issue till some time after the war had started when Lincoln issued *"The Emancipation Proclamation"* which he did because the North at the time was losing the war and he felt the issue of slavery would help the cause of the North. There may have been a second reason he issued the proclamation. The British Prime Minister Lord Palmerton wanted to try to offer to mediate the conflict between the North and South. The ruse was that if the North should say no, then Britain would recognize the Confederacy. But Lincoln just may have trumped Palmerton, because he knew that public sentiment was strongly against slavery and the British people would not support an action against a government which was fighting against slavery. For this and other reasons Britain's involvement was limited to indirect actions such as financial support from sympathizers and building ships for the Confederacy, an act which they claimed had nothing to do with the war, because the ships were delivered shy of armaments which were added later. However, after the war ended at the Tribunal of Abington the British paid $5.5M to the U.S. Merchant fleet for damages caused to their fleet and cargo.

But back to our original question of what caused the Civil war? The Answer is that having the South as part of the Union was like having a British colony in our midst.

The South: Stood for free trade, without what it considered the hindrances of tariffs.

The North: Stood for protective tariffs, particularly on British goods.

The North: Held the majority in Congress so the South couldn't easily change those policies.

The North: Primarily exported industry.

The South: Primarily exported cotton and tobacco, primarily to Britain.

If the South were free from the North they could buy cheap goods from Britain with no tariffs.

The Civil War Was About: The American System of high tariffs and protectionism of the Northern industrialized states VS The British Free Trade System of no tariffs, cheap goods of the South. Is it any wonder the British supported the South and considered The American System to be a mortal threat to their Empire? A True History of the U.S. http://www.youtube.com/watch?v=RgcdRCWEt4Q&feature=channel

Gramps: Erick let's fast forward to 1883 and Lincoln's assassination. It is extremely important that you see this historical event for what it really was a coup attempt. I think there is scarcely an American who does not know that actor John Wilkes Booth shot Abraham Lincoln while he was attending a performance of Our American Cousin at the Ford's Theater. Most know Booth was a British sympathizer. Some know that the Federal Government convicted eight individuals and hung four on charges of conspiring with British agents. The most important fact about the assassination ironically is much less known, which is that it was in fact a **coup attempt.** The plan was that Booth would kill Lincoln, Lewis Powell would kill Secretary of State William H. Seward, and George Atzerodt would kill Vice President

Andrew Johnson, and in the resulting chaos they planed to overthrow the Federal Government of the U.S. The plot failed when Seward though wounded survived and Johnson's would be assassin got cold feet and fled Washington D.C.
http://en.wikipedia.org/wiki/Abraham_Lincoln_assassination

What I want to leave you with here is the realization that the British Empire [the Moneyed Elite I call the Money Manipulators] are the mortal enemy of free people all over the world. During this period their objective was to overthrow America and impose The British Free Trade System.

They finally gave up on overthrowing America because we were by now too powerful, but as we shall later see they never gave up their goal of World Dominance. They just changed their strategy to one they had a better chance of winning. They disappeared into the shadows where to this day they control world affairs through their pawns.

The United States Centennial Celebration:
Showcase for the American System of Economics!

In the time immediately following the Civil War, **The American System of Economics** was emerging as the great hope for the world. Henry C. Carey, economics adviser to Abraham Lincoln put it this way: *"Two systems are before the world.... One is the English system; the other we may be proud to call the American system ... the only one ever devised the tendency of which was that of **elevating while equalizing the condition of man** throughout the world...."*

Let's go to 1869 when the transcontinental railroad was completed! At that moment America become the first nation in the history of the world to be able to fully exploit its economic potential by connecting the country from North to South, from East to West, from border to border, from coast to coast. The moment the last spike was driven signaling the completion of the railroad, the U.S. became the greatest threat The British Free Trade System would ever experience. Having developed a domestic policy of tariff protection and being able to transport goods from coast to coast America was literally free from exploitation by the British Free Trade System, which depended on control of the sea ways, and was poised to experience the greatest economic growth in the history of the world. The American System was launched and it would soon be embraced by a world eager to escape the slavery of the British.

PAY CLOSE ATTENTION! Fast forward to 1876: The Civil War is over and Henry C. Carry has organized *"The United States Centennial Celebration,"* and the world is invited to witness the technological marvels of human ingenuity and see how America the youngest nation in the world had become the most prosperous. Nine million visitors attend including official foreign delegations of scientist, engineers, industrialist, and economists. They saw a potential for the uplifting of the human condition such as had never been seen before and it was all attributable to The American System of Economics which prized human creativity as the key to material wealth, as opposed to control of natural resources, and imposed high tariffs as a form of protectionism necessary to allow economic development to flourish in opposition to The British Free Trade System.

Erick: Gramps you have mentioned the need for high tariffs several times now. Why is that so important?

Gramps: The key to allowing a nation to withstand the cheap goods of the Free Trade System was to *"impose high tariffs as a form of domestic protection"* which protects wages while allowing for the development of manufacturing capability and long term infrastructure projects all of which lead to economic stability and a higher standard of living. McKinley put it this way:

"We ... are opposed to British political economy.... Free trade shaves down (the workingman's labor first, and then scales down his pay by rewarding him in a worthless and depreciated State currency."
   – Oct. 4, 1892, William McKinley Governor of New York Later to
        become 25th President of the United States (1897-1901)

America's Policy of Intentionally Losing Trade!

Gramps: Erick, pay close attention.

This Should Be A Wow Moment!

PAY CLOSE ATTENTION! Based on what I just told you if any nation in the world understood the importance of having tariffs to protect the balance of trade it was the U.S. yet prior to Americas economic collapse, of 138 major manufacturing nations the U.S. was the only nation that didn't have a "Value-Added Tax" [VAT] in order to protect its manufacturing base and maintain a favorable balance of trade. **Simply put America was sold out by our politicians. This is why we must reinstate the high tariffs of the American System.** Erick, think about it. From roughly the 1970s through the turn of the century America was systematically stripped of its manufacturing base! China was allowed free access to American markets [No Tariffs] and the open borders policy with Mexico slashed shipping cost to the bare bones. The net result was that an intentionally losing trade policy was imposed on the American people by its own government who were acting on behalf of the Money Manipulators using China as their distribution arm. This was done largely through unfair trade agreements like NAFTA. As a result the U.S. incurred massive trade deficits, wages dropped, the currency was devalued and the economy eventually collapsed. More on this later. In order to restore the Republic these events must be reversed.

ACTION STEPS: **8) Reinstate The American System of Economics:** and you can restore self determination and prosperity not just to America but to the world! Remember "The American System of Economics" was the only one ever devised *"the tendency of which was that of elevating while equalizing the condition of man throughout the world."* Most of the wars of the 20th century have been caused by Communism/Free Trade. It pits the lower class and middle class against one another and takes the limited wealth of the middle class and redistributes it to the lower class eventually resulting in a two class system, the Poor Working Class who is dominated by the Elite Moneyed Ruling Class. World peace will only be possible when: the nations of the world join together to equalize and elevate all of mankind, not just a select few. The key to this seemingly impossible goal is to: **9) Establish An International Develop Fund:** to develop global infrastructure projects as the basis of true wealth. This requires international cooperation, low interest rates specifically for long term infrastructure projects, and high tariffs to protect domestic markets. More on how this can be achieved later.

Gramps: Erick if that answers your question let's get back to our discussion of The American System.

Erick: That's fine.

The American System Was Adopted By Countries All Over The World!

Gramps: Seeing America's success the world realized that they could emulate The American System, escape from the oppression of the British Free Trade System and transform their national economies. With that realization American technology was exported all over the world and the world held the promise of a better tomorrow.

In Russia: The Russian Transportation minister imposed a system of high tariffs, and worked with American engineers to construct a Trans Siberian Rail System modeled after the American Transcontinental rail system. By 1890 there were plans for a Bearing Straight bridge to connect by rail to America.

In France: Tariffs were also imposed and plans were made for development of the Nile River area, and perhaps most important was a plan to connect to the Russian Trans-Siberian project.

In Germany: German Chancellor Otto Von Bismarck wholeheartedly embraced The American System and transformed Germany into Europe's leading industrial power. He also began plans to connect to the Russian Trans-Siberian rail System and to develop a rail line from Berlin to Baghdad.

The American System Held Promise of: International Cooperation, Peace and Prosperity!

Clearly the world was changing. Instead of fighting over natural resources nations were cooperating in developing rail systems to connect the four corners of the earth. The world saw the promise of the American System to *"elevate while equalizing the condition of man throughout the world."* The future held the promise of an era of prosperity and peace as nations joined together in mutual cooperation and mutual benefit. Once completed the network of rail systems promised a cheap efficient way to transport goods around the world and would significantly diminish the world's dependency on maritime shipping.

World War I Was Perpetrated To: End The American System and Destroy The Nations That Adopted It!

While the rest of the world rejoiced at the prospects for the future the powers behind the British Empire [The Money Manipulators] laid plans to make absolutely certain that no such future would ever be realized. There was only one hope for the Money Manipulators. It was risky, but they were desperate. They would orchestrate a World War. In this game of international chess Prince Albert Edward, nephew of Queen Victoria of England was the chief strategist. *If the wealth and power of The British Empire was to be maintained all the nations that had adopted The American System had to be destroyed and plans for an interconnecting multinational rail system connecting the four corners of the globe had to be sabotaged.* Over a period of 24 years he would manipulate circumstances slowly but steadily toward the check mate that would be known as World War I. The over all game plan was to maneuver political events in such a fashion as to create an alliance between Russia, France and Britain against Germany. Edwards objective was not that there would be a victor in the War, but rather that all of Europe would be destroyed, effectively putting an end to the American System while in particular destroying the manufacturing might of Germany and the threat of the Russian Trans-Siberian Rail System. In effect the only winner in the war would be Britain who would use its enemies to destroy each other while ironically placing them once again under the oppressive grip of the British Free Trade system. Equally ironic was the fact that by entering the war on the side of the British, America actually helped to bring an end to The American System and with it the dream of a better world! Erick if you want to know the details leading to World War I go to: http://www.youtube.com/watch?v=RgcdRCWEt4Q&feature=channel

McKinley Was Assassinated and Replaced By Roosevelt:

In Order to Destroy The American System Here in The U.S.!

Gramps: Erick though I am not going to go into the details leading to the outbreak of World War I in 1914, I do want you to know what was happening in America in the time leading up to the war. With that in mind let's jump forward to 1901 and the assassination of President William McKinley. It is September 6, 1901 at the Pan-American Exposition and Leon Czolgosz an anarchist shot President McKinley who died of his wounds six days later. With McKinley's assassination, [other than for Abraham Lincoln] died this nation's staunchest supporter of the American System, both of which were assassinated. McKinley supported high tariffs and wanted to unite North and South America by constructing a rail road through Mexico and South America. Had this project been completed along with Russia's plans to build a bridge across the Bearing Strait it would have been possible, by the 20th century, to travel by rail through Europe to the U.S. and all the way to the tip of South America. This would have effectively broken Britain's strangle hold on trade as her control of the sea ways would have been of limited strategic importance. On September 5, 1901 McKinley made a speech at the Pan-American Conference in Buffalo to 50,000 North and South Americans espousing the virtues of the American Plan. The next day he was assassinated. Erick let me read you a quote from that speech:

"Thirty years of protection have brought us to the first rank in agriculture, mining and manufacturing development. We lead all nations in these three great departments of industry. We have outstripped even the United Kingdom which had century's head start on us ... Tried by any test, measured by any standard we lead all the rest of the world. Protection has vindicated itself."
 – President William McKinley, 25th U.S. President 1897-1901

Gramps: Prior to McKinley's assassination the British already had their hand pick replacement poised to take his place and change the course of history. In 1899 then Vice President Garret Hobart died in office and Theodore Roosevelt was forced on McKinley as his VP for the next election. Roosevelt was as far as you could get from being a Lincoln Republican and McKinley knew it. He would never have chosen Roosevelt if presented with any other choice. For example McKinley was for high tariffs while Roosevelt favored lower tariffs. <u>When Roosevelt became president, upon McKinley's assassination, he shot down McKinley's Pan-American railway system and instead pursued the development of the Panama Canal.</u> According to John Perking author of the best selling book <u>Confessions of an Economic Hit Man</u> Roosevelt attempted to negotiate for rights to the canal from the Colombian Government and when they refused he [illegally without approval of the Congress] sent the U.S. Battleship Nashville and a contingent of Marines into Columbia seized the canal and declared Panama an Independent Nation.

Roosevelt had close ties to England. In 1886 he visited England to be tutored on naval war strategy by his exiled uncle James Dunwoody who had been the head of the Confederate Secret Service during the Civil War and had been responsible for securing the Confederate Navy from the British. Roosevelt was also an admirer of Alfred Thayer Mahan a friend of Prince Edward and author of <u>The Influence of Sea Power on History</u> which effectively endorsed the British Empire's Free Trade System. According to the documentary 1932, A True History of the U.S. **Had McKinley not been assassinated America would have very likely united the world under the rallying point of the American System.**

WWI Resulted In Destruction of All of Europe:

Ended The American System and Sowed The Seeds For WWII!

Gramps: Erick let's get back to events leading up to World War I. On June 14, 1914 the heir to the Austro-Hungarian throne Arch Duke Ferdinand was assassinated and as history records thus started World War I, but as we discussed the groundwork for the war had been in the making for over twenty years, ever since plans were announced in 1890 to build a Trans-Siberian Rail System. Erick I want you to stop for a second and ask yourself a question. <u>If the British Empire [The Money Manipulators of Old] would start WWI, a war that killed nearly 15 million people, in order to protect their banking dynasty what do you think they would be willing to do in the 21st Century to realize their dreams of achieving a One World Government?</u> Remember Pearl Harbor was a False Flag event given that the military had cracked the Japanese code and knew in advance about plans to attack Pearl Harbor. So if they would start two world wars what wouldn't they do? Wars are profitable and they further political agendas. With this in mind let's jump to the end of WWI and see how events favored the British agenda. Remember the British goal was to put an end to the spread of The American System in Europe, so all the countries which embraced the American System had to be destroyed, but most particularly Germany, because she had been most successful in modernizing, and she, other than the U.S. represented the biggest threat to the British Empire. So the question is: Did WWI accomplish the British objective? Absolutely! As they say *"The Proof is in the pounding"* so let's look at the outcome of the war and see to what extent Britain's goals were achieved.

The 1919 Peace Conference in Paris excluded Germany from negotiations:

<u>Highlights of the Peace Accord</u>: The controversial War Guilt Clause forced Germany to accept full responsibility for causing the war and forced them to pay a staggering $132 billion gold Marks in retribution. All of Germany's army and navy were dismantled. All the locomotive and train cars were removed from the country. The merchant marine ships were stripped away. Key border areas such as The Alsace Loraine Region, with its canals, iron and coal went to France and Poland got upper Silesia with its industry and transport system. http://en.wikipedia.org/wiki/Treaty_of_Versailles

The outcome of such a harsh treaty left Germany crushed. With high reparations to pay and much of its manufacturing and transportation stripped away the outcome was that by 1921 the country was experiencing run away inflation. Given Germany's economic situation Russia agreed per the Rapallo Treaty to forgive the portion of the war reparations owed them. This was not to be tolerated. Two months after the signing of the Rapallo Treaty the Russian Foreign Minister Walter Rathenau was assassinated. Coincidence? I think not? Germany was to be crushed pure and simple. By 1923 Germany, facing hyperinflation and unable to pay war reparations was invaded by allied forces which occupied the Rhineland the country's key industrial region. The result was that by 1923 Germany was crushed economically, its people in poverty and despair and the seeds of WW II were planted.

Erick: Did the Money Manipulators start WWII as well?

Gramps: In a matter of speaking, but it is too involved to get into right now. Let's just say they underestimated Hitler's ambition. For purpose of our discussion about the American System what is more important is the outcome of World War II and how it determined the political landscape for the second half of the twentieth century. Erick at the end of WWII FDR was still President of the U.S. and Winston Churchill was Prime Minister of England though Roosevelt died in office and was replaced by his Vice President Harry S. Truman.

WWII Peace Talks Failed To End Free Trade!

Erick: I thought Henry Wallace was V.P. under FDR.

Gramps: He was up till the 1944 election. As the war drew to an end Roosevelt's health was failing. It looked to the world like Roosevelt had hand picked Henry Wallace to succeed him as the next President of the U.S. but then in a surprise move Roosevelt dumped Wallace as his running mate in the 1944 election and replaced him with Harry S. Truman.

When something like this happens you have to stop and ask why? So Erick here is my unofficial interpretation of the history surrounding these events. This is an example of where you have to be very careful about believing what a man says and the official accounts of history. As the Bible says you judge a man by the fruit that he bears. So let's take a quick look at the public image of FDR versus what I believe was the truth about him and then we will be able to understand why Wallace was dumped and Truman was brought in. FDR was billed as *"a man of the little people,"* but in reality he had been hand picked by Wall Street interest. Remember he assumed office in March 4, 1933 during the depths of the Great Depression and his first official act as president was to declare a bank holiday. The Money Manipulators had worked hard to bring about the Great Depression and they certainly would not have allowed just anyone to manage their man made crisis. Remember what Congressman McFadden said of the crash and depression:

"It was a carefully contrived occurrence. International bankers sought to bring about a condition of despair, so that they might emerge the <u>rulers of us all.</u>"

Roosevelt was by no means *"a man of the little people."* The truth was that Roosevelt's family had been involved in New York banking since the eighteenth century. FDR's uncle Fredric Roosevelt served on the board of the original Federal Reserve. FDR attended Groton and Harvard, and worked on Wall Street in the 1920's where he set on the board of directors of eleven different corporations. He also took America off the gold standard allowing the Fed to expand the money supply as they wished and drive both inflation and devaluation of the dollar. And don't forget, his signature legislation, The New Deal, was funded by massive borrowing from his friends at the Fed.

FDR's son-in-law Curtis Dall recounted in his book: <u>My Exploited Father-in-law:</u> *"...Most of his thoughts, his political 'ammunition,'... were carefully manufactured for him in advance by the [Council on Foreign Relations] CFR-One World Money group. Brilliantly...he exploded that prepared 'ammunition' in the middle of an unsuspecting target, the American people—and thus paid off and retained his international political support."*

During FDR's time in office he served his CFR handlers interest with impunity. CFR members were appointed to key positions of influence including Treasury Secretary Morgenthau, Secretary of State Edward Stettinus, War Secretary Henry Stinson and Assistant Secretary of State Summer Welles. And since then the CFR has held key positions of power in every administration. For example, most United States Secretaries of State, all Secretaries of War or Defense, from Henry L. Stimson to Richard Cheney have been CFR members. Another key position controlled by the CFR has been the Central Intelligence Agency [CIA]. The CFR's control of the CIA started with Allen Dulles a founding member of the CFR and brother of Secretary of State [under President Eisenhower] John Foster Dulles. John Foster Dulles was also a founding member of the CFR and coincidently he was an in-law of the Rockefellers, Chairman of the Board of the Rockefeller Foundation, and Board Chairman of the Carnegie Endowment for International Peace. Erick, we will discuss the CFR in detail at a later time but between now and then I want you to ask yourself this question? If you wanted to control a government, its economy and issues of war and peace wouldn't it be helpful to have men in the types of key positions we have been discussing?

So getting back to the question of why Wallace was dumped and Truman was brought in. I believe that toward the end of the war FDR like Wilson who preceded him came to regret having sold out the American people to the interest of the Money Manipulators and would have liked to have seen WWII mark the end of The British Empire's Free Trade System. I believe Wallace was committed to that objective and for that reason he could not be allowed to become president.

Erick let me read you an excerpt from a speech by Wallace, May 8, 1942. It will give you an idea of what I am referring to.

"If we really believe we are fighting for a people's peace the rest becomes easy... This is a fight between a slave world and a free world. Just like the U.S. in 1862 could not remain ½ slave and ½ free, so in 1942 the world must make its decision for a complete victory one way or the other. We in the U.S. may think there is nothing very revolutionary about freedom of religion, freedom of expression, freedom from the fear of secret police, but when we begin to think about the significance of the freedom from want for the average man then we know that the

revolution of the last 150 years has not been completed, either here in the U.S. or any other nation in the world. We know that this revolution cannot stop till freedom from want has been attained."

The bottom line is, if Wallace really believed what he said he was dangerous to the Money Manipulators and he had to go and go he did. With Roosevelt's health failing party leaders pressured him into replacing Wallace as his running mate in the 1944 election with a man they knew they could control, Harry S. Truman. The rest is history. Truman submitted to Churchill's post war plans, resulting in the cold war and continuation of The British Colonial Empire. Once again the British by replacing Wallace with Truman had manipulated U.S. politics to their advantage. We were left with a cold war between the U.S. and Russia and the spread of Communism around the globe.

Erick as the war drew to a close Roosevelt had several meetings with Churchill during which they discussed their visions of a post war world. Erick I am going to get a cup of coffee and while I am gone I would like you to read these transcripts made by FDR's son Elliot of conversations between Roosevelt and Churchill. I think they reflect FDR's change of heart, but more importantly they tipped Roosevelt's hand to Churchill who then had time to see to it that Truman was brought in to replace Wallace and make sure British interest were protected.

Erick: OK Gramps.

Franklin talking to his son Elliot: *"When we have won the war I will work with all my might to see to it that the United States is not weaseled into the position of accepting any plan that will further France's Imperialistic ambitions or that will aid or abet the British Empire in its Imperial ambitions. Winston has got to listen to me this time."*

Franklin talking to Churchill: *"Those Empire trade agreements are a case in point. It is because of them that the people in India and Africa and all the colonial Near East and Far East are still as backward as they are."*

Churchill talking to Roosevelt: *"Mr. President England does not propose for a moment to lose its favored position amongst the British Dominions. The Trade that has made England great shall continue under conditions prescribed by England's ministers."*

Roosevelt talking to Churchill: *"Alexander Hamilton's reports prove that our American System strengthens the economy through developing the population. This is what has always worked and will work. It's principled."*

Roosevelt talking to Churchill: *"I am firmly under the belief that if we are to develop a stable peace it must entail the development of backward countries, backward peoples."* Roosevelt goes on to describe how England's policies rather than enriching other nations impoverish them. *"...your ministers recommend a policy which returns nothing to the people of that country in consideration. 20th century methods involve bringing industry to those colonies. 20th century methods include increasing the wealth of the people by increasing the standard of their living, by education, by bringing sanitation, and by making sure they get a return for the raw wealth of their community. Take India Winston. I can't believe we can fight a war against fascist slavery and at the same time not work to free people all over the world from a backward colonial policy."*

Churchill talking to Roosevelt: *"There can be no tampering with the Empire's economic arrangements. ...they are the foundation of our greatness. Mr. President I believe you are trying to do away with the British Empire. Every idea you entertain demonstrate it. But in spite of that we know that you constitute our only hope and you know that we know it. You know that we know that without America the Empire won't stand."*

Roosevelt talking to his son after Churchill had left: *"...we have a chance to use our influence in favor of a more united cooperating world. This nation has a rendezvous with history."*

Gramps: Based on their conversatons Churchill realized that Roosevelt hoped that the big four [the U.S., Britain, The Soviet Union and China] would under the principals of the Atlantic Charter form the United Nations which would take the responsibility to banish Colonialism/The Free Trade System world wide and bring the power of technological development to nations across the globe. That obviously isn't what happened.

For all practical purposes it appeared that the British Empire was done for. That is because we think in terms of Sovereign Governments not Shadow

Governments. The British Empire/Money Manipulators simply went underground. Europe was devastated and the United Nations founded The International Bank for Reconstruction and Development (IBRD), with headquarters in Washington, D.C., also called the *World Bank*.

Erick: Why is this significant?

World Bank Helped Continue Free Trade By: *Intentionally Bankrupting Resource Rich Nations and Taking Their Resources!*

Gramps: Erick, this is important because it provides a crucial piece of the Global Empire Jigsaw Puzzle. The World Bank is to the World what the Federal Reserve is to the U.S. which is the vehicle by which to transfer wealth from a sovereign nation(s) into the hands of the elect few known as The Money Manipulators. The World Bank was ostensibly established to help Europe rebuild from the devastation of WWII, which it did. But you need to see it for what it really was and how it fit into the *long term agenda of Globalization.* Post WWII, India the crown jewel of the British Empire, and most of the rest of the Colonial Colonies gained their freedom which meant the Money Manipulators needed to find new sources for cheap labor and resources. This is where the World Bank came in. They would loan exorbitant sums of money to resource rich developing nations ostensibly to develop infrastructure, but the intent was to get them to default on the loans and get control of their natural resources.

Erick: What you are telling me doesn't make sense. On the one hand you told me that Britain emerged from World War II a shadow of her former self, too weak to retain control of her Colonial Empire with India and other Colonies eventually declaring Independence. Then on the other hand you are telling me that Britain seized the natural resources of the world and controlled the world's economy by rationing those resources and controlling the monetary system of the world and relentlessly moving the entire world toward the global economy that eventually destroyed the National Sovereignty of the U.S., Europe and nations all over the world resulting in the Global One

World government which currently oppresses us. How can it be both? It seems to me it has to be one or the other.

Gramps: No, Erick it was both. The reason you are having difficulty coming to grips with this dichotomy is that you are looking at things from the conventional world view of Sovereign Nation States with dually elected heads of state. That isn't how it worked. First of all I may have confused you with all the names I have been bantering around. So let me clarify. What I started out calling the British Empire goes by many names depending who you are talking to and what era of history you are referring to. All of the following names are in fact interchangeable and refer to the original British Empire or facets of it: Let's start with my favorite The Money Manipulators. Then there is The Colonial Empire, The Free Trade System, Imperialism, The Liberal Movement, The Progressive Movement, The Trilateral Commission, The Council on Foreign Relations, The Bilderberg Group, The Federal Reserve, The World Bank and the International Monetary Fund [IMF].

PAY CLOSE ATTENTION! From the viewpoint of governance it is important to remember that The British Empire originated as a Monarchy with an Oligarchial Elite Ruling Class which enslaved the working class surfs. It was a two class society, the ultra rich and the poor which is just another name for Communism. Its goal was always to establish a One World Communist Government ruled by them the Moneyed Elite. Though their ends may be furthered by war the preferred model for transition was to conquer nations from within by; placing their operatives in key positions and then patiently begin the long process of incrementally, step by step dismantling their monetary system, their corporate structure, their institutions and their political system, till they simply collapsed from within. That is exactly how they toppled America, from within!

Erick, the key to the power of the British Empire is the wealth it amassed during the height of its Colonial Empire when she ruled over 1/3 of the world's land mass and population. It is just like when you won the Monopoly game because you owned most of the real estate which eventually meant you had all the money and it is like what Henry Kissinger said: *"Who controls money controls the world."*

PAY CLOSE ATTENTION! Erick, follow the money. That is what is important. That is how they get their claws into the under belly of a nation and eventually devour it from within. For example it was the immense wealth of the British Empire which funded the Industrial Revolution and gave them the foothold they needed in order to eventually devour America from within. <u>J.P. Morgan was the front man in the U.S. for the British Central Bank now referred to as The World Bank.</u> Just imagine how much money they had to wield after centuries of plundering the wealth of the world. By the 1920s The House of Morgan had a hand that reached into literally thousands of companies. He controlled Wall Street and Presidents and wielded his power with ruthless disregard. Once they had a foothold it was just a matter of time till they could find a man who was greedy enough to sell out his country in exchange for the power of the Presidency. As I said earlier they found such a man in Woodrow Wilson who in exchange for backing in his election bid agreed in 1913 to institute the corrupt Federal Reserve which is just another name for the Central Bank of England. <u>From that point forward Both houses of Congress and the President were irrelevant controlled by a shadow government who put whom they want into the White House as their puppet leaders.</u> It didn't matter if he was a Republican or Democrat. One would suit their purpose as well as the other, as long as they could control him, obstruct him or if necessary kill him. The object was to wield power effectively by any means, using anyone who suited their purpose at the moment. The American people simply didn't get it. If their leaders seemed to be making decisions that weren't in the best interest of the country they didn't stop and ask why, they just voted that person or party out of office without realizing that both parties were contaminated, that the entire system had been corrupted and as long as the Moneyed Elite were in control it didn't matter who they voted into office. It was the culmination of the European Plan of Empire where the slave masters have freed themselves from the burden of caring for labors because wages control the labors.

PAY CLOSE ATTENTION! The moment the Federal Reserve was instituted the Revolutionary War, long thought to be over actually ended and contrary to the annals of history the victor was the British Empire who at long last gained control of the U.S. Monetary System. All that remained was to assimilate America into the British Empire and then use America's immense wealth and military dominance to continue its Imperial ambitions of world domination.

Gramps: Erick, did I answer your question?

Erick: Totally! I finally get it and I can see why people were not able to figure it out till it was too late. The only thing now is I don't see how we can ever take the country back from such a powerful adversary!

Gramps: Erick, it's premature to have that conversation now, but as we discuss the manuscript, where appropriate I will continue to tell you what people need to do and then when we are completely done we can put together a strategic battle plan. Erick I promise you this! The last thing I would ever want to do is give you false hope. I love you too much to do that to you. There are two things I want you to put in your spirit. The first is that little David the Shepard boy slue Goliath the mighty giant and this story is no different.

VITALLY IMPORTANT: Secondly I want you to read the Bible I gave you and when you do you will find out that God cannot lie. The ending of our story has already been written and I promise you the bad guys don't win. The captives are set free but there is a condition to our freedom. **We have to surrender to God and repent for our greed.** America and most of the world turned their backs on God and worshiped mammon (material possessions) and in so doing we were willing to see our fellow man put into bandage as long as we could live the good life. No more will that be tolerated! None of what we have gone through has been by accident. It has been purposed to soften our hearts and develop compassion and love for our fellow man. No longer will it be tolerated that one group oppresses another. All this is meant to refine us, to purify us and to bring us to the point where we finally realize that the key to our victory lies within each of us and in the principled, ethical plan of The American System to equalize while elevating all of mankind. Just think about it; the darkness always gives way to the light. When men, all men treat each other with brotherly love and when we all look to God for guidance then the wars propagated by man's greed will end and we will all learn to live together in peace. I know that sounds idealistic, but it isn't. It is factual. **God will not release us from our bondage till we learn to walk in brotherly love and that is a promise too.**

The Enemies Fatal Error: Erick, I also want you to read the story of Gideon. God used him in order to demonstrate that through him all things are possible, but in the process God wanted to make sure that the odds against Gideon and his men were so great that there was no way that they could claim that the victory was by their might. In the end God confused the enemy and they turned on themselves and literally destroyed themselves. I tell you this story because there is a fatal error in the plan of the Money Manipulators and in the end that error will cause them to turn on themselves and literally defeat themselves. <u>You see from the very beginning they have lied to their followers.</u> Here in America they pitted the lower class against the middle class with the promises that the state would take money from the greedy middle class and give it to the lower class who viewed themselves as oppressed, which they were, just not by the middle class. They were oppressed by the elite ruling class who actually hoarded all the money and oppressed both the lower class and the middle class. When people realize the truth they will join together and rise up against the true oppressors the Money Manipulators.

The Enemies Fatal Error: <u>The fatal error in their strategy is that they think that they have freed themselves from the burden of caring for the labors because wages control the labors.</u> Well things have gotten so bad that, that illusion is no longer saleable. The people finally realize that they have been oppressed and their freedom was never anything but an illusion. Here is where the story takes a twist and like in the story of Gideon God steps in and confuses the enemy. The slave masters never stopped to contemplate what happens when the slaves stand up and refuse to work for them. When that happens then the slave masters will understand that without the slaves they are nothing because a parasite cannot live if they don't have a host to feed on.

God's Promise: Having said what I have I would hasten to add that you also need a practical battle plan, but at the same time I want to assure you that this is not a battle you can win by yourself. If humanity does not submit and learn to live together, God will absolutely not come to our aid and we cannot defeat the forces of evil without his help. We will have to have the courage to stand up and fight and we will need leaders, but God will provide them when they are needed. He will keep them hidden and safe till it is time for the battle to begin then he will reveal them. I don't claim to be such a leader, but God has given me insight and made me a strategist. By the time we finish our discussions I promise that you will have a basic outline for the battle. It can be refined and as the battle progresses and the leaders step forward. I know the author of the story and I know the end, and in the end when we have submitted and learned what we are supposed to learn like the Israelites and the Exodus we will be set free. That is a promise!

Gramps: Less we end our discussion without me getting my point across there is a crucially important lesson in this story.

ACTION STEPS: No longer will it be tolerated that one group oppresses another. Our oppression is meant to refine us, to purify us and to bring us to the point where we finally realize that we must: **10) Surrender To God And Repent For Our Greed:** because God will not release us from our bondage till we learn to walk in brotherly love. It will take courage to stand up and fight and we will have to be willing to go through hardship and stay the course, but if we do he will send us leaders and we will be victorious. From a practical view point the key to victory is to once again implement the principled, ethical plan of The American System to equalize while elevating all of mankind. No system of government works where people expect hand outs. With this in mind **11) We Must Reform The Welfare System:** so people are given dignity. Only the indigent will be given aid without working. All others will be given training so they can be productive members of society and then if they still can't make it they will be given assistance, but they will be expected to work if at all able. It never works to give anyone something for nothing. More on this later.

Excerpt from The Declaration of Independence!

"We hold these truths to be self-evident, that all men are created equal, that they are endowed by their Creator with certain unalienable rights, that among these are life, liberty and the pursuit of happiness. That to secure these rights, governments are instituted among men, deriving their just powers from the consent of the governed. That whenever any form of government becomes destructive to these ends, it is the right of the people to alter or to abolish it, and to institute new government,

laying its foundation on such principles and organizing its powers in such form, as to them shall seem most likely to effect their safety and happiness. "

Erick, this is a good place to stop and tomorrow we can discuss the role of the World Bank in continuing the Free Trade System of Slavery and Imperial Empire.

Chapter 5

The Shadow Government Emerges: [The Carter Era]

Secret Agenda of the Bilderberg Group, Council on Foreign Relations and Trilateral Commission!

"In the long history of the world only a few generations have been granted the role of defending freedom in its hour of maximum danger. I do not shrink from this responsibility, I welcome it."
                                                    – President John F. Kennedy

PERSONAL NOTE: Stepping out of character once again: In keeping with the format of the book the dialog in this chapter is projected into the year 2030 at a time when the U.S. has fallen to Communist oppression, but as you read this chapter I want you to think in terms of current day America. I am writing this in early 2010 and even though it is my opinion that America has already become a Socialist State and is dangerously close to succumbing to a Communist Regime at the present we still have the semblance of a free society and we have to rally as our forefathers did and fight for freedom and liberty for future generations. If we lose this battle I can assure you our children will grow up in the society in which Erick finds himself.

"We have the power to make this the best generation of mankind in the history of the world or to make is the last."
                                                    – President John F. Kennedy

That is, the last generation free of oppression!

Please keep in mind that the data and most importantly the names of the people I expose in this chapter are current and represent those we must target for removal from office. Please also pay attention to the offices these men hold and reflect on the power they wield. These positions must be vacated and filled with patriots. Make no mistake we are at war with forces from within our government, [The Shadow Government which I am about to expose] but I want to stress that **"IT MUST BE A PEACEFUL MOVEMENT!"** If we resort to violence I assure you they will clamp down on us, declare martial law and we will lose our freedom.

PAY CLOSE ATTENTION! Throughout this chapter I will be quoting our Founding Fathers on key political issues related to freedom and liberty and contrasting them with quotes from contemporary politicians so you can see how dangerously close we are to losing our liberty. And when it comes to exposing the agenda of the Shadow Government I will be quoting members of the Bilderberg Group [BG] Trilateral Commission [TC] Council on Foreign Relations [CFR] as well as key government officials regardless of whether or not they are affiliated with one of these organizations.

I will use their own words to convict them so there can be absolutely no doubt as to their intentions and treasonous actions.

Gramps: Erick today I am going to keep a very important promise which I made to you when we first started these conversations.

Erick: What promise is that?

Identifying The Enemies of Freedom: Gramps: I promised that I would give you the knowledge you needed to launch a successful counter offensive against the enemies of freedom and liberty, the men I call the Money Manipulators. Today I will remove their masks, expose the Shadow Government from behind which they operate, reveal their strategic game plan and put names to the cast of traitorous criminals so we know exactly who needs to be removed from power.

Step One: Identify the organizations which breed the vipers that would enslave us. They are The Bilderberg Group [BG], The Trilateral

Commission [TC], and The Council on Foreign Relations [CFR]. We will learn more about them momentarily.

Step Two: Is to understand exactly what their objectives are and their plan of execution.

Step Three: Is to put names to the cast of characters so we can make sure they are removed from power, never to return.

"Remember that a government big enough to give you everything you want is also big enough to take away everything you have."
– Senator Barry Goldwater

Erick: Gramps, I have had conversations with my friends and the consensus is that they are just too powerful and there is nothing we can do to fight them.

Gramps: Erick if that is truly the way you feel I guess I better back up and come at this from another direction. The whole idea of this conversation is to arm you to fight back, but if you feel you are defeated even before you begin to fight then I assure you are, but I assure you they are not invincible!

KNOW THY ENEMY, BUT FEAR HIM NOT!

"Since I entered politics, I have chiefly had men's views confided to me privately. Some of the biggest men in the United States, in the field of government and manufacturing. They know there is a power somewhere, so organized, so subtle, so watchful, so interlocked. So complete, so perverse that they better not speak above their breath when they speak in condemnation of it."
– Woodrow Wilson President (1913)

Gramps: As long as you believe that crock you are defeated before you start. Yes we are dealing with a formidable enemy but he is not invincible. He would just like us to think he is. As long as he can scare us into inaction he wins by default. What a strategy, but it is a lie from the enemy.

Erick: Gramps I am excited about our discussion today! I want to believe that America can once again be a free society!

Gramps: The great sorrow of my life is that my generation lacked the courage to preserve liberty for your generation. That is why I wrote my manuscript. It is my sincere desire to inspire your generation to be the one to take liberty back. Erick please remember what I am about to say and pass it down to your children. Ronald Reagan saw the truth when he said: *"Freedom is never more than one generation away from extinction. We don't pass it to our children in the bloodstream. It must be fought for, protected, and handed on for them to do the same."*

Erick: The attitude amongst most of my friends is that there is nothing we can do, that the iron grip is too powerful and there is no hope of ever getting our freedom back.

Gramps: Erick, Erick! That is exactly what they want you to think. As long as they can convince you that you are beaten you are. That kind of talk is nothing more than propaganda. Thomas Jefferson knew the real truth: *"When the people fear their government, there is tyranny: when the government fears the people there is liberty."*

Ronald Reagan was speaking of our foreign enemies when he said: *"**Above all, we must realize that no arsenal, or no weapon in the arsenals of the world, is so formidable as the will and moral courage of free men and women, It is a weapon adversaries in today's world do not have.**"* It saddens me that today the enemy we are talking about defeating is our own government, but Ronald Reagan's words are no less true in our situation.

Gramps: Erick, can you imagine what it must have been like to be one of the founding fathers of America, meeting to propose a plan to declare their independence from the strongest power on the planet?

I tell you this: America would never have come into existence without a few brave men of courage, men of honor, of faith, of conviction! Men who were willing to leave the comfort of their homes and fight a war that if lost would cost them their homes, their families and their lives. Men such as these cannot be defeated by men of greed who sit in their footraces and order their minions to do their fighting for them. Their minions simply don't have the heart to win and I might add that when that critical decisive moment comes, that moment when all hangs in the balance they won't have God by their side to save the day.

No, evil will not prevail! That is not the way God wrote the story.

This evil we fight will purify us. It will make us better more compassionate human beings. It will reveal to us the price to be paid for our greed! It will teach us the meaning of humanity and brotherly love and it will develop the love of God within us!

Thomas Jefferson said that: *"The spirit of resistance to government is so valuable that I wish it to be always kept alive..."* Erick I want to make myself perfectly clear **I am <u>NOT</u> proposing violence. I am proposing Peaceful Resistance in the spirit of Martin Luther King and Gundy.**

Gramps: Erick as our conversation progresses I will show you exactly what the enemies Achilles' Heal is and how we can defeat him. Just bare with me! The war has just begun. We are by no means defeated, and we will not be, not as long as we have the will to resist evil.

Gramps: Erick, are you ready to get to it?

Erick: What do you mean?

Gramps: Why the battle plan of course, the all important strategic game of Chess. Before any war, peaceful or otherwise can be fought you must first know your enemy, not only who he is, but what motivates him, what he thinks, how he is likely to react and most importantly what his weaknesses are.

Erick: How can we ever hope to fight an enemy that hides in the darkness and the shadows?

Gramps: You cast the light of truth on him, expose him for what he is and his greatest weapon is immediately taken away. That is exactly what we are going to do today. We are going to expose the Shadow Government to the light of day. Erick just who do you think the shadow government is?

Erick: Well you have repeatedly referred to them as the Money Manipulators of the British Empire, which you describe as a group of corrupt International Bankers who manipulate world events from the shadows and who have for generations been nibbling away at our liberty in small incremental steps which they hoped were so small as to not be noticed.

Gramps: Erick your answer tells me what the Shadow Government is and that they use secrecy as a strategic weapon but you haven't told me who they are. This is a very big and secretive organization and we will probably never know the complete cast of players, but that is ok. We know enough to effectively fight back. Our battle plan is comprised of three simple steps.

Our Battle Plan!

Step One: Identify the organizations which breed the vipers that would enslave us. They are The Bilderberg Group [BG], The Trilateral Commission [TC], and The Council on Foreign Relations [CFR]. We will learn more about them momentarily.

Step Two: Is to understand exactly what their objectives are and their plan of execution.

Step Three: Is to put names to the cast of characters so we can make sure they are removed from power never to return.

Step One: Remove The Cloak of Secrecy: I refer to the Bilderberg Group [BG] as the super secret Strategic Planning/Executive Branch of the Shadow Government, while The Trilateral Commission [TC] and The Council on Foreign Relations [CFR] can be thought of as the feet on the ground which carries out the day to day initiatives of the organization.   Meetings for all three entities are conducted under what is referred to as *"Chatham House Rules"* which specifies that nothing discussed in the meeting is to be repeated or quoted outside the meeting or in the press. I should note that directors of The Washington Post, The *New York Times* and *Time* Magazine [Three Coconspirator Corporations] have attended meetings over the years and felt no obligation to inform the public of what was discussed. I guess they answer to someone other than the general public.

"We are grateful to the Washington Post, the New York Times, Time Magazine and other great publications whose directors have attended meetings and respected the promises of discretion for almost 40 years. It would have been impossible for us to develop our plan for the world if we had been subject to the light of publicity during those years. But,

the world is more sophisticated and prepared to march toward a world government. The super national sovereignty of an intellectual elite and world bankers is surely preferable to the National Auto-determination practiced in past centuries."

— Nelson Rockefeller, Council Foreign Relations

If this isn't Treason what is?

PAY CLOSE ATTENTION! The BG, TC and CFR are comprised of influential power brokers representing governments and royal families around the world, as well as leaders from the fields of industry, banking, the media, academia, and the military. Such notable organizations as: The United Nations [UN], North Atlantic Treaty Organization [NATO], World Trade Organization [WTO], World Bank, Federal Reserve, International Monetary Fund [IMF], and Central banks from around the world including the Bank of England are members of the BG, TC and CFR. The BG holds an annual strategic planning meeting of approximately 150 of the world's most influential power brokers and then the TC and CFR carry out their directives. This brings us to Step Two:

Step Two: Understand Their Objectives and Their Plan of Execution: I would remind you that my manuscript repeatedly points out efforts on the part of *"The Moneyed Elite"* to usurp the power and authority of Sovereign Nations all over the world including and most especially the United States of America. Yet our government officials elected by the people and sworn to uphold the Constitution of The United States of America see no problem **meeting in secrecy** with these people. If this conclave of Globalist doesn't constitute a shadow government I don't know what would. Further in my opinion, as I said a second ago, it constitutes *"Treason or at the least Sedition."* Erick according to the dictionary TREASON is: Disloyalty or Treachery to one's country or government. SEDITION is: Any act, writing, speech, etc., directed unlawfully against state authority, the government, or the Constitution.

PAY CLOSE ATTENTION! It is one thing to have a closed door session of Congress which by the way that has only happened five times in the history of the U.S., but it is another matter entirely to meet in regular secret sessions with a group on international bankers and foreign government officials whose purpose is to replace our Sovereign National Government with a One World Government. The following quote is nothing less than a **threat against American Sovereignty** and again I say that to consort in private with such subversives is **nothing less than Treason**!

"We shall have world government whether or not you like it. The only question is whether World Government will be by conquest or consent."
   – James P. Warburg [Representing Rothschild Banking Concern, while speaking before the United States Senate, Feb. 17, 1950]

Of course the official position of the BG, TC and CFR is that they are by no means a subversive organization that would undermine the sovereignty of individual nation states. No, according to them they are humanitarians. Matter of fact according to Denis Healy, Bilderberg founding member, and steering committee member of thirty years:

"To say we are striving for one-world government is exaggerated, but not wholly unfair. Those of us in Bilderberg felt we couldn't go on forever fighting for nothing and killing people and rendering millions homeless. So we felt that a single community throughout the world would be a good thing."

So the admission is that they are striving for a one world government, but it is okay because they have our best interest at heart. Erick, in my day we would call that putting lipstick on a pig. Any way you look at it, it is still a pig or you could call it a bald-faced lie.

Let's see at the opening of this chapter President Wilson referred to:
"...a power somewhere, so organized, so subtle, so watchful, so interlocked. So complete, so perverse that they better not speak above their breath when they speak in condemnation of it."

I don't suppose he was talking about the humanitarian BG-CFR-TC group! Well according to the CFR Journal 1974, P558 it certainly sounds like they could have been: *"The New World Order will be built...an end run on national sovereignty, eroding it piece by piece will accomplish much more than the old fashioned frontal assault."*

PAY CLOSE ATTENTION! Eric, to paraphrase Zbigniew Brzinski, Nation States are obsolete and society will be dominated by an elite unrestricted by traditional values, or in other words we can expect to be slaves. That certainly doesn't sound humanitarian to me. Matter of fact it sounds down right frightening and it sounds like Wilson's warning hit home. In all fairness I should quote Brzinski less I exaggerate what he said: *"National States as a fundamental unit of man's organized life has ceased to be the principal creative force: International banks and multinational corporations are acting and planning in terms that are far in advance of the Nation States..."*

*"The Techtronic era involves the gradual appearance of a **more controlled society** that would be dominated by an elite **unrestricted by traditional values**.*" – Between Two Ages: Americas Role In The Technetronic Age By Zbigniew Brzinski CFR Member, Founding Member TC, Secretary of State Carter Administration and Security Adviser to five Presidents.

Erick I have several more quotes which I could read to you but I think I have just about proved my point so I will start to wrap up:

"The case for government by elites is irrefutable."
                                                   – William Fulbright U.S. Senator

"The Council on Foreign Relations is the American branch of a society which originated in England ... [and] ... believes national boundaries should be obliterated and one-world rule established."
                          – Dr. Carroll Quigley, CFR member, college mentor of
                                       President Clinton, author of Tragedy and Hope

PAY CLOSE ATTENTION! Erick, regardless of what their propaganda machines say these men stand convicted by the words of their own mouths of being part of a Shadow Government and as for those who are elected officials of the United States sworn to uphold the Constitution I charge them with Treason! Those things which men hide from other men are hidden for a reason and that reason is always to serve vested interest not to serve the interest of those from which they are hidden.

"It is difficult for common good to prevail against the intense concentration of those who have special interest, especially if the discussions are made behind closed doors."   – President Jimmy Carter

"The liberties of a people will never be, secure, when the transactions of their rulers may be concealed from them."

– Patrick Henry

To those who categorize discussions about the BG-TC-CFR as nothing more than conspiracy theory not only have these men convicted themselves by the words of their own mouths but Congress investigated them and concluded that they overwhelmingly propagandizes the globalist concept... and are virtually an agency of the government. In the 1950's Congress formed the Reese Committee to investigate the CFR. According to Rene A. Wormser, Chief Counsel to the Reece Committee: *"The Council on Foreign Relations, another member of the international complex, financed by the Rockefeller and Carnegie Foundations, overwhelmingly propagandizes the globalist concept. This organization became virtually an agency of the government when World War II broke out..."*

Gramps: Erick I don't know about you but to me they look as guilt as hell!

ACTION STEPS: These men whose names and positions I am about to reveal [both elected and appointed officials] must go or our liberty is doomed. It is imperative that we realize that our Congressmen and Senators in Washington have by in large sold out to the moneyed interest. Only a few, for example Ron Paul and Michele Backmann can be trusted to serve the American people and not the moneyed interest or their own vested interest. **12) It Is Imperative That [with only a few exceptions] All Incumbents, Both Republicans And Democrats Be Voted Out Of Office. Additionally: 13) Our Elected Officials Must Be Prohibited By Penalty Of Law From Participating In Secret Meetings With Those Outside Our Elected Government!** We need to wipe the slate clean and start over and it is imperative that all those we vote into office: **14) Sign A Pledge To Support A Reformation Platform; including among other things election reform or otherwise the seat of government will continue to be controlled by the Moneyed Elite who will continue their influence peddling.** As mentioned before we cannot regain control of the Government or the Economy unless we get rid of the FED. THAT IS IMPERATIVE! More on this later.

Erick: Gramps before we go any further I need to understand: *"How and When"* the *[Shadow Government-BG-TC-CF]* got control of the government and our economy in the first place?

Gramps: At a basic level the answer to your question *is* that money talks. As we have been discussing throughout all our conversations the Money Manipulators used their vast fortunes to gain control of Government Officials, The Media, Wall Street, Academia and the Military Complex.

PAY CLOSE ATTENTION! This is mostly a review, but it will help set the stage for exactly who we have to get rid of and why! Specific to the government: influence peddling was legalized through Lobbying and then thanks to gerrymandering and lack of term limits once the Money Manipulators helped their candidate of choice to get in office they could expect him or her to serve their special **interest** for a long time to come. In terms of Wall Street J.P. Morgan literally funded the industrial revolution. Then thanks to President Wilson selling out to the bankers we got the corrupt Federal Reserve, which issued money at interest to the U.S. Government which in turn ballooned the National Debt as well as birthing the Federal Income Tax as a means to repay that debt. Then when the Fed orchestrated the Great Depression the Money Manipulators bought most of the nation's assets for pennies on the dollar. Then thanks to their crony President FDR the very banking interest that caused the depression were put in charge of managing the recovery. Erick, you may recall from earlier conversations that through the National Recovery Act [NRA] banking interest headed by Hugh Johnson a member of the Council on Foreign Relations was actually put in charge of managing the recovery. The NRA was based largely on FDR'S NEW DEAL which coincidently relied heavily on borrowing from the Fed which of course drove up the National Debt further burdening an already impoverished nation. All of these things were thanks to the Money Manipulators and their influence peddling and control of the Monetary System. WWII further increased the National Debt as we borrowed from the Fed to fund the war and Munitions Companies, Energy Companies and other Key Industries made vast fortunes off the war as well, that is as long as they were on the *"preferred venders list"* which meant that they were either owned by the right people like say the Rockefellers or they contributed to the right political campaign funds. Graff is great. It really works.

The CFR was imbed into the government during the Presidency of FDR and its control was greatly expanded at the outbreak of WWII when the government assimilated the CFR's international intelligence network into the government. In terms of the TC they infiltrated the government through appointments made by TC controlled Jimmy Carter.

President Carter was the first President groomed for the presidency by the Trilateral Commission. Three years prior to the 1976 election he was introduced to David Rockefeller, Chairman Emeritus of the CFR, and Zbigniew Brzinski, CFR Member, Founding Member TC, who openly acknowledged that he had helped groom Carter for the Presidency. Incidentally his V.P. Walter Mondale was a member of the TC as well. Once in office Carter appointed 26 TC Members to key positions in his administration. I will list a few of the more important ones starting with Zbigniew Brzinski–National Security Advisor a position he held under five U.S. Presidents, Michael Blumenthal–Secretary Treasury, Fred Bergsten–Under Secretary of the Treasury, Cyrus Vance–Secretary of State, James Schlesinger–Secretary of Energy, Harold Brown-Secretary of Defense, Andrew Young-Ambassador to the UN, Elliot Richardson–Delegate to Law of the Sea and most importantly labor leader Leonard Woodcook was appointed Chief Envoy To China etc.

From Carter on the Office of President of the United States has been controlled by the Shadow Government. Of Carters 26 TC appointees far and away the most important was labor leader Leonard Woodcook to the position of Chief Envoy to China.

Erick: Why was that particular appointment so important?

Gramps: Remember the Money Manipulators chief objective was to establish a One World Government and to do that the U.S. industrial complex had to be dismantled so the U.S. population would become compliant and go along with their agenda. The door to Global Free Trade was opened in 1972 when Richard Nixon opened diplomatic relations with China. <u>Now under the TC controlled Carter administration they would walk through that door and begin the systematic dismantling of the U.S. Economy.</u>

Carter went down as one of the worst Presidents in U.S. history, but I contend that he wasn't the fool he was painted to be. He was just following the play book of his handlers. During his administration, coincidently exactly at the time we were opening trade with China, the U.S. experienced an **oil embargo.** The official account in the history books was that in response to the Yom Kipper War in Israel and the decision of the U.S. to supply the Israelis with armaments OAPEC, Egypt, Syria and Tunisia declared an oil embargo thrusting the U.S. in a crisis. Erick you may notice that every time the U.S. takes a drastic turn in a direction that is not in our national interest it seems to be associated with a **crisis.** It is like Henry Kissinger said some time later during the 2008 economic melt down:

*"He Obama can give a new impetus... to develop an overall strategy for America in this period when really a **New World Order** can be created. It is a **great opportunity given such a crisis.***"
– Henry Kissinger Former Secretary of State and Member Council on Foreign Relations, June 2006, Ottawa Canada

Erick: So gramps what was the result of the oil crisis?

PAY CLOSE ATTENTION! Gramps: Before I answer your question let me say that the book The Oil Non Crisis by Lindsey Williams contends that the U.S. has now and has always had vast reserves of oil and any shortages are propagated for profit and or political reasons pure and simple. Based on my research I agree with him. So now to answer your question: The oil embargo provided the Fed the excuse it needed in order to be able to tamper with the economy. We experienced a period referred to as **Stagflation,** which is an economic term referring to a period of inflation occurring simultaneous to a period of stagnant business activity. How coincidental the U.S. enters into unfavorable Free Trade Agreements with China and then suddenly the U.S. experiences the perfect financial crisis where it encounters both inflation and stagnant business activity at the same time. The oil crisis aside there was one other requirement to create this perfect economic storm and that was high interest rates. Never you mind, the Fed was there to accommodate their masters, the Money Manipulators. According to *Time* Magazine March 24, 1980 President Carter announced a crisis in which both Inflation and Interest exceeded 18%.

Erick: What was the result of the coupling of such high interest and inflation rates?

Gramps: Well as you might imagine the U.S. Economy came to an abrupt halt. We were setting ducks and the U.S. economic infrastructure was systematically dismantled over the next couple of decades!

Erick: How so?

PAY CLOSE ATTENTION! Historically trade policy had been established through **[Treaties negotiated by the U.S. Senate]** and requiring a 2/3 vote of all those present. Thanks to the influence of the Trilateral Commission our trade policy was put on a "***Fast Track Program***" which took control away from the Senate. For example Trade Agreements such as NAFTA, CAFTA and FFAA are negotiated by the Administration, require only a ½ vote of all those present, allow no amendments and must be ratified in thirty days or less. Even worse **[Regulations]** such as the [SPP] Security and Prosperity Partnership intended to engineer a North American Union between the U.S., Canada and Mexico **can be implemented by Unelected Bureaucrats.** And then there are the vicious **[Executive Orders]** which are issued by the President solely at his discretion.

The net result is that all of the customary checks and balances have been circumvented and they are able to ramrod things through which would normally never be tolerated.

Fast Track: was instituted under President Gerald Ford and Vice President Nelson Rockefeller [Founder Trilateral Commission] who was appointed when Nixon resigned. It was used to engineer the New Economic World Order by for example pushing through GATT Tokyo Round, U.S. Israel Free Trade Agreement, Canada – U.S. Free Trade Agreement, NAFTA, GATT General Agreement Tariffs and Trade and the really important one was GATT Uruguay Round.

Erick: Why was GATT Uruguay Round so important?

Gramps: It created The World Trade Organization which opened the flood gates to World Wide Free Trade and was particularly damaging to the United State's balance of trade.

"The liberties of a people will never be, secure, when the transactions of their rulers may be concealed from them." – Patrick Henry

The Money Masters:
http://www.youtube.com/results?search_query=the+money+masters +full+movie&search_type=&aq=0

Erick: What was the outcome of all this?

The Intentional Collapse of The U.S. Economy!

VITALLY IMPORTANT: Gramps: Trade Liberalization agreements gutted the U.S. manufacturing sector! Entire industries simply ceased to exist, lost to China and India. The Fed made sure that there was **no credit to promote capital growth projects** which meant that the capital American entrepreneurs needed to modernize and compete in the global market was not available. That coupled with the fact that the U.S. practiced intentionally losing trade policies by being the only industrialized nation without a value-added tax or tariff to protect our trade balance resulted in massive trade deficits which systematically drained the economic life blood out of the U.S. As if that wasn't bad enough, Savings and Loan banks [S&L's] barred by Roosevelt from speculative investing found themselves unable to compete in the high interest rate environment of that era and protective regulations were systematically stripped away opening the door to predatory lending practices which caused a collapse of the S&L's and yet another **crisis.** Financially sound corporations were purchased and systematically sold off piece by piece rendering them a non threat in the emerging global market. Erick I could go on. But I think you get the picture. **I want to punctuate the fact that none of this was by accident.** It was a carefully choreographed set of **staged crises** coupled with implementation of policies designed to render the U.S. economically impudent and it could never have been accomplished if the corruption had not come from the President down through the entire political system. The apple barrel is rotten and the crooks have to go!

VITALLY IMPORTANT: In summary, a number of things had to come together simultaneously in order to create the perfect financial storm. It took a staged oil crisis, imposition of unfavorable free trade agreements, intentionally losing trade policies, deregulation of the S&L's, dismantling of sound corporations, massive unfunded entitlement programs, ongoing budget deficits and most importantly the imposition of inordinately high interest rates by the Fed. The outcome of this manipulation of the U.S. economic super structure was a devastating trade imbalance, dismantling of U.S. manufacturing capability, job losses, lower salaries, inflation, and devaluation of the dollar accompanied by **DEBT-DEBT-DEBT till the system collapsed under its weight!** The once wealthiest nation in the world destroyed from within and eventually brought to its knees financially, morally and politically, and all without ever firing a shot. That is how the land of the free and the home of the brave became the land of tyranny and oppression. A true story, so help me God.

Erick: Gramps how did the Trilateral Commission do as you call it an end run around U.S. trade policy and do the things you just described.

According to Congressman Duncan Hunter (R-CA) in an interview with *Human Events* Dec. 4, 2006:

"We practiced what I call 'losing trade' – deliberately losing trade over the last 50 years. Today, other countries around the world employ what they call a value-added tax, in which foreign governments refund to their corporations that are exporting goods to the United States the full amount of their value-added taxes that that particular company pays in marketing a product...When American products hit their shores, they charge a value-added tax in the same amount. So they enact a double hit against American exporters. One is that they subsidize their own imports going out, and the second is that they tax us going in. [Tariff] The United States doesn't do this."

The Office of The President Has Been Compromised!

I hope I have conveyed that the Office of President of the United States of America has been compromised! The power of that office now resides with those who would destroy the Sovereignty of our Nation. The result is that the balance of power which normally exists between the Executive, Legislative and Judicial Branches of government is nullified and our government is no longer capable of functioning as our founding fathers designed it and as a result **"Our Constitutional Republic Is At Risk."** I will elaborate more on this momentarily.

Both Houses of Congress Are Irrelevant!

When our Congressmen and Senators have been infiltrated by the same special interest as the office of the President our last bastion of hope has been overrun and we must realize that it is as Senator Barry Goldwater warned in the 1960's that: *"...both houses of congress are irrelevant. America's domestic policy is now being run by...[The Chairman of the FED] and the Federal Reserve. America's foreign policy is now being run by the International Monetary Fund."*

The End Game is to Destroy America From Within!

I contend that all of those in the shadow government are guilty of Sedition for consorting to establish a New World Order which by their very admission would do: *"...an end run on national sovereignty, eroding it piece by piece..."* Council on Foreign Relations Journal 1974, P558. And as for our **elected officials** who have sworn an oath to uphold the Constitution of the United States I contend that by virtue of their participating in secret meetings with seditionists they are **guilty of Treason.** They should be impeached, but for the sake of the Republic it is better to just vote them out of office and bar them from holding public office ever again.

The Question Is What Do We Do About It?

ACTION STEPS: 15) We Must Withdraw From [or renegotiate] All Free Trade Agreements: The most important of which is The World Trade Organization [WTO] which is the vehicle for proliferation of Free Trade around the globe. Additionally we must **16) Oppose The Security And Prosperity Partnership [SSP] And The North American Union:** which would merge the U.S., Canada and Mexico. According to David Rockefeller's memoirs: He gave credit to the TC for creation of the European Union which stripped the individual nations of Europe of their sovereignty. We want no part of any such agreement that would take away U.S. Sovereignty! More later.

Step Three: Name The Traitors and Remove Them From Power:

PERSONAL NOTE: Stepping out of character: In the pages that follow I hope to give you some idea of just how deeply the Shadow Government of the Bilderberg Group, Trilateral Commission and Council on Foreign Relations has entrenched itself in our Government, Media, Corporations, Academia and Military. All in all there are approximately 4,000 members of the TC and CFR so I cannot possibly expose all of them. What I want to convey in the following pages are the names of men in key positions and even more important than their names are the positions of power which they hold. And lastly where appropriate I will give examples of how they have corrupted our system of government!

Gramps: Erick please take a look at the following chart. It gives a high level overview of how deeply the CFR has infiltrated the top positions in our government.

Roster of CFR/Trilateral Commission Members

LEGEND:

CFR = Member of the Council on Foreign Relations
TC = Member of the Trilateral Commission
BG = Member of the Elite Bilderbergs

**Source: CFR/Trilateral Commission Members
http://www.apfn.org/apfn/cfr-members.htm**

Key Members Council Foreign Relations and Trilateral Commission			
David Rockefeller, Chairman Emeritus		CFR	TC
Peter G. Peterson, Chairman of the Council on Foreign Relations		CFR	TC
John D. Rockefeller, IV	(D-WV)	CFR	TC
William Roth, Jr.	(R-DE)	CFR	TC

NOTE: Members of the Council on Foreign Relations and the Trilateral Commission dominate key positions in the U.S. Government, Military, Industries, Media and Academia.

INFLUENCE OF TRILATERAL COMMISSION

Members Include: Six out of eight World Bank Presidents, eight out of ten U.S. Trade Representatives, Presidents and/or Vice-Presidents of every elected administration since the Carter Admin., seven out of twelve Secretaries of State and nine out of twelve Secretaries of Defense.

THROUGH THESE POSITIONS THE TC'S AGENDA OF ACHIEVING A ONE WORLD GOVERNMENT IS PROPAGATED ON AMERICA!

Erick: Now that I see this chart I have a better idea of exactly how the Shadow Government was able to use the office of Trade Representative to impose Free Trade Agreements on the country. I guess it doesn't hurt your cause if you have the U.S. President, Secretary of State, Secretary of Defense and President of the World Bank all in collusion either.

LABOR UNION LEADERS			
NAME	TITLE	CFR	TC
Jay Mazur	International Ladies' Garment Workers Union	CFR	TC
Jack Sheinkman	Amalgamated Clothing and Textile Workers Union	CFR	
Albert Shanker	Pres., American Federation of Teachers	CFR	TC
Glen E. Watts	Communication of Workers of America	CFR	TC

Gramps: A person doesn't have to be a member of the TC or CFR to wield power. Sometimes all you need is to have those in power beholding to you. Point at hand is how in 2010 President Obama joined forces with Andy Stern, President of SEIU the largest union in the country and they rammed an unpopular healthcare bill, which represented 1/6 of the U.S., GDP down the throats of the American people. Obama said: *"Before debating Healthcare I talk to Andy Stern of SEIU."* Then to Obama's embarrassment SEIU came out with a movie entitled <u>LABOR DAY: When Winning Is The Only Option</u>. The movie claimed that SEIU got Obama elected. Kind of looks like influence peddling to me. Any way it is an example of how a TC connected White House can reach out and help their friends.

Listen to this: In terms of our conversations about the Shadow Government wanting to intentionally bankrupt the U.S., it turns out the Obama administration had several appointees who were self convicted Communists. For example there was Manufacturing Czar, Ron Bloom who said: *"We know that the free market is nonsense. We kind of agree with Mao that political power comes largely from the barrel of a gun."*

Gramps: Is it any wonder U.S. manufacturing fell apart when you have people advising the president who think that The Free Market Capitalist System is "NONSENSE" and espouse violence. These comments are very similar to those of SEIU President and friend and advisor to President Obama. Andy Stern who said:

*"There are opportunities in America to share better in the Wealth to <u>redistribute the power</u> and unions and government are part of the solution...We're trying to use the power of persuasion and if that doesn't work we are going to use the <u>Persuasion of power</u> because there are government and there are opportunities to change laws that effect these companies...****We took names. We watched how they voted. We know where they live.****"*
– Andy Stern President SEIU, Glen Beck Show, November 2009

Gramps: <u>It seems that both Andy Stern and Ron Bloom believe that force is the great persuader.</u> Their comments remind me of the old Communist slogan *"Workers of the world unite."* We know how that worked out. Work Camps are never a good thing.

Well that is in keeping with other rhetoric coming out of the Obama White House. For example there was White House Communication Director, Anita Dunn who said: *"Mao Tse Tung and Mother Teresa, not often coupled with each other, but the two people that I turn to most."*

Erick: What are you getting at Gramps?

Gramps: Erick I want you to see what you are up against when you oppose the Federal Government. When members of our government speak openly about force coming from the barrel of a gun and praising Mao Tse Tung a man who killed approximately 67 million of his own people then you know you are opposing pure evil and your strategy cannot be the same as you would use when dealing with honest fair minded people. That raises the specter of strategy and how do you take on such an adversary, but that is a topic we will discuss later.

Getting back on topic, what you have here is an example of how the power of the Presidency is disseminated far and wide and can do immeasurable damage if it has a subversive agenda such as exemplified by the Communist quotes just sited. For example former Fed Chairman Alan Greenspan came out after the healthcare bill was passed, after it was conveniently too late and posed an hypothetical question as to, *"What if the bill costs more than expected."* **He inferred it could bankrupt the country**, which was exactly what the politically astute had been saying from the get go. Remember the agenda of the Shadow Government was to **create crisis,** because crisis can force people to do things they normally wouldn't do. Things like: **ACCEPT A ONE WORLD GOVERNMENT!**

But they are right, crisis does create opportunity. For example **Zbigniew Brzezinski had this to say of President Obama:**

"I think there needs to be a fundamental rethinking of how we conduct world affairs, AND Obama seems to have both the guts and the intelligence to address the issue and to change the nature of America's relationship with the world."

What a wonderful endorsement! Too bad it came from Zbigniew Brzezinski: The man whose idea it was to give arms, funding and training to the Mujahideen in Afghanistan: Zbigniew Brzezinski, CFR member and cofounder along with David Rockefeller of the Trilateral Commission, July 1, 1973. Also National Security Advisor to five presidents and member [NCS] Defense Department Commission on integrated long-term strategy – Reagan Administration Co-chair.

The Influence of The TC and CFR Goes Deep!

Brzezinski also had this to say:

"The Techtronic era involves the gradual appearance of a more controlled society would be dominated by an elite unrestricted by traditional values."

– Between Two Ages: America's Role In The Technetronic Age
By Zbigniew Brzinski

Sounds like Slavery to me! What do you think?

KEY GOVERNMENT POSITIONS: Gramps: Erick, take a look at the next chart. What I want you to notice is how deeply the tentacles go, how much power the shadow government exerts over our legitimate government if indeed we have a legitimate government left. They all have to go!

"The real menace of our republic is the invisible government which like a giant octopus sprawl its slimy length over city state and nation. Like the octopus of real life it operates under cover of a self created screen. At the head of the octopus are the Rockefeller Standard Oil interest and a small group of powerful banking houses generally referred to as international bankers. The little coterie of powerful international bankers virtually run the United States government for their own selfish purposes. They practically control both political parties." – John F. Hylan, Mayor of N.Y. [1918-1925]

Key U.S. Government Positions Held By CFR and TC Members (Current & Recent)

NAME	POSITION	CFR	TC	BB
Paul Volker	N. American Chairman Trilateral Comm.		TC	
George H. Bush	U.S. President	CFR		
William Clinton	U.S. President	CFR	TC	BB
Jimmy Carter	U.S. President	CFR		
Dick Cheney	U.S. Vice President	CFR		
Walter Mondale	U.S. Vice President		TC	
John McCain	Senator (Arizona) former Presidential candidate	CFR		
Albert Gore, Jr.	U.S. Vice President	CFR		
Hillary R. Clinton	Secretary of State Obama Admin		TC	
Condoleezza Rice	Secretary of State Bush Admin	CFR		
John Kerry	Senator, Chairman Foreign Relations Committee	CFR		
Colin L. Powell	Chairman Joint Chiefs of Staff	CFR		
James Woolsey	Director Central Intelligence Agency	CFR		
Robert M. Gates	(Set of Defense, former Director Central Intelligence)	CFR		
Henry Cisneros	Secretary of Housing and Urban Development	CFR		
Donna Shalala	Secretary of Health & Human Services	CFR	TC	
Bruce Babbitt	Secretary of Interior	CFR		
Dick Thornburgh	Asst. Sec. for Administration, United Nations	CFR		
Anthony Lake	National Security Advisor	CFR		
Sandy Berger	National Security Advisor	CFR		
Lee Aspin (Deceased)	Secretary of Defense	CFR		
Laura Tyson	Chairman, Council of Economics Advisors	CFR		

continued next page

NAME	POSITION	CFR	TC	BB
Hudson Institute	Project for the New American Century (PNAC) signatory	CFR		
Robert Kagan	Cofounded Project for the New American Century	CFR		
ENVIRONMENTAL PROTECTION AGENCY				
James M. Strock	Asst. Adm., Enforcement & Compliance	CFR		
OFFICE OF MANAGEMENT & BUDGET				
Alice Rivlin	Deputy Director	CFR		
OFFICE SCIENCE & TECHNOLOGY				
William R. Graham, Jr.	Science Advisor to President & Director	CFR		

JUDICIARY: Gramps: This is just a short/partial list I put in to drive home a point, which is that without an impartial and separate Judicial System our balance of power breaks down, our constitutional rights are jeopardized and the Republic itself is in parole!

"All the rights secured to the citizens under the Constitution are nothing, and a mere bubble, except guaranteed to them by an independent and virtuous Judiciary." – Andrew Jackson

"The Trilateral Commission is intended to be the vehicle for multinational consolidation of the commercial and banking interest by seizing control of the political government of the United States... They rule the future." – Felix Frankfurter, Justice of the Supreme Court

JUDICIARY

NAME	TITLE	CFR		
Sandra Day O'Connor	Assoc. Justice, U.S. Supreme Court	CFR		
Steve G. Breyer	Chief Judge, U.S. Court of Appeals, First Circuit, Boston	CFR		
Ruth B. Ginsburg	U.S. Court of Appeals, Wash., DC Circuit	CFR		
Laurence H. Silberman	U.S. Court of Appeals, Wash., DC Circuit	CFR		

FEDERAL JUDICIAL CENTER

William W. Schwarzer Director		CFR		

Gramps: Erick, I want you to see how our founding fathers have revered the Constitution as the key to enduring freedom and how by contrast contemporary politicians have viewed it as an obstacle to their quest for unrestrained power.

Founding Fathers:
"Don't interfere with anything in the Constitution. That must be maintained, for it is the only safeguard of our liberties."
– Abraham Lincoln

"The Constitution is not an instrument to restrain the people, it is an instrument for the people to restrain the government – lest it come to dominate our lives and interest." – Patrick Henry

Contemporary Leaders:
"The illegal we do immediately. The unconstitutional takes a little longer." – Henry Kissinger

"The Constitution is just a God Damn piece of paper."
– George W. Bush, Nov. 2005, Capital Hill Blue

"You can fool some of the people all the time, and those are the ones you want to concentrate on."
– President George W. Bush

The Supreme Court [The highest Court in the land]: Ruled in eight separate cases that The Federal Income Tax is Illegal!

SO HOW IS IT POSSIBLE THAT AN UNCONSTITUTIONAL FEDERAL INCOME TAX IS IMPOSED ON AMERICAN CITIZENS?

Gramps: Erick, there are many examples of subversion of The Judicial System and the Constitution, but I know of none that was more vile than that regarding the imposition of an **UNCONSTITUTIONAL FEDERAL INCOME TAX** on the American people. In 1894 the government tried to impose a Federal Income Tax. In 1895 The Supreme Court ruled that a tax on income or wages was illegal. In response to this ruling the government drafted the 16th Amendment to the Constitution. But in Brushaber V.S. Union Pacific R.R. Co., 204 U.S. 1 The Supreme Court rejected any claims that the 16th Amendment granted any new taxing authority *"when they ruled it created no new power of taxation and that it did not change the constitutional limitations which forbid any direct taxation of individuals."* According to Article 1, section 9 of the Constitution **it is unconstitutional for the U.S. to directly tax wages salaries or earnings.** All in all there were eight separate cases filed and in all eight cases The Supreme Court ruled that though the Federal Government "Could Tax Profits and Gains" but it ***"Could Not Tax Labor and Wages."*** By the way the Supreme Court's decision was never overturned so it would seem quite clear that we should not have to pay Federal Income Taxes, but we do! Why?

Enter The IRS, The Government's Version of The Nazi's Gestapo! You see the government needs the Income Tax in order to pay the [privately owned] Federal Reserve Banks, the debt they owe for the printing of U.S. currency which it creates out of thin air with a simple computer entry. Erick, by the way when you get home go through your canceled checks and find your last Federal Income Tax check. Turn it over and I think you may be surprised that your money was not deposited in the U.S. Treasury per the endorsement on the check, but instead it was deposited in a Federal Reserve Bank. Why do you suppose that is?

Tax Protesters Win Tax Evasion Cases: Government VS Whitey Harrel: Mr. Harrel was acquitted on four counts of not filing a Federal Income Tax Return because when the jury asked Judge Kahn to provide them with a copy of the law requiring Mr. Harrel to file a 1040 Tax Return the Judge was unable to do so. Unwilling might be a more accurate statement. The Judge responded to the jury: *"I will instruct the jury according to the law...You have everything you need."* Obviously the jury disagreed with the judge. They felt the question of guilt or innocence rested on the law so absent a law saying that Mr. Harrel was required to file a 1040 the jury returned four not guilty verdicts. Subsequently 24 people were charged with not filing 1040s. All 24 were acquitted. Then the government changed the rules and denied American citizens their rights under the Constitution. It simply would not do to have people think that they could defy the government even when the government's actions were illegal. **The new law of the land became Might over Right and that rule stands to this day!**

The New Headline Became Tax Protesters Found Guilty! In the Case of The Federal Government VS Irwin Shift: Federal Judge Dawson Presiding: Mr. Shift was found guilty and was sentenced to 13 years in prison, not for breaking the law [because there is no law requiting the filing of a 1040] but guilty for standing up for his Constitutional rights. Erick, if you have any doubts that America is a **Democratic Dictatorship** consider these comments from Mr. Shift's trial.

Irwin Shift: "but The Supreme court said..."

Judge Dawson: "Irrelevant–Denied."

Irwin Shift: "The Supreme Court is Irrelevant."

Judge Dawson: "Irrelevant–Denied."

Source: Documentary, *America Freedom to Fascism,*
Producer Aaron Russo

Erick: We need to reflect on the words of Abraham Lincoln, and more than that we need to act on them.

"We the people are the rightful masters of both Congress and the courts, not to overthrow the Constitution but to overthrow the men who pervert the Constitution." – President Abraham Lincoln

The American people need to stand up in mass and say to the Federal Government you are our servants and you will abide by the Constitution of the United States of America. You swore a sacred oath to do just that and failure to uphold that oath is Treason. By the way we shouldn't forget Mr. Shift and others who are in prison for standing up for their constitutional rights.

IT IS TIME WE THE PEOPLE STAND UP AND TAKE BACK THE RIGHTS WHICH WERE GRANTED US BY THE CONSTITUTION OF THE UNITED STATES!

MILITARY/POLICE STATE: Gramps: Erick, you once asked me how the government was able to impose a police state and lock us down. Several pieces of legislation were slipped through often piggybacked on other legislation which gave the government the right, **at their discretion** to declare an emergency which allowed them to **impose Martial Law.** From that point all they had to do was **create a crisis and** impose martial law. Here are a couple of examples of such legislation.

H.R.5122: amends Posse Comitatus and The Insurrection Act to: Allow the Federal Government to unilaterally take control of State National Guards and position Federal Troops anywhere in the country during a public emergency. – Source: Morals, Frank. Bush Moves Toward Martial Law *Toward Freedom* Oct. 26, 2006 http://www.towardfreedom.com/home/content/view/911

Gramps: This was in stark opposition to Congress' position that: *"...you can't ever use our military for domestic law enforcement ... We don't want you using military to arrest citizens. We don't want Marshall Law."* – Barbara Ol Shansky, Deputy Legal Director Center for Constitutional Rights

But as had increasingly become the case it didn't matter what Congress wanted or what the Constitution said. All that mattered was that the puppet masters who were pulling the strings in Washington wanted to make previsions to control the U.S. people in case of **Civil Disobedience,** because they were committed to obtaining their goal of a One World Government as they had put it by *"Conquest or Consent."*

EO #11921: Provides that when a state of emergency is declared by a President Congress cannot review the action for six months.

PAY CLOSE ATTENTION! Gramps: This provision allowed for the transition to our present dictatorship. Again it was just like Hitler had done in Nazi Germany. With the Legislative and Judicial neutralized all they had to do was **create a crisis and impose martial law** and then they had six months to dismantle the government and **impose a dictatorship.** But before they could impose Martial Law there was one last objective they had to accomplish. They had to disarm the American people so they couldn't resist the take over.

PAY CLOSE ATTENTION! Then in 2008 Attorney General, Eric Holder [Obama Administration] argued before the Supreme Court in DC Gun Ban Case Columbia VS Heller, for the complete disarming of the American people and that only the military should own firearms.

PAY CLOSE ATTENTION! Then President Obama pushed for a million man domestic military force reporting directly to him. The public not knowing their history didn't realize that, that was exactly what Hitler had done in Nazi Germany during his rise to power.

Obama Said: *"We cannot continue to rely only on our military in order to achieve the national security objectives that we have set. We have to have a **Civilian National Security Force** that is just as powerful, just as strong, just as well funded."*

Gramps: All of this is in sharp contrast to the liberties our Founding Fathers provided in the Constitution. What a shame we didn't preserve those rights. If we had America would be a much different country.

Our Founding Fathers said:
"The Constitution preserves the advantage of being armed which America possesses over the people of almost every other nation where the governments are afraid to trust the people with arms."
– James Madison

"Firearms are second only to the Constitution in importance; they are the peoples' liberty teeth." – George Washington

"No free man shall ever be de-barred the use of arms. The strongest reason for the people to retain their right to keep and bear arms is a last resort to protect themselves against tyranny in government."
– Thomas Jefferson, Third U.S. President (1801-1809)

Gramps: Erick, take a look at the next chart and you will see just how deeply the Money Manipulators have penetrated our military. Then we need to discuss another military issue, namely that War is big business. Tomorrow we are going to discuss the topic of *"Wars For Profit"* but I want to touch on the subject briefly now so you can reflect on what I say as you look over the next chart.

U.S. MILITARY
DEPARTMENT OF DEFENSE

NAME	TITLE	CFR
Les Aspin	Secretary of Defense	CFR
Charles M. Herzfeld	Dir. Defense Research & Engineering	CFR
Frank G. Wisnerll	Under Secretary Policy	CFR
Andrew Marshall	Dir., Net Assessment	CFR
Henry S. Rowen	Asst. Sec. International Security Affairs	CFR
Michael Stone	Secretary of the Army	CFR
Judy Ann Miller	Dep. Asst. Sec.	
	Nuclear Forces & Arms Control	CFR
Donald B. Rice	Secretary of the Air Force	CFR
Bruce Weinrod	Dep. Asst. Sec., Europe & NATO	CFR
Franklin C. Miller	Dep. Asst. Sec.	
	Nuclear Forces & Arms Control	CFR
Adm. Seymour Weiss	Chairman, Defense Policy	CFR

U.S. ARMS CONTROL
AND DISARMAMENT AGENCY

Thomas Graham	General Council	CFR
Richard Burt	Negotiator On Strategic Defense Arms	CFR
William Schneier	Chmn., General Advisory Council	CFR
David Smith	Negotiator, Defense & Space	CFR

Nine out of twelve Secretaries of Defense have belonged to either the TC, CFR or both. There are also a large number of high ranking military officers I could have listed but the list would be too long.

Erick: Gramps based on what I learned in school every war the U.S. has been in was started by an enemy intent on aggression and all we were doing was defending our country. America has a reputation of being the world's peace keepers.

Gramps: That is the bill of goods they sold the public, but in reality every war since WWI was propagated on the American people by the propaganda machine of the Money Manipulators and the wars benefited them financially and strategically, but that is the topic of tomorrow's conversation.

As we have discussed repeatedly during our conversations if you want to know the truth of something follow the money trail and it will lead you to the culprit, and it is no different in this instance. Erick, bear with me. I am going to repeat excerpts from a quote I cited just a few minutes ago, but it punctuates my point here, which is that to the Moneyed Elite the public are nothing more than pawns to be used to achieve their goals. Our lives mean nothing to them.

"The real menace of our republic is the invisible government... At the head... are the Rockefeller Standard Oil interest and a small group of powerful banking houses generally referred to as international bankers. The little coterie of powerful international bankers virtually run the United States government for their own selfish purposes. They practically control both political parties."
                              – John F. Hylan, Mayor of N.Y. [1918-1925]

By point of example Rockefeller's Standard Oil supplied both U.S. forces and the Vietcong in the Vietnam War, and had war been officially declared [remember it was officially a police action] I assure you his actions would have resulted in him being charged as a war criminal. But that didn't happen, but what did happen was that he made a fortune off of the war at the expense of the lives of thousands of American solders whose mothers were left to morn the death of their children!

Most Americans don't realize that while America sits on its moral high horse spouting about human rights violations and condemning political leaders all over the world **"AMERICA IS THE NUMBER ONE ARMS DEALER IN THE WORLD."** We may spout moral platitudes but at the end of the day it is American made weapons which are responsible for the carnage and mass murder and it is the likes of Rockefeller who are getting rich off the blood money.

And if you think for a second that our highest political leaders aren't sharing in the profits you are wrong. For example according to author Dan Briody in his book The Iron Triangle: Inside the Secret World of the Carlyle Group, after President Ronald Reagan [one of the few modern day presidents I had any respect for] got out of office in 1987 he and Secretary of Defense Frank Carlucci founded the Carlyle Group. The intent was to bring together former military and government officials to form a Capital Investment Group that would, use their contacts in order to leverage investments in Defense Industry Projects. Who says war isn't profitable and who says government officials don't profit from their positions. So Erick let me ask you a question. If you were one of these rich and powerful men we have been discussing how motivated do you think you would be to promote peace?

Erick: Well gramps I see where you are coming from. You are suggesting that these men not only didn't promote peace they did everything they could to promote war.

Gramps: You're dam right! That is exactly what I am saying and that isn't all. They sold America out as well!

Erick: What do you mean they sold America out?

Gramps: In March 2006 the Carlyle Group website announced that: The Carlyle Group, by now a global private investment equity firm headquartered in Washington DC, was forming an eight man investment team. Their stated objective was, to raise a multi-billion dollar fund the purpose of which was **to purchase U.S. Infrastructure Projects**, including U.S. highways which would become toll roads. The Team was headed by Robert W. Dove formerly of Bechtel Enterprise and Barry Gold former Managing Director of The Structured Finance Group of Citi-Corp. Salomon Smith Barney. [According to Corsi]

Erick, this is nothing less than the planned dismantling of the U.S. infrastructure. Public assets, paid for with tax payer money sold off to international investors without any input from the public. Public assets which would become profit centers for international investors, not to mention the National Security issues of having foreign investors operating say a water plant or an airport.

According to Corsi who sites The Guardian, former President George W. Bush gave speeches and advised on various Carlyle Group projects for which he received substantial compensation. This is yet another instance of corruption and influence peddling where the office of the President is used by the Money Manipulators to undermine the best interest of the American people and it has to be stopped.

Their opinion of our solders is that: Military men are: *"...dumb, stupid animals to be used as pawns for foreign policy."*
– Woodwars and Berstein, <u>The Final Days</u>.

To you moms out there, America needs a strong defensive capability, but it is time to stop letting these war criminals send our children to their deaths to serve their financial and political agendas!

The Media: "THE WATCHMEN ON THE TOWER"
Gramps: By the turn of the century, other than for Fox News virtually every major news outlet was owned by the Moneyed Elite and their organizations were full of TC and CFR members who took their marching orders from their masters in the Shadow Government! Matter of fact it really goes back much further than that. Virtually everything we were told about foreign and domestic affairs was nothing more than propaganda. They infiltrated the schools and rewrote our history books. They launched a campaign to undermine the influence of Christianity. They lied to us about the financial condition of the economy and even facilitated the predatory lending practices that eventually brought the economy to its knees. They created false flag events and misinformation to get us into WWI, WWII, The Vietnam War, and The Wars in Iraq and Afghanistan which profited them and cost us the lives of our children, but that is tomorrow's topic.

Erick I apologize because I know I have used this quote before, but it really punctuates just exactly the degree to which our media was and is controlled by the Shadow Government.

"We are grateful to the Washington Post, the New York Times, Time Magazine and other great publications whose directors have attended meetings and respected the promises of discretion for almost 40 years. It would have been impossible for us to develop our plan for the world if we had been subject to the light of publicity during those years...."

Gramps: Erick please look over the next chart and then we can finish our conversation.

THE MEDIA

NAME	TITLE	CFR	TC
CBS			
Laurence A. Tisch	CEO	CFR	
Roswell Gilpatric		CFR	
James Houghton		CFR	TC
Henry Schacht		CFR	TC
Dan Rather		CFR	
Richard Hottelet		CFR	
Frank Stanton		CFR	
ABC			
Thomas S. Murphy	CEO	CFR	
Barbara Walters		CFR	
John Connor		CFR	
Diane Sawyer		CFR	
John Scall		CFR	
BALTIMORE SUN			
Henry Trewhitt		CFR	
NBC/RCA			
John F. Welch	CEO	CFR	
Jane Pfeiffer		CFR	
Lester Crystal		CFR	
R.W. Sonnenfeidt		CFR	TC
John Petty		CFR	TC
Tom Brokaw		CFR	
David Brinkley		CFR	
John Chancellor		CFR	
Marvin Kalb		CFR	
Irving R. Levine		CFR	
Herbert Schlosser		CFR	
Peter G. Peterson		CFR	
John Sawhill		CFR	

THE MEDIA

NAME	TITLE	CFR	TC
DOW JONES & CO (WALL STREET JOURNAL)			
Richard Wood		CFR	
Robert Bartley		CFR	TC
Karen House		CFR	
READERS DIGEST			
George V. Grune	CEO	CFR	
William G. Bowen	Dir.	CFR	
SYNDICATED COLUMNISTS			
Georgia Anne Geyer		CFR	
Ben J. Wattenberg		CFR	
NATIONAL REVIEW			
Wm. F. Buckley, Jr.		CFR	
WASHINGTON TIMES			
Arnaud De Borchgrave		CFR	
PUBLIC BROADCAST SERVICE			
Robert Mcneil		CFR	
Jim Lehrer		CFR	
C. Hunter-Gault		CFR	
Hodding Carter III		CFR	
Daniel Schorr		CFR	
CHILDREN'S TV WORKSHOP [SESAME STREET]			
Joan Ganz Cooney	Pres.	CFR	
CABLE NEWS NETWORK			
W. Thomas Johnson	Pres.		TC

THE MEDIA

NAME	TITLE	CFR	TC
U.S. NEWS & WORLD REPORT			
David Gergen			TC
ASSOCIATED PRESS			
Stanley Swinton		CFR	
Harold Anderson		CFR	
Katharine Graham		CFR	TC
REUTERS			
Michael Posner		CFR	
TIME, INC.			
Ralph Davidson		CFR	
Donald M. Wilson		CFR	
Henry Grunwald		CFR	
Alexander Heard		CFR	
Sol Linowitz		CFR	
Thomas Watson, Jr.		CFR	
Strobe Talbott		CFR	
NEW YORK TIMES CO.			
Richard Gelb		CFR	
William Scranton		CFR	TC
John F. Akers	Dir.	CFR	
Louis V. Gerstner, Jr.	Dir.	CFR	
George B. Munroe	Dir.	CFR	
Donald M. Stewart	Dir.	CFR	
Cyrus R. Vance	Dir.	CFR	
A.M. Rosenthal		CFR	
Seymour Topping		CFR	
James Greenfield		CFR	
Max Frankel		CFR	

THE MEDIA

NAME	TITLE	CFR	TC
Jack Rosenthal		CFR	
John Oakes		CFR	
Harrison Salisbury		CFR	
H.L. Smith		CFR	
Steven Rattner		CFR	
Richard Burt		CFR	
Flora Lewis		CFR	

NEWSWEEK/WASHINGTON POST

Katharine Graham		CFR	
Deb. Katzenbach		CFR	
Robert Christopher		CFR	
Osborne Elliot		CFR	
Phillip Geyelin		CFR	
Murry Marder		CFR	
Maynard Parker		CFR	
George Will		CFR	TC
Robert Kaiser		CFR	
Meg Greenfield		CFR	
Walter Pincus		CFR	
Murray Gart		CFR	
Peter Osnos		CFR	
Don Oberdorfer		CFR	

Erick it is time the American people wake up and realize what has been done to us. Americans are a peace loving people and if we knew the truth we wouldn't go along with either America's foreign or domestic policies because we would understand that they are not in our best interest and they are not in the best interest of other nations either. We have been used to promote Global Empire and we didn't even realize it.

"If a nation expects to be ignorant and free, in a state of civilization, it expects what never was and never will be."   – Thomas Jefferson

Along these lines consider what Henry Ford had to say about the way our monetary system is controlled: *"It is well enough that the People of the nation do not understand our banking and monetary system for if they did, I believe there would be a revolution before tomorrow morning."* – Henry Ford, Founder Ford Motor Co.

The following quote provides insight as to just how completely we are controlled, and that control is not just financial. The control extends to the false information we are provided and how it influences most of our day to day decisions. As the following quote demonstrates we are a thoroughly controlled and manipulated society and it is time we woke up and realize it so we can begin to come to our senses, realize who the enemy is and begin to fight back.

"For a long time I felt that FDR had developed many thoughts and ideas that were his own to benefit this country, the United States. But he did not. Most of his thoughts were carefully manufactured for him in advance by the Council on Foreign Relations – One World Group. The United Nations is but a long range international banking apparatus clearly set up for financial and economic profit by a small group of powerful One-World Revolutionaries, hungry for profit and power. The One-World government leaders and their very close bankers have now acquired full control of the money and credit of the privately owned Federal Reserve Bank."
                    – Strob Talbott Former U.S. Deputy Sec. of State

During Obama's Presidency we saw a full court press put on suppression of the media and our Constitutional rights of freedom of speech. For example consider what Marl Lloyd, Obama's Diversity Czar [a communist term] had to say about freedom of speech:

"Pressure, pressure, pressure...we need to apply pressure and direct that pressure not at the government, but through the government at our true opposition the broadcasters ...my focus here is not freedom of speech or the press...this freedom is all too often an exaggerated... blind reference to freedom of speech or the press...serves as a distraction from the critical examination of other communications policies."
                    – Prolog To A Farce: Author Mark Lloyd

Then there was this wonderful inspiring quote: *"Any serious effort to*

reform the media system would have to necessarily be part of a revolutionary program to overthrow the capitalist system itself."
 – The Monthly Review 2008: Robert McChenny Founder Free Press

Gramps: All I can say is if that doesn't scare you nothing will. They pretty much came out and said the American people are the enemy and they have to be controlled and their speech suppressed! Erick just in case you have any illusions left that our media reports the news openly and honestly consider this quote.

"The Central Intelligence Agency owns everyone of any significance in the major media." – William Colby [Former CIA Director]

I am afraid that with the notable exception of Fox our media is nothing more than an organized **Misinformation Propaganda Machine** run by the Money Manipulators and our own CIA who if we only knew have been behind many atrocities. Again that is the subject of another conversation.

The Monetary System: **Gramps:** Erick we have already talked a lot about how the strategy of the Money Manipulators is to control Sovereign Nation States by getting control of their monetary system, manipulating the value of the currency and eventually collapsing the economic system. There isn't a lot I need to add. I do however want you to read a couple of quotes that will help you understand exactly what has to be done to save America.

"The government should create, issue, and circulate all currency. Creating and issuing money is a supreme prerogative of government and its greatest creative opportunity. Adopting these principles will save the taxpayers immense sums of interest and money will cease to be the master and become the servant of humanity."

Well we gave up the right to create currency, and exactly what President Thomas Jefferson said would happen, happened. He said: *"The Central bank is an institution of the most deadly hostility existing against the principles and form of our Constitution...if the American people allow private banks to control the issuance of the currency, first by inflation and then by devaluation the banks and corporations that will grow up around them will deprive the people of all their property until their children will wake up homeless on the continent their fathers conquered."*

And now in hindsight we know Senator Barry Goldwater was right as well when he said: *"The Income tax created more criminals than any other act of government."*

Erick, since the Fed got control of issuance of our currency there has been approximately 96% devaluation in the value of the dollar. And when the government rammed the Stimulus down our throats it was a repeat of 1929 all over. It was just like Congressman McFadden said in 1934: *"It was a carefully contrived occurrence. International bankers sought to bring about a condition of despair, so that they might emerge the **rulers of us all**."*

*"The Bill [referring to the Stimulus] was actually a **Coup De Ta by Wall Street**. The bill didn't just give $700 Billion to the banks. It was a blank check. As of Feb. 2009 $9.7 trillion has disappeared into a black hole."* – U.S. Tax Payers Risk 9.7 Trillion on Bailout Program by Mark K. Pittman and Bob Ivry

Gramps: So Erick do you agree with the quotes you just read?

Erick: Yes of course!

Gramps: Then the $64,000 question is what are you going to do about it?

Erick: Honestly gramps I don't know what to do. Based on what you have told me Lincoln, McKinley, Kennedy and McFadden all tried to get rid of the Fed and they were all killed.

Gramps: Yes you are correct, but you forgot about President Jackson. He got rid of the Central Bank of his day so it can be done. The others tried to stand up against the Money Manipulators alone. Jackson did it in public with the support of the public. You can do the same thing. You need to rally popular opinion and organize mass peaceful protest like the Tea Party did when they rose up in the 2010 elections. Remember you are dealing with a parasitic organization and no matter how much it wants you to believe you can't defeat it you have to **remember a parasite can't exist without its host**. You have the power you just don't realize it. Take a look at the following charts and when you are done I will tell you how to get rid of the parasite once and for all!

INTERNATIONAL MONETARY SYSTEM
WORLD BANK PRESIDENTS

Since 1968 all but one of the Presidents of The World Bank have been members of the Trilateral Commission.

NAME	POSITION & Term In Office
Robert McNamara	President (1968-1981)
A.W. Clauson	President (1981-1986)
Barbara Conable	President (1986-1991)
Lewis Preston	President (1991-19950
James Wolfenson	President (1995-2005)
Paul Wolfowits	President (2005-2007)
Robert Zeellick	President (2007-Present)

WORLD BANK PRESIDENTS ARE APPOINTED BY THE PRESIDENT OF THE UNITED STATES!

FEDERAL RESERVE SYSTEM
[PAST & PRESENT - PARTIAL LIST]

NAME	POSITION	CFR	TC
Paul Volcker	Chairman	CFR	TC
Alan Greenspan	Former Chairman	CFR	TC
Sam Y. Cross	Manager, Foreign Open Market Acct.	CFR	
Robert F. Erburu	Chmn. San Francisco Fed. Res. Bank	CFR	
Robert P. Forrestal	Pres. Atlanta Fed. Res. Bank	CFR	
Bobby R. Inman	Chmn., Dallas Fed. Res. Bank	CFR	TC
Robert H. Knight Esq.	Unknown	CFR	
Steven Muller	Unknown	CFR	
John R. Opel	Unknown	CFR	
Anthony M. Solomon	Unknown	CFR	TC
Edwin M. Truman	Staff Dir. International Finance	CFR	
Cyrus R. Vance	Unknown	CFR	
E. Gerald Corrigan	V. Chmn./Pres. NY Fed. Res. Bank	CFR	
Richard N. Cooper	Chmn. Boston Fed. Res. Bank	CFR	

TREASURY DEPARTMENT

NAME	POSITION	CFR	TC
Henry Paulson	U.S. Treasury Secretary	CFR	
Robert R. Glauber	Under Sec., Finance	CFR	
David C. Mulford	Under Sec., Intntl Affairs	CFR	
Robert M. Bestani	Dep Asst Sec., Intntl. Monetary Affairs	CFR	
J. French Hill	Dep. Asst. Sec., Corp Finance	CFR	
John M. Niehuss	Dep. Asst. Sec., Intntl. Monetary Affairs	CFR	
Roger Altman	Deputy Sec	CFR	

BANKING INSTITUTIONS

NAME	POSITION	CFR	TC
CHASE MANHATTAN CORP			
Thomas G. Labrecque	Chairman & CEO	CFR	
Robert R. Douglass	Vice Chairman	CFR	TC
Willard C. But	Cher, Dir.	CFR	
Richard W. Lyman	Dir.	CFR	
Joan Ganz Cooney	Dir.	CFR	
David T. Mclaughlin	Dir.	CFR	
Edmund T. Pratt, Jr.	Dir.	CFR	
Henry B. Schacht	Dir.	CFR	
CHEMICAL BANK			
Walter V. Shipley	Chairman	CFR	
Robert J. Callander	President	CFR	
William C. Pierce	Exec.Officer	CFR	
Randolph W. Bromery	Dir.	CFR	
Charles W. Duncan, Jr.	Dir.	CFR	
George V. Grune	Dir.	CFR	
Helen L. Kaplan	Dir.	CFR	
Lawrence G. Rawl	Dir.	CFR	
Richard D. Wood	Dir.	CFR	
Michael I. Sovern	Dir.	CFR	

CITICORP			
John S. Reed	Chairman	CFR	
William R. Rhodes	Vice Chairman	CFR	
Richard S. Braddock	President	CFR	
John M. DeuTch	Dir.	CFR	
Clifton C. Garvin Jr.	Dir.	CFR	
C. Peter Mccolough	Dir.	CFR	
Rozanne L. Ridgeway	Dir.	CFR	
Franklin A. Thomas	Dir.	CFR	
MORGAN GUARANTY			
Lewis T. Preston	Chairman	CFR	
BANKERS TRUST NEW YORK CORP.			
Charles S. Stanford	Chairman	CFR	
Alfred Brittain III	Dir.	CFR	
Vernon E. Jordan	Dir.	CFR	
Richard L. Gelb	Dir.	CFR	
Patricia C Stewart	Dir.	CFR	
BANK AMERICA			
Andrew F. Brimmer	Dir.	CFR	
Ignazio E. Lozano, Jr.	Dir.	CFR	
Ruben F. Mettler	Dir.	CFR	
FIRST NATIONAL BANK OF CHICAGO			
Barry F. Sullivan			TC
SECURITIES & EXCHANGE COMMISSION			
Michael D. Mann	Dir Int. Affairs	CFR	
MANUFACTURERS HANOVER DIRECTORS			
Cyrus Vance		CFR	
G. Robert Durham		CFR	
George B. Munroe		CFR	
Marina V. Whitman		CFR	TC
Charles J. Pilliod, Jr.		CFR	
FIRST CITY BANCORP, TEXAS			
A. Robert Abboud	CEO	CFR	

ACTION STEPS: In addition to the other recommendations we have already discussed you need to: **17) Organize A Mass Boycott of The Nations Largest Banks.** Any bank that is "Too Large To Fail" needs to be broken up. That is why we have anti trust laws. If you have a credit card with one of them get rid of it. It is not as easy to change mortgage companies but if you are in a position to, then by all means do so, but certainly if you buy a new property in the future do not use one of super banks.

According to Simon Johnson and James Kwak authors of 13 Bankers the following banks have combined assets equal to 60% of the countries Gross domestic Product. These are the banks you need to boycott: Bank of America, J.P. Morgan, Chase, Citigroup, Wells Fargo, Goldman Sach and Morgan Stanley.

How To Minimize Influence Peddling!

VITALLY IMPORTANT: Gramps: Erick remember there are approximately 4,000 people in the TC and CFR, so all we have discussed are those in the highest profile positions. Those able to do the most harm, like for example those who can drive our energy and healthcare policies, those who can undermine our Constitution, those who affect our National Security etc. I should add that almost all major corporations [especially our banks, energy companies, pharmaceutical companies, armaments companies and media] have Top Executives who belong to the TC and or CFR. They spend billions buying influence of our legislators and it has to stop. We can't vote them out of office so the next best thing is to clean out Washington by **voting out all incumbents and impose sweeping election reforms** including abolishing all Lobbyist! That will cut off the head of the snake and put the American people in a position to have the interest of the people represented for the first time in decades!

The State of The Union!
A Eulogy For America!

PERSONAL NOTE: Stepping out of character and time line I want to close this chapter by giving you current financial figures so you know just how bad our economic situation is and just how guilty of <u>Fiscal Malfeasance</u> our Legislators in Washington are! If these men were in Corporate America this type of financial mismanagement would land them in prison, which is where they rightly belong. They are not stupid. They are corrupt and America needs to wake up to that fact!

Remember in order to usher in <u>The New World Order</u> the U.S. must fall! Well David Walker has a good idea of just how that can be accomplished and it would seem the folks in Washington not only know about it but are quietly supporting it from behind the scenes.

David Walker the Controller General of The United States. [An appointed not elected position] said:

*"That the numbers were so bad and the **government so disinterested** that he resorted to taking his message to the American tax payer and opinion makers in what he called: 'A Fiscal Wake Up Tour.'"*

"...the survival of our Republic is at stake!"

"... the most serious threat facing the U.S. isn't someone hiding in a cave in Afghanistan or Pakistan, but our own fiscal irresponsibility."

"We have been in 13 cities outside Washington with this fiscal inventory. People are absolutely starved for two things—the truth and leadership."

Walker's fiscal disclosures have been called: **"The dirty little secret everybody in Washington knows...A Senate financial truth so inconvenient that no one wants to talk about it."**

According to Walker:

"As serious as the Social Security problem is, the Medicare problem is five times more serious. The problem is that people keep living longer and medical costs keep rising at twice the level of inflation, but instead of dealing with the problem the President and Congress made things worse when they included prescription drug coverage under

the Medicare Program in what Walker called the most fiscally irre-
sponsible piece of legislation since the 1960's. We promised way more
than we can afford..." http://www.youtube.com/watch?v=OS2fl2p9iVs
The Andy Court Show Documentary IOUSA: http://www.youtube.com/
watch?v=O_TjBNjc9Bo

The numbers I am about to share with you are available on www.
whitehouse.gov. They come from the Office of Management and Budget so there can be no question the government knows full well the
road they are leading us down.

Fiscal Year	Total Federal Debt	Fiscal Year	Total Federal Debt	Fiscal Year	Total Federal Debt
2009	$12.219 T	2013	$17.509 T	2017	$22.095
2010	$14.087 T	2014	$18.648 T	2018	$23.272
2011	$15.276 T	2015	$19.773 T	2019	$24.505
2012	$16.388 T	2016	$20.930 T		

Numbers are in trillions of dollars

**If the idea of a $24 Trillion National Debt isn't bad enough there
is more. If we figure in current unfunded entitlement programs
our National Debt as of 2019 will be $117 Trillion or $390,000 for
every man woman and child in the country which is $1,560,000
for a family of four.** Let me put that in perspective for you. Let's
assume you made $50,000 a year and worked for 40 years your life-
time earnings would be $2,000,000 and your family's portion of the
National debt comes to $1,560,000. But wait these numbers don't
include the entitlement programs the government is still pushing. By
the time you factor in National Healthcare and Cap and Trade we may
well be paying the government for the privilege of working. That is of
course sarcasm, but I trust you get my point. I ask you to stop and seriously contemplate what I have just disclosed! **I don't see how anyone
Conservative or Liberal, Republican or Democrat could conclude
other than this level of debt is unsustainable. The only conceivable
outcome is: Economic Collapse which is exactly what Obama and
the crew in Washington want. A Crisis of sufficient magnitude to
usher us into their One World Government. The Empire of Evil,**
which just happens to be our topic for tomorrow! Good night. See you
tomorrow.

Chapter 6

The New World Order —
THE EMPIRE OF EVIL:

The American People Fight Back –
Developing Our Tactical Strategies!

"History records that the money changers have used every form of
abuse, intrigue, deceit, and violent means possible to maintain their
control over governments by controlling money and its issuance."
     – James Madison, 4th President of the United States (1809-1817)

If you believe the above quote to be true as I do, then the question
becomes how do you fight back and break the cycle of oppression,
break the chains that bind us, invisible though they be, and set society
free to experience real freedom? That is what this chapter is about. It
is about setting the captives free!

"Efforts and courage are not enough without purpose and direction."
                              – President John F. Kennedy

Gramps: Kennedy was right you have to have purpose and direction. That said the purpose of this chapter is to make sure that before
you and your friends take on the Government and Banks that you are
fully aware of what you are up against and have properly prepared and
planned. <u>I can assure you that your adversary knows everything there
is about **how to bend the public to its will.**</u> So our objective is to get

into their heads just like they have gotten into ours. We have to learn how to be immune to their lies and know how to wage a successful long term campaign designed to put control of this great nation back in the hands of the people where it belongs. Let's start with a quote from Obama: *"If a people cannot trust their government to do the job for which it exist – to protect them and to promote their common welfare – all else is lost."*

Gramps: Like so many politicians before him Obama was a master at telling us what we wanted to hear and then doing something quite different. We are having this conversation precisely because we cannot trust our government to promote our common good so we need to figure out how to get the crooks out of power and install people of integrity, people who haven't been bought and paid for by forces counter to our interest.

PERSONAL NOTE: Stepping out of character I want to speak to you from my heart. I believe that there are millions, hopefully billions of hard working, honest people in America and around the world who are concerned about what is happening in the world today. We can see that things are headed in a direction that could well end up in a one world dictatorship but we either don't know what to do or we don't believe there is anything we can do. Hopefully by the time you finish this chapter you will be of the opinion that we can make a difference. Hopefully by the time you finish this book you will know exactly what we need to do and you will be prepared to step out in faith and courage and join in the fight for a free world where we can all live in peace and harmony. I have two sons and I want them to have a chance to live in a free society. I don't want to think that in 2030 I will actually be talking to my grandson telling him about how America lost her freedom.

I am a little reticent to say what I am about to because I know that not everyone who reads this book believes in the supernatural, but I do. I believe in a supernatural God that can and will deliver us if we will drop to our knees and surrender to him. I believe I and many others have been called by God to deliver a Clarion call to the world. The world is at a crossroads and before us are two paths. One leads to slavery and oppression and the other to freedom and salvation. This has become am immoral world ruled by greed and materialism and if we continue down this path the outcome will surely be slavery and oppression. It will be like the children of Israel who suffered 300 years of bondage in Egypt and 40 years in the wilderness while God taught them to surrender to his will. If on the other hand we will drop to our knees now and surrender to his will we can be spared all that pain and suffering. The choice is ours.

I know that we are up against a global empire of unimaginable power that is willing to do what ever it takes to enslave us, but I believe with all my heart that they can be defeated by a unified, committed morally resolute citizenry with a plan and with God on our side.

Erick: So what do we do next?

Gramps: Well I thought we might do something a little different today. This is a pretty intense subject so I thought we might lighten things up by playing a game.

Erick: What kind of game?

Gramps: A strategy game. It will put you on your toes and bring clarity to the material we have already covered while teaching you to better understand you adversary and be able to anticipate his actions. The objective of the game is to become your adversary, think as he thinks, act as he acts and learn how to use his strengths and weaknesses against him in order to defeat him. In effect you are assuming an alter ego for purposes of strategizing. By the way I call this game Anticipatory Thinking. It teaches you to analyze any situation by asking a series of probing questions about [what, where, when, how and why] your opponent does what he does. It yields amazing insight.

Anticipatory Thinking!

Answering The What Question: Erick I know you play chess so as we get into our strategizing sessions I want you to think like a chess master. Gramps what are you getting at? You may not know this but Chess was invented by a Chinese general who used the game to teach his officers war strategy. That is exactly what we are learning today, war strategy. The first thing a Chess Master does is memorize the board and then plan his next several moves in advance while at the same time anticipating his opponents counter moves. In our case that relates to the fact that we have to know what has occurred in the past in order to be able to anticipate the future. That is why we had to go through all that boring history: *"so we could learn to anticipate what our opponent will do before he does it."* It keeps us from making the same mistakes over and over.

Answering The Why Question: gives you vitally important insight as to *"what motivates your opponent"* which in turn reveals a lot about how resolute he is, which sheds light on his character and morality or lack thereof. Without this perspective you will invariably underestimate your adversary in which event you have lost the war before it even starts.

Answering The Who Question: Any good military strategist knows that in a battle the opponent you have to defeat isn't so much the troops on the ground as it is the general behind the scenes who is calling the shots. That is what we have to keep in mind as we develop our strategy. We can remove the President of the United States and all the Congressmen and Senators and all the CFR and TC appointees within our government, but if we don't get rid of the puppet master **[The Federal Reserve]** who pulls their strings he will just rise again, buy new puppets and come at us over and over again until he finally defeats us. That is exactly what has been happening to us for the last 200 years. For example in 2008 the public was fed up with Republican President Bush so they naively turned to a charismatic Democratic Candidate, Barack Obama and voted him into office not understanding that the puppet master saw their frustration and simply switched isles and bought the Democratic candidate. The name may have changed but the agenda went on unimpeded.

With this in mind it is crucial that we focus our strategy on the head of the beast, the puppet masters of old who originated from the Oligarchical Ruling Class of Europe which our founding fathers fled from when they came to America. These men are obsessed with power and they see themselves as an Elite Ruling Class that believes that all the resources of the world are theirs to control, to meter out to whom they please. It is crucial that we understand how they view us. To them we are nothing more than their slave labors. We have no value other than what they assign to us. **The point is we cannot think of these men in terms of our morality. We have to understand they are capable of committing any atrocity in order get what they want.** If we cannot see them in this way we will grossly underestimate them and miscalculate their actions and they will surely win. In order to win this war we have to have a two pronged strategy which simultaneously gets rid of the puppets and the puppet master, or in military parlance we have to realize that the war has to be fought on two fronts simultaneously.

Answering The How Question: Once we understand Who our enemy is and What he is willing and capable of doing to get what he wants our next objective is to understand *"How"* he goes about achieving his objectives. In large part that question was answered by identifying exactly who we are up against. Our enemy will use the power of all the political offices they have infiltrated so we have multiple enemies to deal with. In terms of tactical analysis, we have to determine our enemy's modus operandi which is to say: is he brash and impulsive or is he patient and plodding? Is he direct and frontal with his attack, or does he use misdirection and subterfuge? Is he careful and does he play it safe or is he a risk taker? How does he handle defeat, which is to say does he give up, withdraw and regroup or does he go on the offensive and double his efforts? And as strange as it may seem, does he exhibit all of these actions at different times? That is not only possible but almost certain, which points out our need to answer the when and where questions.

Answering The When and Where Questions: is about determining at which stage of the war you are at. Is it at the <u>covert stage</u> where one party is trying to overthrow the other from within, without the other even realizing they are under attack? Has the <u>fist skirmish</u> just happened and both sides are just feeling each other out to determine strengths and weaknesses and determine future strategies. Is the war nearing a <u>pivot point</u> where one of the parties feels victory is within reach and is ready for a full frontal attack designed to force surrender of the opponent? **If you don't understand at <u>what stage of war</u> your adversary considers himself to be your counter offensive tactics will almost certainly be ineffective because a military strategist employs different strategies at different point in a war.**

<u>**Identifying Your Opponents Strengths and Weaknesses**</u>: Once we

have answered the Who - Why - What - Where - When - and How Questions we have to determine the enemies strengths and weakness which includes *"His Assets and Resources,"* This might include money or people under his direct control or hidden assets that he controls indirectly such as [mercenaries or spies] which is to say people who he has paid for services to be rendered when and where necessary. Mercenaries and Spies are generally hidden assets which function most effectively if no one knows who they are. That is why we had to identify all the organizations which have been infiltrated by the TC and CFR and why we have to assume all our politicians in Washington have been compromised.

Putting it all together and formulating our strategy: Anticipatory Thinking is like a video game. It has beginner and advanced levels. As we get ready to go to the advanced level where we actually plan and execute the battle we have to be able to combine everything we have learned which means we have to be able to combine the What - Where - When - How - Why - and Who Questions along with the assessment of strength and weaknesses in order to be able to extrapolate or anticipate not only our adversaries next move, but his next several moves and our counter moves. The player who can think most like his opponent and think the furthest into the future generally wins.

It's like they say, *"the best defense is a good offense."* At the present the American public is almost 100% in a defensive mode, which means we are losing the war. We have to get up to speed. The Tea Party represents our first attempt to field an offensive team, but our play book is woefully deficient because we have allowed the enemy to confuse us, misdirect us, intimidate us, out maneuver us and worst of all we have allowed him to divide us. A house divided can't stand. Our objective here is to become a **united fighting force** capable of out thinking and out maneuvering our enemy and likewise capable of using his strength against him.

Either We Stand Together Or We Will Lose The War and Along With It Our Freedom!

Erick I know we discussed this yesterday but it is crucially important so I am going to repeat myself. Our greatest weakness is that we are a house divided and that has to stop! We see ourselves as Republicans VS Democrats, Liberals VS Conservatives, Black VS Whites, Moslems VS Christians and the most dangerous division of all is between those who want the government to take care of them VS those that want the government to get out of our way and let us take care of ourselves. The truth is that it is the government who has held us back and oppressed us. It is their unfair taxes which are impoverishing us. They and no one else are our enemy. **Once they fully execute their take over we can expect them to kill or imprison anyone who they deem to be nonproductive individuals who constitute a drain on what they consider to be their valuable resources.** This means the following groups will be primary targets: The elderly, physically and mentally impaired and any and all lower socioeconomic groups which mean anyone who depends on government services like, welfare recipients, those on social security etc. The second targets will be anyone who they view as a threat to their take over. This group includes protesters, certain religious groups, certain ethnic groups, intellectuals and entrepreneurs etc. All in all they are prepared to imprison or kill millions of us. Remember the ad from a few pages back. They are setting up **internment camps** to imprison American citizens and **at their own admission they believe political power comes largely from the barrel of a gun!** Their intentions couldn't be any clearer! If we don't want to be led like Sheep to the slaughter we have no other choice but to stand together and fight back! **We have to understand that our only hope of defeating them is to come together as a united resolute force committed to regaining our freedom** through every form of peaceful protest possible!!!

Reviewing Our Intelligence Information

Now we have a basic understanding of what *"Anticipatory Thinking"* is, but we are still not quite ready to profile our adversary or develop a strategic battle plan. In military parlance we are at the Strategic Command Center near the front lines and all the commanders are assembled to plan the assault. We are waiting for the latest Intelligence Reports so we can make the best most informed decisions. With this in mind I have assembled a selection of excerpts from previous quotes which I would like you to read before we begin our strategy session. I want us to have a fresh image in our minds of exactly who our enemy is, what he is capable of, some of the tactics he has used in the past, and some of the resources he has at his disposal. **NOTE:** I also paraphrased the quotes in order to accentuate their intent. Paraphrases are in [ ] and I did not site references because all the quotes are excerpts of previous quotes or quotes further down in this chapter.

Selected Quotes and Paraphrases:

- *"A crisis is an event that forces democracies to make decisions they wouldn't otherwise make."* [A tool, real or staged, used by people in power to manipulate political events.]

- *"Give me control of a nation's money supply and I care not who makes the laws."* [Describes the means by which the shadow government wields power and enslaves nations and individuals!]

- *"We shall have world government whether or not you like it."* [Declaration of war!]

- *"An Oligarchy which extends the rights of an elite ruling class over those who exist to serve them."* [Self appointed Ruling Class who view us as their slaves and nothing more!]

- *"Use economic power to gain control of first America then the rest of the world."* [Plan to bankrupt U.S. and declare global dictatorship.]

- *"The dirty little secret is that both houses of Congress are irrelevant."* [Shadow government is in control and will remain in control unless we take back the seat of power!]

- *"Fed Chairman said: ...no other agency of government can override actions that we take."* [The people have no voice in the political system and political leaders are puppets of Moneyed Elite!]

- *"International banks virtually run the U.S. for their own selfish purposes."* [A Monetary Dictatorship: run by The Federal Reserve, World Bank, IMF & UN]

- *"It is difficult for common good to prevail against the intense concentration of those who have* <u>special interest</u> *especially if the decisions are made behind closed doors."* [Unless we make a clean sweep of Washington, get rid of the FED, CFR and TC appointees, and ban lobbyists and secret meetings we will never regain control of our government!]

■ *"Freedom gradually disappears from every country over which England is enabled to gain control."* [Strategy of Free Trade System where they destroy a nation from within step by step, a little at a time! Sometimes called incrementalism.]

■ *"A gradual appearance of a more controlled society dominated by an elite unrestricted by traditional values."* [Threatens imposition of a tyrannical dictatorship!]

■ *"The free market is nonsense. We kind of agree with Mao that political power comes from the barrel of a gun."* [Admitted Communist faction within Obama Administration which is willing to use force to achieve its agenda of establishing a Communist Dictatorship!]

■ *"National Sovereignty wasn't such a great idea."* [Faction in Clinton Administration which discloses loyalty to New World Order not U.S. Republic.]

■ *"New world order is hybrid Capitalist/Communist Society."* [U.S. Republic will be replaced by Communist dictatorship! Conspiracy is global in reach.]

■ *"The UN regards 2/3 of human population as excess baggage."* [Can expect forced population reduction!]

■ *"Climate Bill will help bring in Global governance."* [Staged crisis to force us into One World Government!]

■ *"NATO is major stepping stone to New World Order."* [Potential occupation force!]

■ *"The Trilateral Commission is intended to be the vehicle for multinational consolidation of the commercial and banking interest by seizing control of the political government of the United States."* [Treasonous rogue element operating covertly within the government from president down.]

- *"It is ignorance to consider the UN's interest to be anything other than world political and military power."* [Military occupation force masquerading as peace keepers!]

- *"Our task of creating a Socialist America can only succeed when those who would resist us have been totally disarmed."* [Implementation of police state by usurping our Constitutional rights and taking away our means to defend ourselves against a corrupt government!]

- *"Surrender of U.S. sovereignty is key to one world order."* [Declaration of War against U.S. Republic!]

- *"The CIA owns everybody of any significance in the major media."* [Admission that media is propaganda machine and cannot be trusted.]

- *"The world order will be built by doing an end run on national sovereignty, eroding it piece by piece."* [Incremental unrelenting covert assault on our Republic!]

- *"We are not going to achieve a new world order without paying for it in blood as well as words and money."* [Declaration of war!]

- *"The Illegal we do immediately. The unconstitutional takes a little longer."* [Treasonous Revolutionary Rogue Element that must be removed from power!]

PERSONAL NOTE: Stepping out of character once again, this next section is not occurring in 2030 but rather in 2010 and therefore represents current events that are unfolding now or are anticipated to occur in the near future. This section is simply an effort to fully comprehend who our adversary is, what he is capable of, and therefore the level of commitment that will be required in order to defeat him. By the way the last chapter of the book is a comprehensive political platform. I have been inserting high level overviews of bits and pieces of that plan throughout the book, but I will bring it all together in a detailed step by step plan once we have covered absolutely everything.

Formulating Our Tactical Strategy!

Reflecting on the quotes you just read should give you a good idea of exactly what we are up against. We need to put aside our naiveté, cast aside all illusions and look into the black soul of the enemy and see the pure evil that is resolutely committed to enslaving us and ruling over us with utter disregard! We have to unmask him and see him for the many headed beast which he is.

Naming The Enemy and Identifying The Many Headed Beast = The WHO: We have to assume that The President and most of our Senators and Congressmen as well as their counter parts in Nation States all over the world have sold out to the Money Manipulators and are doing their bidding. In addition to our elected officials other heads of the beast can be found to reside in the Federal Reserve and other Central banks, the World Bank, IMF, WTO, UN and NATO as well as the Media and major corporations especially in the fields of energy, munitions and pharmaceuticals and imbedded within all these organizations we will find members of the Trilateral Commission and Council on Foreign Relations who are there to make sure that the New World Order Agenda of their masters is relentlessly pushed on those they see as their slave labors. For now we can't be concerned with all these entities. Our objective here is to Profile the people who are pulling the strings of all these men and organizations, the likes of the Rothschild's who are reportedly worth over $100 Trillion and the Rockefeller's who are reportedly worth over $10 Trillion and the other world leaders in the Bilderberg Group. **The Wealth of the world is consolidated in the hands of a select few men and the world will never know peace or prosperity till we take away their fortunes and prevent them from being able to issue currency to sovereign nations** whose sole right it is to issue currency. We don't need to be concerned with exactly who all these men are. What we want to do is develop a kind of group profile so we get an image of how the enemy thinks and what he is capable of.

VITALLY IMPORTANT: By the way they would have us believe that the key to financial prosperity is to take from the middle class and give to the lower class. No my friends the answer is to take the ill-gotten gains from the Banking Cartels and the Government which will prevent the predatory lending practices and oppressive taxes which are impoverishing us all and will allow true economic growth so we can all prosper and not at the expense of one another, but as a natural expression of a truly free open market system which generates enough wealth for all. This is the basis of the American System which made America great in the first place and can do so again!

Strategic Analysis: Hopefully we can finally figure out the rules of engagement.

Our 1st step: Stop the delusional belief that our elected officials in Washington are there to serve the public interest. Nothing could be further from the truth. For example the public is dependent on a bankrupt Social Security System, but Congress has a separate solvent retirement program. We are forced on an unpopular Universal Health-care Plan, but Congress refused to participate opting to keep their Private Cadillac Options. No they are there to serve their vested interest and to expedite the agenda of the special interest groups who have in one manner or another bought and paid for their services. Tactically this means that as they come up for election we have to vote out all incumbents and bring in new representatives who will commit to term limits and to do away with lobbyists. The apple barrel is rotten and all the apples have to go and we have to start over. Anything short of this is guaranteed to fail.

Our 2nd step: Target the head of the beast, which **means we have to take away from the Money Manipulators the means to create money.** It is therefore essential that the Federal Reserve be put out of business. We will discuss how to remove the Fed at a later time.

PAY CLOSE ATTENTION! This is the acid test of our resolve. If we are not prepared to do the two things enumerated above the war is over and we might as well just surrender.

<u>Understanding The Enemy and His End Game = The Why and Part of The How:</u> It is vitally important to understand that these men see themselves as innately superior to the masses. They are in many instances descended from the Ruling Oligarchy of Europe, the very men whose tyranny our founding fathers fled. They have a sense of entitlement, in that they view themselves as an elite ruling class! <u>In their minds **they own the world and all of its resources** and the rest of us only exist to do their bidding.</u> We have no inalienable rights, none what so ever. We are their Surfs, Peasants, Minions and Slaves and nothing more.

<u>Matter of fact in certain instances we are seen as</u> **liabilities not assets,** and liabilities are expendable. So as we have discussed before, anyone who cannot produce more than he consumes will be eliminated along with anyone who opposes their authority. But it doesn't stop there. <u>We are consuming their resources at what they view as</u> **an unsustainable rate**! In nature the answer to such an over population problem might be to say for example thin a deer herd. After all it is humane. Kill off the deer population and there will be more food for the remaining deer and fewer will starve. Or in our instance kill a few million or billion of us and there will be more resources for them in order to sustain their opulent lifestyles.

But it goes beyond resources. In the final analysis it is about power. Power is like opium. At first it exhilarates you, then it numbs you, then it controls you and finally it consumes you. These men are consumed by power and it is as the saying goes *"power corrupts and absolute power corrupts absolutely."* After all was not Caesar a God and cannot a God do what ever he wants without the petty concerns of man's morality? And did not Marie Antoinette say of the peasants who had no bread *"let them eat cake."* No my friends make no mistake; we are but livestock to be dealt with, with no regard.

<u>Strategic Analysis</u>: Many Europeans understand just exactly how evil the forces behind the New World Order are, but I believe most Americans are virtually clueless. We are still scratching our heads wondering how our elected officials could be so dumb, or why we can't get the Republicans and Democrats to put aside their differences and come together for the good of the nation. News flash! These men are not dumb, or inept, or incompetent; far from it! They are intelligent and they know exactly what they are doing. I shall shortly review the key highlights of the Presidential Administrations from Carter to Obama and it will become clear that there is a definite strategy at work. Each President lays the ground work for the agenda of the next. Like runners in a relay race they pass the baton from one administration to the next, never dropping it and never missing an opportunity to create the next **crisis** for the next administration to take advantage of in order to drive us relentlessly closer and closer to the day when they create the ultimate crisis—declare martial law, lock us down and implement their New World Order Dictatorship! My point here is, that this is all out war and we can scarcely afford to lose! Please read the following quote and really reflect on its meaning.

"Is life so dear, or peace so sweet, as to be purchased at the price of chains or slavery? Forbid it, Almighty God! I know not what course others may take but for me; give me liberty or give me death."

– Patrick Henry

VITALLY IMPORTANT:

<u>Our greatest weakness is:</u> We are a house divided and if we hope to have a chance in this war we have to come together as one voice, one mind and one body!

<u>Our second greatest weakness is:</u> Our lack of resolve! We fail to understand that if we lose this war we will live out our lives in oppression or worse we may well be killed! I stand with Patrick Henry and say give me liberty or give me death.

I still believe that most Americans are looking for a soft landing. They naively hope that all this will just go away. They don't want to see this National Debt Crisis for what it really is, an intentional plan to bankrupt the nation and make us believe that the only choice we have is to willingly submit to the New World Dictatorship. If we do that we will be giving up our freedom and submitting to the chains of oppression. **We must face the reality that there is no soft landing!** We waited too long to wake up and face reality. There are only hard choices left.

VITALLY IMPORTANT: Either we submit and live in poverty under communist oppression or we fight back. **Either way we will endure serious financial hardships,** but at least if we fight back we have a chance [I believe a good chance] to regain control of the reins of power and rebuild the nation hopefully as a Wiser More Godley Society. God doesn't want us to suffer but he does want us to turn away from materialism, turn to him and learn to live together in peace. Either way we will learn the lesson. The only question is will we willingly submit or will we have to suffer the chains of slavery.

I don't want to seem melodramatic, but things are truly that bad and these are truly our only choices. For my part I chose freedom at any cost. I have some more quotes for you to ponder as you consider your choices.

"The Man who trades freedom for security does not deserve nor will he ever receive either." – Benjamin Franklin

"When the people fear their government, there is tyranny: when the government fears the people there is liberty."
          – Thomas Jefferson Third U.S. President [1801-1809]

VITALLY IMPORTANT: We have discussed the fact that our biggest weakness is that we are a house divided and we have up to this point underestimated our adversary, but to this point our adversary has relied on these two weaknesses. If we can come together as a united, resolute force who truly understands what our adversary is capable of **we may force him into underestimating us** just like we did him, and with equally devastating effects. The war isn't over. Matter of fact it has just begun and I am betting on a people who are fighting for their freedom as opposed to an arrogant over confident totalitarian regime who relies on buying loyalty. There are a lot more of us than there are of them and we cannot afford to lose!

Understanding The Mechanism of Enslavement = The How:

This battle has been going on since the U.S. won the Revolutionary War! You say how can that be? We defeated the British and America emerged a free nation, free to pursue its dream of building a nation of free men and women dedicated to liberty and justice for all. Our founding fathers knew better. The annals of history are full of warnings from them, but over time we allowed the trappings of materialism to lull us into a false security and we became complacent. The enemy was so arrogant that he even told us exactly how he would return to rule us, but we didn't listen.

The following two quotes tell us in no uncertain terms the vehicle of our slavery and what we have to do if we want to end the slavery once and for all and declare our independence.

"I care not what puppet is placed on the throne of England to rule the Empire. ...The man that controls Britain's money supply controls the British Empire. And I control the money supply."
                                    – Baron Nathan Mayer Rothschild

How much clearer could it be? The U.S. President is a puppet of the Moneyed Elite. All you have to do is look at the actions of the last several presidents and there can be no doubt that this is a true statement. Well today the Rothschild's and their elite friends control the money supply of America [That has been a fact since 1913 when they installed The Federal Reserve Bank] and most of the world, which means they control our government and most of the governments of the world through the Puppet leaders they have installed to rule over us and do their bidding. This single quote gives us the Who and the How of our enslavement. The next quote tells us what we have to do if we want to be free to live our lives without oppression from the elite ruling class.

"Banking was conceived in iniquity and was born in sin. The bankers own the earth, Take it away from them, but leave them the power to create deposits, and with the flick of a pen they will create enough deposits to buy it back again. However, take it away and all the great fortunes like mine will disappear and they ought to disappear, for this would be a happier and better world to live in. But if you wish to

remain the slaves of bankers and pay the cost of your own slavery.
Then let them continue to create deposits. "
– Sir Josia Stamp, President of the Bank of England in the 1920's
and the second richest man in Britain

Strategic Analysis: I hope this explains why I have said repeatedly
that we have to get rid of the Fed. The Fed and for that matter all the
central banks around the world must go. They must be abolished and
the creation of currency must be put back in the hands of individual
Nation States. And as Josia Stamp said we must make sure they never
again *"have the power to create deposits."* Not only must the banks
go, but their minions must go as well. That means, as I said before,
we say goodbye and good riddance to the President of the U.S. and all
our Congressmen and Senators. Vote the puppets out never to return
which means the lobbyist who bought their services must go as well.
In addition we ban CFR and TC members from holding public office.

From a more current perspective we previously discussed the fact that
with the advent of international corporations the Money Manipulators
decided that the most effective way to establish an unchallenged economic monopoly was to go political so they formed the CFR and TC
and placed operatives in governments and major corporations around
the world. Thus was born the global shadow government which
became the real power behind the U.S. Government and most of the
major industrialized nations of the world.

**VITALLY IMPORTANT: <u>Understanding At What Stage We</u>
<u>Are In the Take Over = The Where and When</u>:** So, why does
the U.S. have to fall before they can birth The New World Order?
Simply put the U.S. is the most powerful military and economic
force on the planet. **If the American people were to wake up
and figure out what is happening and take back our government and military and unleash the creative genius that made
us great we could nix their global take over, so we have to fall**.
On the other hand if they can collapse the U.S. economy first and
get control of our military they can use it to force would be resist-
ers into the fold of the New World Order. So at what stage of the
take over are we?

The First Stage: They have patiently pursued their plans from the shadows for over 200 years, but the systematic bankruptcy of the U.S. didn't really go into full force till Wilson sold out his country and put the Illegal Federal Reserve into power giving the Money Manipulators the means to systematically cause the boom bust cycles which they have used to so skillfully siphon off the wealth of America.

The Second Stage: Then for nearly 100 years they have patiently nibbled away at our Republic a little at a time, bit by bit, attacking and then retreating into the shadows and then attacking again in an unrelenting series on incremental mostly unnoticeable steps. It is important that we realize that the attacks were not just financial. They had to condition us psychologically to be prepared to accept a Communist government. They had to assail the uniquely American sense of self reliance and ever so gradually get us to depend ever increasingly on the government as our provider. They herded us into cities, made us dependent on their corporations for our livelihood, systematically infiltrated our schools and reshaped our concept of self reliance and rugged individualism making each generation more and more pliable to their will. They took control of the media and used it as a propaganda machine to hide from us the truth of whom and what America was becoming. They desensitized us with, ever increasingly more and more sexually immoral desensitizing movies and music venues. And in the name of Social Justice they began the process of establishing a system of Social Entitlement Programs designed to eventually bankrupt the nation. And lastly with the morality of the nation sufficiently diluted they made a full frontal assault on our religious beliefs. This assault on our religious beliefs is crucially important because as our founding fathers knew a Republic form of Government is only suitable for a moral self reliant people who are willing to be ruled by the rule of the Law, the Constitution. That is why they had to relentlessly dismantle and or usurped the Constitution.

VITALLY IMPORTANT: <u>The First Step in the Restoration of America</u>: So in summary they had to mold us into a more pliable people if they hoped to rule us. So part of the restoration of America has to be to regain control of all these institutions. We have to reestablish ourselves as the hard working, fiercely self-reliant, moral, God fearing, law abiding people who founded this great nation and declared their independence from a tyrannical government in England, in order to form a more perfect union based on the inalienable rights of life, liberty and the pursuit of happiness and intentioned on a small central government which existed to protect a governmental system of the people by the people for the people. We have lost our identity and unless we regain it we are doomed. We need to get on our knees and pray to God who hears the prayer of a Righteous Man and surely answers them. We are fighting an unimaginably powerful and veil enemy and if we try to defeat him without surrendering to God and once again becoming a Godly people I can assure you we will lose the battle. We are surely fighting an evil carnal regime, but make no mistake we are also fighting a Spiritual Battle and we need supra-national help in order to win this war. We are coming into times that will make men's hearts faint! **So the very first step in our counter offensive is to get on our knees and pray as we have never prayed before.** God will not tolerate a lukewarm people. Either we surrender or we are in this battle alone, in which event we will surely lose.

<u>**The Third Stage:**</u> They are very close to being able to impose the New World Order and impose a global dictatorship. Having pretty much gained control of all our institutions and conditioned our minds with fifty years of unrelenting propaganda and manipulation they are free to focus almost exclusively on bankrupting us and creating a series of crisis that will make us pliable to their will. But before I get into the details of stage three I need to digress and give you a little more insight as to exactly what we are up against. Consider the following quote from Congressman Larry P. McDonald:

"The Rockefeller File is not fiction. It is a compact, powerful and frightening presentation of what may be the most important story of

*our lifetime – the drive of the Rockefellers and their allies to **create*** ***a one-world government combining super-capitalism and Commu-*** ***nism*** *under the same tent, all under their control.......not one has dared reveal the most vital part of the Rockefeller story: that the Rockefellers and their allies have, for at least fifty years, been carefully following* ***a plan to use their economic power to gain political control of first*** ***America, and then the rest of the world.*** *Do I mean conspiracy? Yes I do. I am convinced there is such a plot, international in scope, gen- erations old in planning, and incredibly evil in intent." On 31 August 1983, McDonald was killed aboard Korean Airline 007 flight which "accidentally" strayed over Soviet airspace and was "accidentally" shot down. The media reporting was scant and short-lived and not a single mention was publicly made about the fact that McDonald had been heading a congressional effort to expose what he called a dan- gerous international conspiracy."*

> – In November of 1975, Congressman Larry P. McDonald
>   spearheaded efforts against the New World Order.

Even what you just read isn't enough to allow you to truly comprehend what we are up against. With this in mind I need to give you a glimpse into the minds of two of the greatest mass murders in history.

*"The size of the lie is a definite factor in causing it to be believed, for the vast masses of a nation are in the depths of their hearts more easily deceived than they are consciously and intentionally bad. The primi- tive simplicity of **their minds renders them a more easy prey to a big** **lie than a small one**, for they themselves often tell little lies, but would be ashamed to tell big lies."*

> – Adolf Hitler: Mein Kampf, 1925

So to paraphrase Hitler: If you want to deceive and manipulate the masses all you have to do is tell a really big lie which by the way means you can commit an unimaginable atrocity like say 9/11 and lie about it and get away with it. Erick we will discuss this tomorrow. I think what I have to tell you will shock you. Now thinking in terms of big lies and manipulating the public here is what Hitler's right hand man Herman Goering had to say:

*"The people can always be brought to the bidding of the leaders. That is easy. All you have to do is **tell them they are being attacked**...It*

works every time." When we discuss **Wars For Profit** tomorrow you will understand that this is exactly what the power mongers have done to the U.S. public on several occasions. What I am trying to convey here is that we cannot trust anything they say. Nothing! Absolutely Nothing!

By the way we have an interesting insight into their play book, which is that they seem to be following Hitler's play book to the letter. Hitler staged a fire at the German Parliament and used it to grab political power and eventually undermine the German Constitution. Then coincidently we had 9/11 and just like Goering describes we are told we have an enemy [**a crisis**] and we have to not only go to war, but we have to relinquish civil liberties which we would have never given up otherwise. Then with these new powers in place our Constitution is nibbled away at bit by bit. Hitler forms youth camps and Obama sneaks a provision in the healthcare program to take over the student loan program so he can tighten the noose on the already government controlled school system. Hitler forms a domestic military force ostensibly for homeland security which is later used to bring the country under his iron grip. Obama calls for a million man domestic army supposedly for, you guessed it, homeland security. Then contrary to our Constitutional right to bare arms he launches initiatives to take away our arms which our founding fathers say is our last defense against a corrupt government. Hitler builds detention camps and uses his domestic military force to herds millions into death camps never to be seen again. FEMA builds internment camps supposedly to house people in the event of national emergency, but then the government runs ads for **"Internment Specialist to quote <u>guard prisoners</u>!"**

<u>Stage Three Continued</u>: Okay, we can finally get back to the time line of the U.S. take over. We established that with our institutions under their control and having largely brainwashed us they were ready to focus on bankrupting us. Let's pick things up with the Carter era. Every president since Carter has set the stage for the next president and with each presidency the national debt increases and their actions become bolder and more egregious as they move steadily closer and closer to the final take over of the U.S. For example Carter completed the unfinished business with China that Nixon left behind when he was forced to resign.

Carter's Legacy: As we discussed earlier Carter's administration was defined by an oil **crisis**. There is nothing like a good **crisis** to drive an economically destructive agenda and make it seem all so innocent. Carter's legacy was a period of what was dubbed Stagflation, which was simultaneous inflation and high interest rates. If that won't stifle economic growth nothing will. But let us not forget that Carter made 26 TC appointments including the position of trade envoy to China and under his TC controlled presidency the devastating Fast Track Trade Program was put in place which resulted in both NAFTA and the WTO which opened the flood gate to the world wide free trade which destroyed the U.S. balance of trade and began the process of intentionally driving up the National debt to unsustainable levels. When Carte entered office our National Debt was $700 Billion dollars, but thanks to his opening of the door to the WTO it began to balloon out of control. Take a look at the chart below and you will see exactly how serious the problem is.

National Debt By President

President	Start Date	National Debt	End Date	National Debt
Reagan	12/31/81	1.029 T	12/31/88	2,684 T
Bush	12/31/89	2.953 T	12/31/92	4.117 T
Clinton	12/31/93	4.536 T	12/31/00	5.662 T
Bush	12/31/01	5.943 T	12/31/08	10.700 T
Obama	12/31/09	12.311 T	04/20/10	12.881 T

NOTE: It took over 200 years to accumulate a $1 Trillion National Debt. Then in just 29 years we go to almost $13 Trillion and by 2019 the National Debt is projected to be $24,505 Trillion, but with unfunded entitlements it is expected to exceed $117 Trillion. How better to drive a Nation Into Bankruptcy?

Reagan's Legacy: Reagan was one of the few modern era presidents which I admired, but my admiration for him aside the fact is that during his term in office the National Debt went from $1.029 to $2.684 Trillion. In just eight years he amassed more debt than America had accumulated in the prior 200 years. 1987 saw the largest one day drop in the DOW in U.S. history [21.6%]. The drop was triggered by the speculative/predatory trading of junk bonds. It seems like repeating patterns drive the market up, crash it and take your profits and run. Reflecting back on the Carter era it is worth noting that Reagan ended the price controls on domestic oil which had contributed to the Oil Crisis during Carter's Presidency and miraculously the fuel shortages went away. Remember I told you earlier that the oil shortages under Carter were not due to any actual shortages at all.

Bush Senior's Legacy: The Persian Gulf War like any war drove the U.S. deeper into debt. Given Hussein's invasion of Kuwait there was provocation, but I believe that if the truth be known the real motivation was not to protect Kuwait, but to protect U.S. oil interests. The war aside Bush continued in the tradition of his predecessors to undermine the U.S. balance of trade. In 1990 he signed the Immigration Act which increased immigration by 40% and negatively impacted unemployment. Though actually signed under Clinton Bush spearheaded the North American Free Trade Agreement NAFTA between the U.S. Mexico and Canada. According to John J. Sweeney of the Boston Globe *"The trade deficit with Canada and Mexico ballooned to 12 times its pre NAFTA size reaching $111 billion in 2004."*

Clinton's Legacy: I commend Clinton for his policies regarding deficit reductions and balancing the budget which certainly contributed to his popularity, but none the less the agenda of the Money Manipulators was advanced during his administration. He signed the NAFTA agreement spearheaded by his predecessor. And though started prior to his term he also signed the repeal of the Glass-Steagall Act which had prohibited commercial banks from being owned by full service brokerage firms [securities companies]. Repeal of the Act allowed merger of banks, securities firms and insurance companies and set the stage for the predatory lending practices which lead to the 2007-08 collapse of the housing market. Had Glass-Steagall remained in effect the predatory lenders would not have been able to combine conventional home mortgages with high risk zero down no-doc loans and adjustable rate mortgages [ARMS] to create the Collateralized Debt Obligations [CDO's] which were bundled together, given fraudulent AAA ratings and sold to unsuspecting investors all over the world.

Had Glass-Steagall remained in place the U.S. would not have experienced what is arguably the worst financial Crisis in U.S. history.

<u>**Bush Junior's Legacy:**</u> Bush presided over the largest increase in national debt of any president in U.S. history with the debt skyrocketing from $5.493 Trillion to $10.700 Trillion. Following 9/11 bush initiated what he called *"the war on terror"* which has us fighting wars in both Afghanistan and Iraq, but <u>what I never could understand was that if he was so concerned about terrorist attacks how could he leave our border with Mexico wide open and support legalization of illegal immigrants.</u>

Bush's efforts to support the agenda of the Money Manipulators were if nothing stellar, not to mention reprehensible and criminal. <u>He blocked efforts from governors from all 50 states to prevent the predatory lending practices which lead to the 2007-08 housing collapse, which has been called the greatest financial **Crisis** since the 1929 depression.</u> By the way it is another coincidence that as the economy went into melt down oil process went through the roof creating one **crisis** on top of another **crisis**. <u>By the way once the Stimulus was passed under Obama the oil Crisis disappeared as mysteriously as it had appeared.</u> Coincidence? <u>He also signed a tough new bankruptcy law which coincidently was written by NBNA the nation's second largest credit card company who was coincidently his largest campaign contributor.</u> I don't suppose this could possibly be considered influence peddling? <u>Most Americans know that Bush signed the Patriot Act which significantly infringed on our civil liberties [one of those things we would not have done minus a **crisis**] but what most do not know is that hours before the bill was to be voted on Bush pulled the Congressional Bipartisan Bill and replaced it with a bill written by the White House which contained provisions which had previously been rejected by Congress.</u> This was just another underhanded power play which in this instance was designed to set the stage for Obama to make it easier for him to impose a police state. <u>Bush also signed EO#12803 expressly allowing privatization of U.S. infrastructure by private international investors. In yet another effort to drive the nation into bankruptcy Bush signed the Medicare Drug Benefit Program that according to Jan Crawford Greenburg resulted in *"the greatest expansion in America's Welfare*</u>

State in forty years." The bill cost approximately $7 Trillion dollars. David Walker Controller General of the U.S. called the bill *"the most fiscally irresponsible piece of legislation since the 1960's."*

Stage Four: The Final Take Over: I believe the following quote accurately describes where they see themselves in terms of implementing their New World Order!

*"The interests behind the Bush administration, such as the CFR, the Trilateral Commission – founded by Brzezinski for David Rockefeller – and the Bilderberg Group have prepared for and are now moving to **implement open world dictatorship** within the next five years."*
 – Dr. Johannes Koeppl [Former official of the German Ministry for Defense and advisor to NATO]

That means we can expect the final take over to come under the Obama administration.

The time is short. We have to put aside our differences and join together.

Obama's Legacy: Obama has broken virtually every campaign promises he made. For openers he said he would not renew the Patriot Act. He lied. He said his administration would be open and transparent and that there would be no earmarks. He lied. The ramming of the healthcare program down our throats was certainly anything but transparent and it contained several under the table deals that could only be described as bribes. Obama said there was no room in his administration for lobbyists. Again he lied. Take a look at the next chart and pay special attention at the bottom to Paul Volker's pedigree.

Obama Appointed Lobbyist

William Lynn: #2 Position @ Department of Defense
✓ **Top Lobbyist Rathion**

Timothy Geithner: Secretary of State
✓ **Former President New York Federal Reserve**

Mark Patterson: Treasury Chief of Staff to Secretary of State
✓ **Former Top Lobbyist Goldman Sacks**

George Mitchell: Lead Middle East Envoy
✓ **Top Lobbyist Saudi Royal Family**

Leon Pannetta: Head of CIA
✓ **King of Wall Street Lobbyist**

Tom Dassal: Head of Department of Health and Human Services
✓ **Top Lobbyist Healthcare Firms**

Paul Volker: Head of Economic Recovery Board
✓ **Former Chairman Board of Governors of the U.S. Federal Reserve System, former President of Federal Reserve Bank of NY and Undersecretary of Monetary Affairs.**

Source: Documentary Obama Deception

So why did I want you to pay attention to Volker? Because he is the key man in terms of understanding what is and is not happening with the economic recovery. I will explain what I mean by that in a second. Read on.

In terms of understanding the plan to bankrupt America there are some interesting similarities between the 1929 crash and the 2007 crash. In previous chapters we established that the Fed caused the Great Depression then the government turned around and put the Fed in charge of the recovery and then they concocted the New Deal which depended heavily on money borrowed at interest from the Fed. **So in other words, the Fed causes the Depression, is put in charge of the recovery and benefits financially from driving us into debt. What is wrong with that scenario?**

In 2007 we had another 1929 crash. We established a short while ago that the collapse would never have occurred had it not been for the repeal of Glass-Steagall under Clinton and for Bush's prevention on the part of Governors to prevent the very Predatory Lending practices which caused the crash. As to the Feds role in the housing frenzy and resulting crash it was flamed by the lowest interest rates since 1945. Now here is the interesting part. <u>Just like in 1929 the Fed who had been instrumental in causing the crisis was put in charge of the recovery</u>. Enter Paul Volker Head of Economic Recovery Board: Former Chairman Board of Governors of the U.S. Federal Reserve System, former President of Federal Reserve Bank of NY and Undersecretary of Monetary Affairs. Then the stimulus was passed which again forced massive borrowing which profited the Fed., the very organization which caused the problem in the first place. Power corrupts!

VITALLY IMPORTANT: We have to get smarter and start connecting the dots if we hope to survive. **They have no intention of creating a recovery.** All they plan on doing is driving us into bankruptcy. According to Obama's budget numbers as of 2019 the National Debt will be $24,505 Trillion and with unfunded Entitlements $117 Trillion. Sorry to say but these are not numbers we can survive. **Building off of the Bush's Legacy Obama is getting ready for the take over.** The stimulus is designed to bankrupt us and if that isn't enough then healthcare should do the job. Healthcare commandeers 1/6 of the U.S. economy but it also gives the government control over our access to medical attention and ultimately who lives and dies. Cap and Trade represents potentially the largest tax increase in history but it also allows the government, through taxes to control virtually every aspect of our lives. Remember when I said that the Money Manipulators considered the world's resources to belong to them. Well through Cap and Trade they will be able to seriously limit resource consumption. **It is like many from the TC & CFR have said in order to birth the New World Order the United States of America must fall and they are willing to shed our blood in order to achieve their objective. The enemy is ruthless. He is using a play book that preaches the bigger the lie the better. And he is using tactics which are identical to the most ruthless regimes the world has ever known.**

Strategic Analysis: Once again they have given us insight as to what to expect.

"We shall have world government whether or not you like it. The only question is whether World Government will be by conquest or consent." – James P. Warburg [Representing Rothschild Banking Concern] While speaking before the United States Senate [Feb. 17, 1950]

They would like us to believe that they are too big and powerful to be defeated, but that isn't true. Remember we established before that they are a parasite and as such they need us to survive. So far we have gone along with what ever they did, like sheep to the slaughter, but it is time to fight back. [Peacefully]

We Can Expect Them To Impose Some Kind of New Crisis: Oil prices could go through the roof, interest rates could go up, we could have major inflation, or there could be another terrorist attack. The possibilities are endless. What ever it is, it is important that we don't allow them to use it as they have used other crisis to force us to do things we would not otherwise do. **We cannot afford to relinquish any more rights or accept and more financial arm twisting.**

PAY CLOSE ATTENTION! The most important thing right now is that we all realize that our freedom and potentially our lives are at stake. We have to **put aside** our differences and form a united resistance. Take a page from the Obama play book—get organized and get politically involved. We have to be resolute and understand that what ever we do there are going to be financial hardships. We have to truly understand and believe that if we do nothing the outcome will be, financial hardship and oppression for generations to come. If we stand up and fight back there will be financial hardship, but we will be free and we will have the hope of a better life. I don't know about you but I owe it to my children to fight for a better life for them.

PAY CLOSE ATTENTION! From a strategic view point we need to take back this government before they are in a position to impose Nationwide Martial Law. The good news is I do not believe they are in a position to do that yet, but don't forget Obama wants a million man army and he is doing everything he can to disarm us. **What ever we do it must be peaceful.** Not only must it be peaceful it must be respectful and patriotic. No disrespectful signs, no bad language and most importantly no violence of any kind. We know we have a President who does not respect freedom of speech so we cannot give him any excuse to vilify us or to prevent us from protesting and absolutely the last thing we want to do is give him an excuse to declare martial law.

I have a special request for all of you in the military. Please remember we are all Americans. We are your mothers, fathers, sisters, brothers and neighbors. We are patriots not enemies. If the government abuses its power and does not protect the interest of the nation or the people we have a Constitutional right to protest. Don't let them use you to take that right away from us. Remember we are Americans one and all. This is your home just like it is ours. All we want is to keep America the land of the free and home of the brave for the next generation and that includes you. God Bless America and God bless you.

As I said it is imperative that we understand just how real and how dangerous the present threat is and how little time we have to respond. With this in mind the balance of this chapter is a selection of quotes from TC and CFR members whose words betray them and quotes from people in a position to know, whose words are a warning for us. I encourage you to take the time to read these quotes. I may not be able to convince you of the dangers but I assure these quotes will. You may want to copy them and pass them on to your friends. We can use all the help we can get.

Americans Are Victims of Media Propaganda:

- *"Media manipulation in the U.S. today is more efficient than it was in Nazi Germany, because here we have the pretence that we are getting all the information we want. That misconception prevents people from even looking for the truth."* – Mark Crispin Miller

- *"The Council on Foreign Relations [CFR] is dedicated to one-world government, financed by a number of the largest tax exempt foundation [i.e. Rockefeller], and wielding such power and influence over our lives in the areas of finance, business, labor, military, education, and mass communication media, that it should be familiar to every American concerned with good government and with preserving and defending the U.S. Constitution and our free-enterprise system. Yet, the nation's right-to-know machinery, the news media; usually so aggressive in exposures to inform our people; remain silent when it comes to the CFR, its members and their activities. The CFR is the establishment. Not only does it have influence and power in key decision-making positions at the highest levels of government to apply pressure from above, but it also finances and uses individuals and groups to bring pressure from below, to justify the high level decisions for converting the U.S. from a sovereign Republic into a servile member of a one-world dictatorship."* – Congressman John R. Rarick

■ *"An agreement was reached; the policy of the papers was bought, to be paid for by the month; an editor was furnished for each paper to properly supervise and edit information regarding the questions of preparedness, militarism, financial policies, and other things of national and international nature considered vital to the interests of the purchasers."* – U.S. Congressman Oscar Callaway, 1917

American Patriots and Their Words of Warning:

■ *"I believe that if the people of this nation fully understood what Congress has done to them over the last 49 years, they would move on Washington; they would not wait for an election....**It adds up to a preconceived plan to destroy the economic and social independence of the United States!**"* – Senator George W. Malone [Nevada], speaking before Congress in 1957.

■ *"I am concerned for the security of our great nation; not so much because of any threat from without, but because of the **insidious forces working from within**."* – General Douglas MacArthur

■ *"The financial system... has been turned over to the Federal Reserve Board. That board administers the finance system by authority of... a purely profiteering group. The system is private, conducted for the sole purpose of obtaining the greatest possible profits from the use of the other people's money."*
– Rep. Charles A. Lindberg [R-MN]

- *"The Trilateral Commission doesn't run the world; the Council on Foreign Relations does that!"* – Winston Lord, Assistant Secretary of State, the U.S. State Department

- *"The one aim of these financiers is world control by the creation of inextinguishable debts."* – Henry Ford, Industrialist

- *"I think there are 25,000 individuals that have used offices of powers, and they are in our Universities and they are in our Congresses, and they believe in One World Government. And if you believe in One World Government, then you are talking about undermining National Sovereignty and you are talking about setting up something that you could well call a **Dictatorship**—and those plans are there!"* – Congressman Ron Paul at an event near Austin, Texas on August 30, 2003

- *"Democracy is not about trust; it is about distrust. It is about accountability, exposure, open debate, critical challenge, and popular input and feedback from the citizenry. It is about responsible government. **We have to get our fellow Americans to trust their leaders less and themselves more,** trust their own questions and suspicions, and their own desire to know what is going on."* – Michael Parenti, Author, Historian

- *"The most powerful clique in these [CFR] groups have one objective in common: **they want to bring about the surrender of the sovereignty and the national independence of the U.S.** They want to end national boundaries and racial and ethnic loyalties supposedly to increase business and ensure world peace. What they strive for would inevitably lead to dictatorship and loss of freedoms by the people. The CFR was founded for "the purpose of promoting disarmament and submergence of U.S. sovereignty and national independence into an all-powerful one-world government."* – Harpers, July 1958

- *"The money power preys upon the nation in times of peace and conspires against it in times of adversity. It is more despotic than monarchy, more insolent than autocracy, more selfish than bureaucracy."* – President Abraham Lincoln

- *"The drive of the Rockefellers and their allies is to **create a one-world government combining super capitalism and Communism**

under the same tent, all under their control. *... Do I mean con-spiracy? Yes I do. I am convinced there is such a plot, interna-tional in scope, generations old in planning, and incredibly evil in intent."* – Congressman Larry P. McDonald, 1976, killed in the Korean Airlines 747 that was shot down by the Soviets.

■ *"Today the path of **total dictatorship** in the United States can be laid by strictly legal means, unseen and unheard by the Congress, the President, or the people. Outwardly we have a Constitutional government. We have operating within our government and politi-cal system, another body representing another form of govern-ment – **a bureaucratic elite.**"* – Senator William Jenner, 1954

■ *"Council on Foreign Relations is 'the establishment.' Not only does it have influence and power in key decision-making posi-tions at the highest levels of government to apply pressure from above, but it also announces and uses individuals and groups to bring pressure from below, to justify the high level decisions for converting the U.S. from a sovereign Constitutional Republic into a servile member state of a **one-world dictatorship.**"* – Former Congressman John Rarick (1971)

■ *"Our government will soon become what it is already a long way toward becoming, an elective dictatorship."* – Senator J. William Fulbright

■ *"If a nation values anything more than freedom, then it will lose its freedom; and the irony of it is that if it is comfort and secu-rity that it values, it will lose that too. Unknown Americans must decide: Are we to be governed by Americans or by an Interna-tional organization? I, for one, owe no allegiance to the United Nations nor will I give it any. **I obey only the U.S. Constitution.** You had better think about this issue, for if the U.N. can violate the Sovereignty of Haiti, Iraq and other countries, it can violate ours...The United States may not be the top dog 15 years from now. U.N. security council resolutions, backed by say Chinese sol-diers, could be aimed at us."* – Charley Reese, Orlando Sentinel

The Plan of Those Who Would Enslave Us:

■ *"The New World Order is a world that has a super national author-ity to regulate world commerce and industry; an international organization that would control the production and consumption of oil; an international currency that would replace the dollar; a World Development Fund that would make funds available to free and Communist nations alike; and an international police force to enforce the edicts of the New World Order."* – Former West German Chancellor: Willy Brandt, former chairman of the Fifth-Socialist International, who chaired the Brandt Commission in the late 1980s

■ *"...This regionalization is in keeping with the Tri-Lateral Plan which calls for a gradual convergence of East and West, ultimately leading toward the goal of "one world government....**National sovereignty is no longer a viable concept...**"* – Zbigniew Brzezin-ski: National Security Advisor to President Jimmy Carter

■ About Mao Tse-tung: *"Whatever the price of the Chinese Rev-olution, it has obviously succeeded not only in producing more efficient and dedicated administration, but also in fostering high morale and community of purpose. **The social experiment in China under Chairman Maos leadership is one of the most important and successful in human history.**"* – David Rocke-feller statement in 1973 [NY Times 8-10-73]

■ ***"The New World Order cannot happen without U.S. participa-tion,*** *as we are the most significant single component. Yes, there will be a New World Order, and it will force the United States to change its perceptions."* – Henry Kissinger: World Affairs Council Press Conference, Regent Beverly Wilshire Hotel, April 19, 1994

■ ***"NAFTA is a major stepping stone to the New World Order."*** – Henry Kissinger: when campaigning for the passage of NAFTA

■ *"What Congress will have before it is **not a conventional trade agreement but the architecture of a new international system....a first step toward a new world order.**"* – 1993-July 18: CFR mem-ber and Trilateralist Henry Kissinger writes in *The Los Angeles Times* concerning NAFTA

■ *"... when the struggle seems to be drifting definitely towards a world social democracy, there may still be very great delays and disappointments before it becomes an efficient and beneficent world system.* **Countless people ... will hate the new world order ... and will die protesting against it.** *When we attempt to evaluate its promise, we have to bear in mind the distress of a generation or so of malcontents, many of them quite gallant and graceful-looking people."* – H.G. Wells, in his book entitled <u>The New World Order</u> [1939]

■ George Soros at the World Economic Forum at Davos, Switzerland, says the world needs a *"new world order,"* and he further warns: *"I am here to alert you that we are entering a period of world disorder."*
   – George Soros: 1995 - Jan 27: Billionaire financier

■ *"We believe we are creating the beginning of a new world order coming out of the collapse of the U.S.-Soviet antagonisms."* – Brent Scowcroft: [August 1990], quoted in *The Washington Post* [May 1991]

■ *"Further global progress is now possible only through a quest for universal consensus in the movement toward a new world order."* – Mikhail Gorbachev

■ *"By the end of this decade [2000 AD] we will live under the first One World Government that has ever existed in the society of nations ... a government with absolute authority to decide the basic issues of human survival. One world government is inevitable."* – Pope John Paul II: quoted by Malachi Martin in the book <u>The Keys of This Blood</u>

■ *"We are at present working discreetly with all our might to wrest this mysterious force called sovereignty out of the clutches of the local nation states of the world."* – Professor Arnold Toynbee, in a June 1931 speech before the Institute for the Study of International Affairs in Copenhagen

Crisis Is A Tool To Control Us and Undermine Our Liberty!

■ *"The whole aim of practical politics is to **keep the populace alarmed** — and hence clamorous to be led to safety — by menacing it with an endless series of hobgoblins, all of them imaginary."* – H. L. Mencken

■ *"We are on the verge of a global transformation. **All we need is the right major crisis and the nations will accept the New World Order.**"* – David Rockefeller: Sept. 23, 1994

■ *"There is a chance for the President of the United **States to use this (9-11) disaster to carry out ... a new world order.**"* – Gary Hart, at a televised meeting organized by the CFR in Washington, D.C. Sept. 14.

■ *"Big Brother in the form of an increasingly powerful government and in an increasingly powerful private sector will pile the records high with reasons why privacy should give way to national security, to law and order, to efficiency of operation, to scientific advancement and the like."* – William O. Douglas 1898-1980, U.S. Supreme Court Justice

■ *"**Out of these troubled times [our objective] a New World Order can emerge?** Today, that new world is struggling to be born, a world quite different from the one we have known."* – George Herbert Walker Bush Sept. 11, 1990

UN's Goal is One World Government:

■ *"It is the sacred principles enshrined in the **United Nations Charter** to which the American people will henceforth pledge their Allegiance."* – President George Bush Sr.: addressing the General Assembly of the United Nations, Feb. 1, 1992

■ *"The United Nations will spearhead our efforts to manage the new conflicts [that afflict our world].... **Yes the principles of the United Nations Charter are worth our lives,** our fortunes, and our sacred honor."* – 1993-April 21: General Colin Powell receives the United Nations Association-USA's Global Leadership Award

- *"Further global progress is now possible only through a quest for universal consensus in the movement towards a new world order."* – Mikhail Gorbachev: in an address at the United Nations, December 1988.

- Vice President Al Gore: as he traveled to Marrakech, Morocco, in April for the signing of the new world trade agreement. Gore appeared hours after U.S. planes enforcing an allied no fly zone over northern Iraq accidentally shot down two U.S. helicopters, killing 15 Americans and 11 foreign officials. Gore said: *"I want to extend condolences to the families of those who died **in the service of the United Nations**."* – Los Angeles Times, 6/12/94

- *"Today America would be outraged if UN troops entered Los Angeles to restore order. Tomorrow they will be grateful. When presented with this scenario, individual rights will be willingly relinquished for the guarantee of their well-being granted to then by the world government."* – Henry Kissinger

I believe this last quote by Henry Kissinger, about the UN is a foreshadowing of what the New World Order proponents have in mind for us. Create ever increasingly **crisis** one after another each worse than the last until they force us to surrender our freedom and liberty to them. We cannot allow that to happen. We have to save America for our children before it is too late!

Chapter 7
America's Secret Imperialist Agenda:
Wars For Profit and Political Exploitation!

Erick: Gramps, I gather from the title of this chapter that your contention is that prior to its collapse the U.S. was what you might call a **"War Monger."** I think of China, Russia and Nazi Germany as being war mongers, but not the U.S. According to what I learned in history class America only entered WWI, WWII and Vietnam because we were attacked, and in terms of Iraq there was the 9/11 terrorist attack and both Iraq and Afghanistan were responsible for promoting terrorism so we had to neutralize the threat they posed to our homeland. So in each instance we were just defending ourselves?

PAY CLOSE ATTENTION! Gramps: The government went to a lot of trouble and expense to keep the truth from the American people because they knew we were basically a moral people who would not go along with their Empire Building Imperialist Agenda of War for Profit, so they had to make us believe, as you say that we were just defending ourselves, but it was a lie!

The public may not have known the truth but historians like myself knew, as did those in positions of power, some of which have given us at least glimpses of the truth. Consider what Author and Historian Michael Parenti had to say: *"The enormous gap between what U.S. leaders do in the world and what Americans think their leaders are doing is one of the great propaganda accomplishments of the dominate political mythology."*

Then there is this quote from Woodrow Wilson: *"Is there any man, is there any woman, let me say any child here that does not know that the seed of war in the modern world is industrial and commercial rivalry?"*

This phenomenon of war for profit is not unique to modern times; it or religious intolerance has been at the source of virtually all wars. Lest we continue to allow our leaders to lull us into unjust wars, kill and maim our children and take away our civil liberties we should consider the words of Julius Caesar.

"Beware of the leader who bangs the drums of war in order to whip the citizenry into patriotic fervor, for patriotism is indeed a double-edged sword. It both emboldens the blood, just as it narrows the mind. And when the drums of war have reached a fever pitch and the blood boils with hate and the mind has closed, the leader will have no need in seizing the rights of the citizenry, [who] infused with fear and blinded by patriotism, will offer up all of their rights unto the leader and gladly so. How well I know? For this I have done. And I am Julius Caesar."

Gramps: Erick by the time we finish our discussion today you will know the truth about each of the wars you just mentioned. In each case America staged a False Flag attack as a provocation for war. I will give you details to support that statement shortly, but in the meantime I need you to understand exactly what they do to us to get us to go along with their wars for profit. While testifying at the Nuremburg War Trials Herman Goering, Hitler's right hand man told us exactly how you get peace seeking people to go to war:

*"Why of course the people don't want war... That is understood. But after all it is the leaders of the country who determine the policy, and it is always a simple matter to drag the people along, whether it is a democracy, or a fascist dictatorship, or a parliament, or a communist dictatorship ...Voice or no voice, the people can always be brought to the bidding of the leaders. That is easy. **All you have to do is to tell them they are being attacked, and denounce the pacifists for lack of patriotism and exposing the country to danger. It works the same in any country."***

Erick that is exactly what they did to us over and over, like Goering said, *"It works every time."*

Erick: Gramps who are you referring to when you say they did it to us?

Gramps: It is like I have said throughout the manuscript. The Puppets are our Elected Officials [particularly our more recent Presidents] and the Puppeteers are the Moneyed Elite. Remember, I said that **America had an Empire Building Imperialist Agenda of War for Profit**. Hopefully the following quote will help you understand exactly what that means.

*"I define **imperialism** as the process whereby the dominant investor interests [The Money Manipulators] in one country bring to bear their economic and military power upon another nation or region in order to expropriate its land, labor, natural resources, capital, and markets—in such a manner as to enrich the investor interests. In a word, **empires** do not just pursue 'power for power's sake.' There are real and enormous material interests at stake, fortunes to be made many times over."* – Michael Parenti Author Against Empire 14 February, 2010 Common Dreams.org

Gramps: Erick as you shall shortly realize America has been absorbed by the Money Manipulators and its primary function has become one of acquiring natural resources from resource rich underdeveloped nations and gaining military control of strategically important regions of the globe.

The Puppeteers are committed to their Wars for Profit and anyone who stands in their way is expendable. Erick, remember when we discussed earlier that the reason John F. Kennedy was assassinated was because he was in the process of doing away with the Federal Reserve. Well that was true, but it was only part of the reason he was assassinated. As the following quote demonstrates he believed fervently in peace.

"Mankind must put an end to war before war puts an end to mankind." – President John F. Kennedy

Kennedy was a man of conviction and for that reason he had to die. Here is what happened.

It began early in his administration when The Joint Chiefs requested troops for Laos, but Kennedy said no and he told his Geneva Conference representative, Averell Harriman:

"Did you understand? I want a negotiated settlement in Laos. I don't want to put troops in."

Tensions between him and the Moneyed Elite worsened steadily as he repeatedly refused to go along with their agenda. He refused to use nuclear weapons in Berlin and Southeast Asia. Then he refused to bomb or invade Cuba during the 1962 missile crisis, saying afterward: *"I never had the slightest intention of doing so."*

Then in June 1963, [a few months before his assassination], he committed an intolerable sin. He decided that in fact mankind must put an end to war and he was going to be the person to initiate it. He called for the abolition of nuclear weapons and general and complete disarmament, which effectively would have put an end to the cold war. October 1963 he signed National Security Action Memorandum [NSAM] 263 to withdraw 1,000 U.S. forces from Vietnam by year end and all of them by 1965. Recognizing the destructive power of the CIA he said he wanted *"to splinter the CIA in a thousand pieces and scatter it to the winds."*

Following JFK's assassination Johnson resumed the escalation of the war in Southeast Asia which eventually included Vietnam, Laos and Cambodia and took somewhere between three and four million lives. But never mind that, the power brokers got their war and they sent a very important message to future U.S. Presidents as to who calls the shots in Washington. Source: <u>JFK and the Unspeakable: Why He Died and Why It Matters</u> By James Douglass

Gramps: Erick I hope this demonstrates that the men in control in Washington are ruthless and will stop at nothing to get what they want, and that includes assassinations and false flag attacks on American citizens. Proof of this will be forthcoming a little later in this chapter.

John F. Kennedy was a man of conviction for which he paid the ultimate price. But I don't want us to focus on Kennedy's death. I would rather we remember his inspiration. I am old enough that I remember the all inspiring speech in which he said:

"Each time a person stands up for an ideal, or acts to improve the lot of others, or strikes out against injustice, he or she sends forth a tiny ripple of hope. Crossing each other a million different centers of

energy and daring, those ripples build a current that can sweep down the mightiest walls of oppression and resistance." He also said: "*Do not pray for easy lives. Pray to be strong men.*"

Given the times we face, my prayer is that we may be men and women such as John F. Kennedy: "*Strong men*" and men such as Patrick Henry who said "*give me liberty or give me death.*" If we are going to save America we have to be willing to pledge our fortunes and our lives as our founding fathers did, because we are fighting the same enemy they fought so long ago. This time we must end the war once and for all.

Erick: Gramps what you said about JFK makes me think back to what Wilson said and it makes me finally understand just how dangerous and ruthless these men are.

Gramps: Are you referring to the quote where he said:

"*Since I entered politics, I have chiefly had men's views confided to me privately. Some of the biggest men in the United States, in the field of government and manufacturing. They know there is a power somewhere, so organized, so subtle, so watchful, so interlocked. So complete, so perverse that they better not speak above their breath when they speak in condemnation of it.*"

– Woodrow Wilson President [1913]

Erick: That's the one. I guess I am really getting an image of just exactly how ruthless these Puppeteers are and just how much power they wield over our Presidents and Congressmen, but I really want to know just how it is you say they staged false flag attacks in order to sucker us into several wars.

Gramps: Erick bear with me just a little longer. I will get to that shortly, but first I want to give you some background so you can see that America is a perpetual war machine, just how big the business of war really is, how large the U.S. Imperial Empire is, who benefits from perpetual war, who ends up picking up the tab and at what cost.

Gramps: Erick once you have read this material I want you to stop and put on your critical thinking cap and honestly and objectively answer the questions which I will pose.

America Is The World's Leading Arms Dealer and Imperial Aggressor:

"From 1945 to 2003, the United States attempted to overthrow more than 40 foreign governments, and to crush more than 30 populist-nationalist movements fighting against intolerable regimes. In the process, the U.S. bombed some 25 countries, caused the end of life for several million people, and condemned many millions more to a life of agony and despair."

– William Blum, <u>Rogue State:</u>
<u>A Guide to the World's Only Superpower</u>

"The U.S. government has given over $200 billion dollars in military aid to some eighty nations since World War II. U.S. weapons sales abroad have grown to about $10 billion a year and compose about 70 percent of all arms sold on the international marketplace. Two million foreign troops and hundreds of thousands of foreign police and paramilitary have been trained, equipped, and financed by the United States. Their purpose has not been to defend their countries from outside invasion but to protect foreign investors and the ruling elite of the recipient nations from their own potentially rebellious populations."

– Michael Parenti: Author, Historian

"America's Permanent War Economy....has endured since the end of World War II....Since then the U.S. has been at war, somewhere, every year, in Korea, Nicaragua, Vietnam, the Balkans, Afghanistan —all this to the accompaniment of shorter military forays in Africa, Chile, Grenada, Panama, and increasingly at home against its own people."

– Seymour Melman author of several books from an article "In the Grip of a Permanent War Economy" Counter Punch, March 15, 2003

Gramps: Erick, when I reflect on the wisdom of two of Americas greatest generals I am all the more convinced that America's motives are purely Imperial Expansion and Profiteering.

"I know war as few other men now living know it, and nothing to me is more revolting. I have long advocated its complete abolition, as its very destructiveness on both friend and foe has rendered it useless as a method of settling international disputes."

– General Douglas MacArthur

"I do not mean to exclude altogether the idea of patriotism. I know it exists, and I know it has done much in the present contest. But I will venture to assert, that a great and lasting war can never be supported on this principle alone. It must be aided by a prospect of interest, or some reward."

— George Washington: General and First U.S. President

Gramps: Erick as the following quotes clearly demonstrate there is plenty of financial reward for those who would support the hell that is war.

Military Profiteering:

"A six year study [1998-2003] of Department of Defense contracts, finds that the ten largest defense contractors all spent heavily on both campaign contributions [a combined $35.7 million] and lobbying [$414.6 million]. The return on their investment was a combined $340 billion in contracts over that time."

— Center for Public Integrity 2004

"Summary: Center Report Finds $362 Billion in No-Bid Contracts at the Pentagon since 1998." – Center for public Integrity; accessed at: http://projects.publicintegrity.org/pns/default,aspx?act=summry On 10 May 2009

Gramps: When I reflect on this kind of gross profiteering I am reminded of the warning given by Dwight Eisenhower in an address to the Nation [January 17, 1961]

He stated: *"We must guard against the acquisition of unwarranted influence....by the military-industrial complex. The potential for the disastrous rise of misplaced power."*

Just How Large Is The U.S. Military Complex?

■   *"According to the 2008 official Pentagon inventory of our military bases around the world, our empire consists of 865 facilities in more than 40 countries and overseas.* – Chalmers Johnson author of Blowback, The Sorrows of Empire, and Nemesis: The Last Days of the American Republic, in an article titled *Dismantling The Empire*, 30 July, 2009, Tom Dispatch.com **Why?**

- With only 4% of the world's population the U.S. allocates more than $711 billion annually to military spending which accounts for 48% of the worlds total military spending. **Why?**

- The U.S. in concert with its staunches allies [The NATO Countries of Japan, South Korea & Australia] spend $1.1 trillion on their combined military, which translates to 72% of the world's total military spending. **Why?**

- The U.S. Armed Forces boast some 1,445,000 active-duty armed services members, 800,000 DOD civilian employees and 1.2 million National Guardsmen plus other Reservist and Mercenary Forces. **Why?**

- The U.S. spends more on military expenditures than the combined totals of the worlds next 46 highest military spending nations. **Why?**

- U.S. Military spending is 5.8 times more than China and 10.2 times more than Russia and 98.6 times more than Iran. **Why?**

Note: The data above is from: The Center for Defense Information at World Military Spending – Global Issues

Gramps: I have to ask myself for what reason other than profiteering by special interest groups or to intentionally bankrupt the nation or both would the U.S. military budget be so much extraordinarily higher than any other nation in the entire world? Especially when we are running a $12 trillion dollar national debt, unemployment is rampant; our infrastructure is in disrepair and trade deficits are out of control. It seems the only sane course of action would be to pull back and focus on domestic issues like rebuilding our manufacturing and restoring our infrastructure.

America Can No Longer Afford To Maintain Its Imperial Dreams of World Domination:

■ *"We are like the British at the end of World War II: Desperately trying to shore up an empire that we never needed and can no longer afford, using methods that often resemble those of failed empires of the past—including the Axis powers of World War II and the former Soviet Union. There is an important lesson for us in the British decision, starting in 1945, to liquidate their empire relatively voluntarily, rather than being forced to do so by defeat in war, as were Japan and Germany."* – Chalmers Johnson author of <u>Blowback, The Sorrows of Empire,</u> and <u>Nemesis: The Last Days of the American Republic,</u> in an article titled *Dismantling The Empire,* 30 July, 2009, TomDispatch.com

■ In his book <u>The Political Economy of U.S. Militarism,</u> Professor Ismael Hossein-Zadeh refers to *"parasitic military imperialism,"* consuming over 40% of the national tax revenue at the expense of unmet human needs.

■ According to Anita Dancs, an analyst for the website Foreign Policy in Focus: *"The United States spends approximately $250 billion each year maintaining its global military presence. The sole purpose of this is to give us hegemony—that is, control or dominance—over as many nations on the planet as possible."*

It is in the best interest of the American people to divert that money to domestic economic restoration.

Gramps: In this situation I am reminded of the words of Dwight D. Eisenhower: General and President [1953]

"Every gun that is made, every warship launched, every rocket fired, signifies, in the final sense, a theft from those who hunger and are not fed, those who are cold and are not clothed. The world in arms is not spending money alone. It is spending the sweat of its laborers, the genius of its scientists, the hopes of its children."

Gramps: We have to put an end to this greed before it puts an end to us!

The only way the wars in Iraq and Afghanistan are going to end is if the American people force the issue. I think it was Chaney who referred to the war on terrorism as a [A phantom enemy] saying we would not see an end to the war in our lifetime. <u>What we have to understand is that these are wars of military occupation for profit and they have no intention of ending them because they are there for the oil and gas.</u> Coincidently, Afghanistan provides the means to control the Caspian Sea with oil estimates of as much as 200 billion barrels which is roughly 15% of the total world's reserves. The region is also believed to contain up to 4% of the natural gas reserves. Per Congressional Research service, an organization supplying bipartisan information to Congress in its report titled, "Caspian Oil and Gas Production and Prospects."

By the way another indication that our government is in the region to stay is the number of battlefield contractors they are putting in place. According to The Congressional Research Service Congress is expected to authorize somewhere between 26,000 and 56,000 additional battlefield contractors in Afghanistan bringing the total number of battlefield contractors to between 130,000 and 160,000 men. Even including the 30,000 U.S. Military personal which Obama has committed to the war the contractors will outnumber regular military approximately 2 to 1. – The Center for Defense Information at World Military Spending – Global Issues

Erick: Gramps why is that important?

Gramps: Hiring mercenaries is an expensive way to fight a war but the government has their reasons. They learned from Vietnam that when our children are forcibly conscripted through drafts that war protest is inevitable. <u>They are in the region to establish permanent military occupation and they realize that, **that is only possible if they avoid a draft,** thus the mercenaries.</u> After all it's not their money they are spending, it's ours.

This strategy reminds me of the plot in a miniseries called <u>Kings</u> that was on TV a while back. In the story the U.S. is engaged in a modern day civil war and instead of our present form of government we have a king. The king is about to sign a treaty that will end a war that has drug on for years and ravaged the nation. A dark figure emerges from the shadows, the true power behind the throne and he informs the king that the war is far too profitable to end. He says I want one more year of war and if you do not give it to me I will remove you from power.

I am also reminded of the War in Vietnam. At the time I read a book [I can't recall the title] but it was written by a retired general. In the book he explained that we could end the war any time we wanted, but we didn't want to. He explained that you cannot fight a war without supplies and he said that you couldn't transport enough supplies on the Ho Che Min Trail to support the war. The only other supply line was the Haiphong Harbor and in order to keep it from filling with silt required a continuous dredging operation. So he said if you want to end the war shut down the harbor and the war is over period. You may recall that when we finally decided to end the war Nixon mined the harbor and the war ended just as predicted. So what is my point? I believe that any strategy that fails to end a war with a quick and decisive victory [especially when the U.S. has such overpowering military superiority] is an indication that the strategy is motivated by profit and the objective is to drag out the war as long as possible rather than to end it decisively. To me it is simple, win the war or end the war, no half measures.

Either you fight to win or you are there for the money and the hell with the lives that are lost. U.S. Senator Barry Goldwater said, *"I could have ended the war in a month. I could have made Vietnam look like a mud puddle."* With our absolute military superiority there is no explanation for why the U.S. has been unable to win a major military conflict since WWII other than because they didn't want to. It is worth remembering that: *"In time of war the loudest patriots are the greatest profiteers."* – August Bebel

Gramps: Erick here are the questions I want you to ponder. Are you ready to put on your thinking cap?

■ If the U.S. is the peaceful non-aggressive nation it would have us believe, then why do we need so much military clout and why does that muscle need to be spread around the entire globe?

■ Does the U.S. have 5 times more enemies than Russia and 10 times more than China or could our military spending be for something other than defense, like say Empire Building?

- Why is our presence particularly concentrated in third world underdeveloped nations which just happen to be literal treasure droves of natural resources?

- If the U.S. is truly facing a foreign terrorist threat as we have been lead to believe [by the events of 9/11] then why don't we concentrate our efforts here at home to protect our borders which any military strategist would tell you should be our first line of defense against a terrorist attack?

- If we truly wanted to stop terrorism wouldn't diplomacy and meaningful foreign aid which benefits a notions citizens seen a better solution than a military occupation which destroyed its cities and villages, and by virtue of our drone technology indiscriminately kills and maims millions of innocent civilians? Wouldn't such tactics only breed hatred and retaliation and make terrorism all the more likely?

- Doesn't it seem fortuitous that the nations being attacked always seem to have either resources which the U.S. covets or they are strategically located in a region of the world that the U.S. wants to control? Coincidence?

Gramps: Erick when I first asked myself these questions I was hopeful that I would be able to find humanitarian justification for the U.S. global military Empire, but what I found instead was that the **U.S. was guilty of hegemony** which is the process where by an aggressor nation establishes military preeminence over weaker nations in order to expand its empire and acquire the resources of the weaker nation for its enrichment.

Erick before we finish our discussion today we will discuss several real world examples of U.S. hegemony but first I want to go back and answer your earlier question about exactly how the U.S. government, did as Goering said and, created several false flag attacks in order to convince a previously unwilling public that they had to go to war in order to protect themselves.

The History of U.S. False Flag Attacks As Provocation For Wars For Profit!

WWI Profiteering:

The Federal Reserve provided the means for the Moneyed Elite to loan enormous sums to the government, income tax provided the means to repay the debt, and the creation of foundations allowed the Moneyed Elite a means to escape paying income tax, so the money machine was in place and then by some happy *"coincidence,"* in 1914 World War I began, and the U.S. national debt rose from $1 billion to $25 billion. While U.S. debt went through the roof enormous profits were made by the politically connected. For example as head of the War Industries Board, Bernard Baruch exercised dictatorial power over the national economy, while coincidently he and the Rockefellers were reported to have made over $200 million in war profiteering. Cleveland Dodge a Wilson backer fortuitously landed contracts to sell munitions to the allies, and with the entry of the U.S. in the war [contrary to campaign promises by Wilson] J.P. Morgan was free to loan hundreds of millions to the allies. Did you ever see so many happy coincidences?

America Enters WWI:

Gramps: Erick what did you learn in school as to why America entered WWI? The passenger ship Lusitania sailed out of New York with 128 Americans on board and was attacked without provocation and sunk by German submarines and the U.S. subsequently entered the war on the side of the British.

Gramps: Well Erick as usual they left out a few pertinent facts so let me set the record straight. For openers an overwhelming majority of Americans wanted no part of a European war, saying it was none of their affair. Knowing this the Germans would never have attacked U.S. interest without provocation. Besides that, **Germany was winning the war so the last thing they would have wanted would have been to draw America into the war and threaten her victory!** If America was to be enticed into the war it would require some type of catastrophic event like the explosion of the battleship Main. Then came another of those oh so convenient coincidences. According to

Colin Simpson, author of "The Lusitania" Winston Churchill [who was at the time head of the British Admiralty] ordered a report to predict the political impact of a passenger ship carrying U.S. citizens being sunk. Then as you said a short time later the Lusitania was sunk by German Submarines, except it wasn't quite as you explained it. Prior to the ships departure full page ads were taken out in the New York papers urging U.S. citizens not to book passage on the ship. This was suspicious to say the least, given that U.S. sentiment at the time was that we wanted nothing to do with the war in Europe, so the Germans would have had no reason to attack the Lusitania. What was not revealed was that the Lusitania was carrying war munitions, to guess who [England], which of course made it a legitimate target for the Germans, thus the ads.

Additionally given that the British had broken the German Naval Codes it would have seemed logical that locations of German U-boats would have been known and the ship could have stayed clear of them. But the plot thickens. According to Simpson, Commander Joseph Kenworthy, of British Naval Intelligence, stated: *"The Lusitania was deliberately sent at considerably reduced speed into an area where a U-boat was known to be waiting...escorts withdrawn."* Additionally it is reported that Colonel House had negotiated a secret agreement with England committing the U.S. to the war.

At the end of the war yet another ulterior motive for war emerged. At the Versailles Treaty President Wilson introduced his famous *"Fourteen Points"* of which point fourteen was a proposal for a General Association of Nations which came to be called *"The League of Nations"* which was intended as a first step toward formation of a one world government. Wilson's official biographer, Ray Stannard Baker, revealed that: *"...not a single idea—in the Covenant of the League was originated with the President. Colonel House was the author of the Covenant, and Wilson had merely rewritten it to confirm to his own phraseology."* The League of Nations was established, but it and its agenda to establish a one world government failed because the U.S. Senate refused to ratify the Versailles Treaty.

America's Entrance Into WWII:

Gramps: So Erick what did they teach you in school as to why America entered WWII?

Erick: Basically the Japanese launched a sneak attack on our fleet stationed in Pearl Harbor in the Hawaiian Islands and left America little choice other than to declare war against Japan. There was a mutual assistance agreement called the Tripartite Pact between Japan, Germany and Italy which committed the three countries to come to each other's aid in the event of an attack on any one of them, so when we declared war on Japan, Italy and Germany were obligated to come to her assistance which meant America was fully committed to WWII.

Gramps: Did they teach you anything that might have suggested that the U.S. intentionally provoked the attack by Japan and that President Roosevelt had advance knowledge of the attack, but allowed it to take place as an excuse for the U.S. to enter the war?

Erick: No. We never studied anything like that in school. Gramps I am sorry but I find it hard to believe that our government would do such a thing. To me that is unfathomable!

Gramps: Well Erick your reaction is pretty normal. They count on the fact that we cannot believe that they would kill our own service men in a ruse to get public support for a war, but don't forget that Goering says, if you want to get the people to agree to go to war all you have to do is tell them they are being attacked. He says it works every time.

With that in mind according to Robert Stinnett in his book <u>DAY OF DECEIT: THE TRUTH ABOUT–FDR–AND PEARL HARBOR:</u> Lieutenant Commander McCollum who was attached to the Office of Naval Intelligence wrote a five page memo in October 7, 1940 addressed to two of Roosevelt's most trusted advisers in which he outlined a plan to get a reluctant American population to join Britain in the European War against Germany. The memo outlined an eight step plan to back Japan into a corner and leave them little choice but to attack American ground, air and naval forces in Hawaii. In his memorandum McCollum outlined eight actions which he predicted would force Japan to attack the United States:

A. Make an arrangement with Britain for use of British bases in the Pacific, particularly Singapore.

B. Make an arrangement with Holland for the use of base facilities and acquisition of supplies in Dutch East Indies [Indonesia].

C. Give all possible aid to the Chinese government of Chiang Kai-shek.

D. Send a division of long-range heavy cruisers to the Orient, Philippines, or Singapore.

E. Send two divisions of submarines to the orient.

F. Keep the main strength of the U.S. fleet, now in the Pacific, in the vicinity of the Hawaiian Islands.

G. Insist that the Dutch refuse to grant Japanese demands for undue economic concessions, particularly oil.

H. Completely embargo all trade with Japan, in collaboration with a similar embargo imposed by the British Empire.

I am not going to go into detail on each of the eight actions, but I do want to make it perfectly clear that Roosevelt was not only aware of the eight provocative actions, he was in charge. According to Stinnett, during secret White House meetings Roosevelt personally took charge of Action D. With reference to the cruisers, Roosevelt called for what he called "*Pop-up*" cruises, of which he said: "*I just want them to keep popping up here and there and keep the Japs guessing. I don't mind losing one or two cruisers, but do not take a chance on losing five or six.*" In Roosevelt's own words he was willing to lose U.S. War ships in order to provoke war with Japan.

I want to discuss just one other of Roosevelt's Actions, namely Action F. which called for keeping the U.S. Pacific Fleet in Hawaiian waters. According to Stinnett, during an oval office luncheon fleet commander, Admiral James O. Richardson was informed of Roosevelt's intentions and exploded saying: "*Mr. President, senior officers of the Navy do not have the trust and confidence in the civilian leadership of this country that is essential for the successful prosecution of a war in the Pacific.*" Richardson opposed Roosevelt because the safety of his men and ships was of paramount importance and for that he was removed from command and was replaced by a more pliable Admiral Husband Kimmel.

Though testimony given at various Pearl Harbor inquiries suggests that Japanese codes were not broken till after the attack on Pearl Harbor there is evidence to the contrary. According to Stinnett; Rear Admiral Royal Ingersoll, Assistant Chief of Naval Operations in a letter dated October 4, 1940 stated that The Navy began tracking the movement and location of Japanese warships in October 1940. *"Every major movement of the Orange [America's code name for Japan] Fleet has been predicted, and a continuous flow of information concerning Orange diplomatic activities has been made available."*

Jumping forward to the attack on Pearl Harbor, Admiral Husband Kimmel who was in charge of the Pacific fleet at Pearl Harbor was intentionally kept in the dark about decryption of Japanese codes. According to Stinnett, The Director of Naval Intelligence Captain Walter Anderson was personally promoted by Roosevelt to Rear Admiral and was placed in charge of all Pacific Fleet Battleships. As Director of Naval Intelligence from June 1939 to December 1940 Anderson had meet regularly with Roosevelt and FBI Director J. Edgar Hoover and he was aware of the success in breaking the Japanese codes and when he reported for duty aboard Kimmel's Flag Ship his first obligation was to inform his commander-in-chief Admiral Kimmel about the decryption success, but he kept quiet and deliberately kept Kimmel out of the loop. After the war a bewildered Kimmel wrote: *"I can't understand, I may never understand why I was deprived of the information available in Washington."* By February Kimmel had sensed his exclusion from the intelligence loop and on March 22 and again on May 26 he requested to be kept informed. *"Inform the Commander-in-chief of the Pacific Fleet immediately of all important developments as they occur by the quickest possible means."* By late July he had been cut off completely from intelligence reports from Washington. Erick as history reports the outcome was the surprise attack on Pearl Harbor which gave Roosevelt the excuse he wanted to enter WWII.

The Vietnam War:

Gramps: Erick what do you know about how the U.S. got in the Vietnam War?

Erick: All I recall was that two U.S. Destroyers the Madix and the Turner Joy were attacked in the Gulf of Tonkin by communist Torpedo boats and President Johnson responded by sending troops to Vietnam. I think it was in 1964.

Gramps: Well Erick that was certainly the official story and it was all we knew about the incident for years, and then on Nov. 2001 the LBJ Library released tapes of phone conversations between President Johnson and Defense Robert McNamara where they openly discussed plans to use the staged Gulf of Tonkin incident as a pretext to expand the war. Then in 2005 the National Security Agency declassified its own official history of the Gulf of Tonkin and admitted that intelligence agency officers had deliberately skewed the intelligence and claimed that Vietnamese boats had attacked U.S. destroyers in August of 1964 when in reality they did nothing even while being fired on by U.S. forces. Following the bogus incident Congress authorized the Gulf of Tonkin Resolution and 58,000 American and 1.5 million Vietnamese went to their death based on a lie. This is the story of the evil which controls our country. The Gulf of Tonkin Declassified http://www.youtube.com/watch?v=KUNQWt9BPKg&feature=related
http://www.youtube.com/watch?v=_RYyLUXuNX8&feature=related

Our founding fathers had great wisdom and insight. It is almost like they could reach through time and see the future. One such example of this is the following quote by *James Madison, Fourth U.S. President 1809-1817:*

> *"If 'Tyranny and Oppression' come to this land*
> *it will be in the guise of fighting a foreign war."*

9/11 And The Introduction of Terrorism:

Gramps: Erick I won't ask you what you know about who perpetrated 9/11 because I know that the only thing that was allowed to be taught in school was that it was Osama Bin Laden and his terrorist organization that perpetrated 9/11. Before I tell you what I believe the facts support, I want to give you an account of the events of 9/11 from the prospective of Rock Star Promoter, Movie Producer, Candidate for Governor of Nevada, and 2004 Presidential Candidate of the Libertarian Party; Aaron Russo who claimed to have knowledge as to who was behind the 9/11 attack. In an interview with Alex Jones; Russo told how he meet and became friends with Nelson Rockefeller [banking mogul and Member of Foreign Relations Council.]

Russo says that one night about eleven months before 9/11 Rockefeller told him that there was *"going to be an event."* Russo says Rockefeller didn't tell him what the event was going to be or exactly when it would occur, but he did say, *"There was going to be an event and out of that event we are going to invade Afghanistan to run a pipeline to the Caspian Sea, invade Iraq to take over the oil fields and establish a base in the Middle East and make it all part of the New World Order.... Then 9/11 happened and I remembered he had said we were going to see soldiers looking in caves for people in Afghanistan and Pakistan and there was going to be a war on terror which is no real enemy and the whole thing is a giant hoax, but it is a way for the government to take over the American people."*

Russo goes on to say: ***"9/11 was done by people in our own government, in our own banking system to perpetuate the fear of the American people to subordinate themselves into anything the government wants them to do. That's what it's about; to create an endless war on terror...Look this whole war on terror is a fraud, a farce.*** *It's very difficult to say that out loud because people are intimidated against saying it, they want to make you into a nut case. But the truth has to come out. That's why I am doing this interview."*

At one point Russo asks Rockefeller, *"What's the point of all this? You have all the money in the world, all the power you need. What's the point?* ***What's the end goal?"*** Rockefeller responded: *"The end goal is to get everybody Chipped* [referring to RFID chips which holds individual medical and financial data] ***to control the whole society to have the banks and the elite people and some government controlling the whole world."***

In respect to Russo's interview regarding Nelson Rockefeller the following quote by David Rockefeller seems quite appropriate and enlightening.

"... The super national sovereignty of an intellectual elite and world bankers is surely preferable to the National Auto-determination practiced in past centuries."

– David Rockefeller Council Foreign Relations

Gramps: Erick, now we have two conflicting theses. On the one hand we have the government saying a group of terrorist headed by Bin Laden is responsible for 9/11 and on the other hand we have an individual claiming to have insider information saying it was the government who was responsible. Let's take a look at the events as they unfolded and the facts as we know them and see which thesis is more plausible, but before we do that let's explore motive and see who had the most to gain or lose?

PAY CLOSE ATTENTION! In regard to Bin Laden the motive can be seen as hatred of America which is seen as an Imperialist aggressor in the Middle East as well as an evil influence which seeks to defile the culture and traditions of Islam. Certainly this is ample motive to perpetrate 9/11. But while they had motive they also had a lot to lose. Given America's past history they could have predicted with certainty that if they perpetrated 9/11 that America's response would be to invade their country resulting in untold destruction of property and potentially millions of lives lost, but given their radical beliefs this might not have been enough to keep them from acting on their hatred. But the one thing they would have wanted to avoid at all cost would be to have their country **occupied** by the very people who they saw as defiling their religious beliefs and culture. So in summary the terrorist had much to lose and little to gain. However once America was naive enough to invade and occupy Iraq and Afghanistan and stir up the Middle East they have nothing to lose by sponsoring terrorist activities against us.

Our actions therefore increased the threat of terrorist activity instead of diminishing it.

As surprising as it may seem the **biggest beneficiaries from the events of 9/11 were right here in America.** For openers the crisis created enormous opportunity for the Money Manipulators to further their agenda of imposing a one world government. As they themselves point out they are always looking to take advantage of or to create crisis in order to further their agenda.

"We are on the verge of a global transformation. **All we need is the right major crisis and the nations will accept the New World Order.** *"*
                                                    – David Rockefeller, Sept. 23, 1994

"The whole aim of practical politics is to keep the populace alarmed —and hence clamorous to be led to safety—by menacing it with an endless series of hobgoblins, all of them imaginary." – H. L. Mencken

"A crisis is an event which can force democratic governments to make difficult decisions.... It's not that I want another 9/11 crisis, but having a crisis would force decisions that otherwise might not get made."
                                                    – Professor Rob A. Pastor credited as Father North American Union
                                                    [Translated from Spanish news paper]

PAY CLOSE ATTENTION! Although we could not have foretold it at the time 9/11 was instrumental in causing the real estate collapse of 2007-08. Following 9/11 the Federal Reserve lowered interest rates to the lowest they had been since WWII and that coupled with the dismantling of The Glass-Steagall Act allowed the toxic CDO's which collapsed the real estate market and resulted in the near collapse of the financial system. The government bail out of the banks created a virtual banking monopoly and left us with a handful of banks who own us because they are perceived to be too big to be allowed to fail. While the banks rallied and paid record bonuses to top executives the American public was left with a staggering debt in the form of money borrowed from the Federal Reserve, money which we must pay back at interest rendering us virtual tax slaves. So if as this book has contended, the objective of the Money Manipulators is to collapse the U.S. in order to bring about their one world government then 9/11 was instrumental in furthering their agenda.

PAY CLOSE ATTENTION! Looking at more immediate events the primary beneficiaries of 9/11 were the Bush Administration, the Pentagon, the CIA, the FBI, the Weapons Industry, the Oil Companies and the Munitions Manufacturers. 9/11 turned President Bush from a weak ineffectual minority President whose party had lost control in the Senate into perhaps the most powerful President since World War II. It is widely recognized that well before 9/11 Bush had plans for a military offensive against Afghanistan in order to replace the Taliban with a government more favorable to the U.S. 9/11 cleared the way for him to invade Afghanistan without appearing to be the aggressor. The invasion of Iraq gave the U.S. Government and U.S. Oil Companies control over what some say is the largest oil field in the world and it gave us an excuse to maintain permanent military bases in the region. The $48 Billion increase to the Pentagon budget which Bush requested in January 2002 was in and of itself more than any other country spent on its entire military budget. The Patriot Act and other similar legislation widely increased the purview of the CIA and FBI and the Arms Manufacturers were given virtual *"Cart Blanche"* with Bush saying, *"they would be given what ever it took to win the war."*

VITALLY IMPORTANT: Rahul Mahajan an outspoken critic of U.S. Imperialism pointed out that a document written in 2000 entitled *"Project for the New American Century"* [PNAC] outlines three major U.S. military objectives all of which were expedited by 9/11. Mahajan says that [PNAC] pointed out: 1) The need for strategically positioned military bases around the world. 2) The need to bring about regime change in countries unfriendly to U.S. policy. 3) The desire to increase military spending by upwards of a Trillion Dollars. **Mahajan also noted that the government's plans to transform the military would probably be unattainable "absent a *catastrophic and catalyzing event like Pearl Harbor."* [9/11]** He adds that within a year the authors of [PMAC] had their Pearl Harbor and a chance to *"Turn Their Imperial Fantasies Into Reality."* Erick how is that for motive?

Erick: I never even stopped to consider that a tragedy like 9/11 could benefit anyone much less our own Government, our Setting President, the Pentagon, the CIA, the FBI, the Weapons Industry, the Oil Companies, the Private Bankers and the Munitions Manufacturers.

Gramps: Now that we have determined who benefited from 9/11 let's see who had the means to actually carry out the 9/11 attack. The sixty four thousand dollar question is how plausible is it that Bin Laden could have orchestrated the most sophisticated terrorist attach in history from half way around the world from his command center in a cave in Afghanistan? He could have funded a group of terrorist and they could have conceivably gotten on the planes and hijacked them, but from that point on he would have been powerless to control events as they unfolded.

If we ask the same question regarding the government we find that they would have had the ability to control literally everything that happened that day and they therefore emerge as the more plausible culprit. Let's look at the events as they unfolded and you will see what I mean. For now let's accept the fact that two planes flew into the twin towers and either the government or a group of terrorist could have pulled that off. When we get to the question of what happened to the Pentagon and to Flight 93 the situation is quite different.

The Pentagon:

Much of the controversy about 9/11 revolved around several incongruous events which raised questions as to what really occurred?

1st Question: Why did NORAD fail to respond on a timely basis?

DAVID GRIFFIN Author The New Pearl Harbor *says that: "According to standard Operating Procedure if an FAA flight controller notices anything that suggest a possible hijacking the controller is to contact a supervisor. If the problem cannot be fixed in about a minute the supervisor is to ask [NORAD] North American Aerospace Defense Command to send up or scramble jet fighters to find out what is going on. NORAD then issues the scramble order to the nearest air force base with fighters on alert.* **Although interception usually occurs within 10 or so minutes in this case [9/11] 80 or so minutes elapsed before fighters were even airborne."**

Government critics point to the failure of NORAD to launch their planes as evidence that 9/11 could not have been carried out by an extremist in a cave in Afghanistan because this event points to a failure in the U.S. defense system that can only be explained by orders given at the highest levels of the military. It was compared to the attempt on Hitler's life during World War II which involved high ranking military officers who used the national emergency plan "Operation Valkvrie" in order to attempt a coup.

Erick: What was the government's explanation for the failure of NORAD to respond to this national emergency.

Gramps: Given the government's control of the media it didn't get much coverage, but not everyone ignored this failure in national security and it lead to the 2nd question.

2nd Question: What role did U.S. War Games play in the events of 9/11?

MICHAEL RUPPERT former Los Angeles Police Officer said: *"Not a single U.S. interceptor turns a wheel till it's too late ... What if they were so confused and had been so deliberately confused that they couldn't respond. The reason they didn't know where to go was because **a number of conflicting and overlapping war games were taking place** that involved the insertion of false radar blips onto radar screens in the NE defense sector."* **It was suggested that the War Games were a cover up for the 9/11 attack.**

This argument was given additional credence by events which took place in London England on 7/7/2005 when 56 people were killed when terrorist bombed three train stations and a bus. PETER POWER, *Visitor Consultants Emergency Management: "It was at half past 9 this morning. We were actually running an exercise for over 1,000 people in London based on simultaneous bombs going off precisely at the same railway stations that happened this morning" DAVID SHAY-LER, Former British Intelligent Agent (MI5) "We were supposed to believe this was some kind of a coincidence there was also an anti-terrorist drill going on, on 7/7 and again just like 9/11 they were talking about attacks on the same kind of tube stations at exactly the same time as the actual attack happened providing some kind of cover for what must be operations orchestrated in some way by the state."*

Critics of the government charged 7/7 and 9/11 were both covert operations. Just imagine two terrorist attacks occurring on the exact day the military conducts training exercises for that exact same scenario and even at the exact same time. I wonder what the odds are of that, not to mention I wonder how the terrorist knew what the government's training schedule was? It seemed more plausible that the government used the exercises as a cover up.

3rd Question: What actually struck the Pentagon?

The government contended that the Pentagon was hit by a 757 jumbo jet, but Tom Haran of the Associated Press was on site immediately after the crash and took a photo which appears on the cover of the book 9/11 The Big Lie [Photos are also available on the internet]. The picture was taken before the facade collapsed and shows a hole approximately 15-18ft in diameter which is way too small to have been made by a 757. This is substantiated by Francois Grangier a French accident investigator who said: *"What is certain when one looks at the photos of the facade that remains intact is that it is obvious that the plane* [the 757] *did not go through there."*

Given the photos of the facade there was conjecture as to what hit the Pentagon. According to Danielle O'Brien Air Traffic Controller at Dulles Airport: *"The speed, the maneuverability, the way that he turned, we all thought in the radar room, all of us experienced controllers, thought that it was a military plane."*

4th Question: How could any plane, commercial or military hit the Pentagon?

You see the Pentagon is protected by five extremely sophisticated missile batteries and is arguably the best protected building in the world, so why wasn't what ever it was shot down? Erick I can only think of two possible answers to this question. Either a stand down order would have had to be given or the aircraft would have had to be equipped with a friendly (U.S. Military) transponder. I can't honestly think of any other explanation can you? Are we to believe that on 9/11 NORAD didn't scramble planes till after the Pentagon was hit and now on top of that the missile batteries didn't respond either? Osama could not have possibly pulled off either of these events!

5th Question: What happened to the wreckage and the bodies?

CNN Live 9/11 America Under Attack: *"From my close up inspection there is no evidence of a plane having crashed anywhere near the Pentagon and as I said the only pieces left that you can see are small enough that you can pick up in your hand...Shortly after the attack government agents picked up debris and carried it off."*

Erick not only did FBI agents break the law by removing evidence from the crash site the entire lawn of the Pentagon was covered with several inches of gravel and dirt completely obliterating any remaining evidence. Any reasonable person would ask why?

Then there was an account on Fox News 9/11 Pentagon Crash Site which echoed that of CNN. *"No seats, no luggage, no bodies, nothing but bricks and limestone. The official explanation is that the intense heat from the jet fuel vaporized the entire plane. Flight 77 has two Rolls-Royce engines made from steel and titanium alloy and weighing 6 tons each. It is scientifically impossible that 12 tons of steel & titanium was vaporized by jet fuel."* The bodies of the passengers were supposedly identified despite the intense heat of the fire but Griffin questioned this account saying: *"We were told that the bodies were able to be identified either by fingerprints or DNA. So what kind of fire can vaporize tempered steel and yet have human bodies in tact?"*

6th Question: Why of all places would they crash the plane into the West Wing and what happened to the surveillance cameras?

Even the part of the Pentagon that was hit seemed to raise questions. According to *The Los Angeles Times*, *"The West Wing of the Pentagon was the only area of the Pentagon with a sprinkler system and it had been reconstructed with a web of steel columns and bars and blast resistant windows to withstand bomb blast. While perhaps 4,500 people normally would have been working in the hardest hit area, because of the renovation work only about 800 were there."*

Under the circumstances the West Wing was the one location assured to **minimize damage** and therefore for a terrorist it was the worst possible place to crash into, but from the perspective of the government and military it assured the minimum amount of damage.

There was even doubt as to whether the hijacker could have flown the plane into the West Wing, reinforcing suspicions that it was a military aircraft or drone missile. According to Air Traffic controllers in order to hit the West Wing the plane had to make an extremely difficult 270 degree spiral turn, made supposedly by a hijacker who was reported to be a terrible pilot, not to mention that he then had to come in at ground level and as the photos of the crash clearly show the aircraft hit cleanly into the building without hitting the ground first.

There was one way most of these nagging questions could have been answered but the government saw to it that they remained unanswered. According to Griffin, *"The videos from security cameras which would have shown what really hit the Pentagon were immediately confiscated by agents of the FBI and the Department of Justice has to this day refused to release them."*

Flight 93:

7th Question: What happened to the bodies, wreckage and flight control transcripts from Flight 93?

Gramps: Erick what do you know about Flight 93?

Erick: What I was taught in school was that the passengers took over the plane and it crashed into a field and never made it to its target which was believed to be the White House.

Gramps: That was the government's official account, but once again eye witness accounts and the facts contradict the government's account. Just like the Pentagon crash sight there was a conspicuous absence of debris, no seats, no fuselage, no engines and no bodies. **When have you ever seen a plane crash that didn't have wreckage and bodies strewn everywhere? I will tell you when never, that's when never.**

Here is what the responding coroner had to say about the crash sight. *WALLY MILLER, Summerset County Coroner at the site of Flight 93 said: "It looks like there is nothing there except a hole in the ground... It looked like somebody just dropped a bunch of metal out of the sky. It looked like somebody took a scrap truck, dug a 10 foot ditch and dumped trash in it... I stopped being coroner after about 20 minutes because there were no bodies there. I have not to this day seen a single drop of blood, not a drop."* GRIFFIN: quoting researcher Thompson pointed out that debris including human remains was found as far away as eight miles from the supposed crash site.

According to *GRIFFIN:* Phone conversations were monitored by the FBI so when Jeremy Glick called his wife at 9:47am and told her *"that the men had voted to attack the hijackers...the hijackers had only knives, no guns... and the conviction that they did not really have a bomb...increased the passenger's belief that they could be success-ful."* Then at 9:58am a passenger talking on the phone with her husband said, *"I think they are going to do it!... They're doing it! They're doing it! But her husband heard screaming in the background followed by a whooshing sound like wind."*

Gramps: Erick, *"A whooshing sound like wind."* Why do you think that was important?

Erick: I don't know. I can't see what that has to do with anything.

Gramps: GRIFFIN reports that one newspaper source claimed: *"That the last thing heard on the cockpit voice recorder is the sound of wind suggesting that the plane had been holed."* **[Shot down by a missile].**

This would have been easy enough to disprove. All the government would have had to do was release the flight control transcripts and we would have known conclusively whether Flight 93 crashed as the result of the attempt by the passengers to take back the plane or if it was shot down by a military fighter.

CBS Television: *"Reported that shortly before the crash two F16 Fighters were reported tailing the plane."* So the government had the means to shoot down the plane, but why would they do such a thing? It was no where near its target and posed no immediate threat? Skeptics of the government story asked if it could be that they couldn't risk the hijackers being captured? The Government's position was that flight 93 crashed as a result of the attempted take over by the passengers, but then there was a slip of the tongue by Rumsfield where he says Flight 93 was shot down over Pennsylvania, so what are we to believe? http://www.youtube.com/watch?v=x6Xoxaf1Al0&feature=related

"On October 16 the government released flight control transcripts of the airplanes except Flight 93."

Erick: This is a lot different than the account I was taught in school. Now I can understand why so many people thought 9/11 was a false flag attack.

<u>8th Question</u>: **Could Flight 93 have been a Coup attempt by factions within our government?**

According to Griffin both Vice President Chaney and National Security Advisor Rice were taken to the White House underground bunker by the Secret Service at 9:03…evacuation of the Capital Building did not begin till 9:48, some 45 minutes later. This was 23 minutes after the traffic controller at Dulles reported a fast flying plane headed toward the White House and it was 7 minutes after the Pentagon was hit. <u>The operative question here is why wasn't the White House evacuated when Chaney and Rice were escorted to the bunker</u>? If they were in danger so were the rest of our political leaders. This time line becomes crucially important when we remember that Flight 93 crashed in a field and never made it to its target, which was believed to be the White House. All of the planes were scheduled to depart relatively close together and it is believed that they were all intended to hit their targets at approximately the same time. Flight 93 was delayed leaving the gate by 41 minutes and it is believed that had it left on time it would have hit the White House prior to 9:48 when the evacuation began. This doesn't prove a coup attempt, but it is certainly suspicious.

If our Congressmen and Senators had died in mass it is probable that Martial Law would have been imposed in which case President Bush would have been given dictatorial power [under provisions of FEMA] and neither the Legislative nor Judicial Branch would have been able to challenge his authority for a period of six months. In six months the government could have been effectively dismantled potentially leaving us with a Dictatorship. 9/11 is eerily similar to events which allowed Hitler, in the name of Homeland Security to suspend Constitutional rights and put in place the infrastructure for the Nazi Police State.

Erick: Gramps, what are you referring to?

Gramps: In 1933 the German Reichstag [Parliament Building] was severely damaged in a fire that was believed to have been a False Flag Attack carried out by the Nazi Party. The goal was to cast blame on the Communist and create an event which would allow Civil Liberties to be sanctioned in the name of Homeland Security. This was exactly what happened in the U.S. with enactment of the Patriot Act and other legislation that followed 9/11. Regardless of who started the fire in the Reichstag or who was responsible for the 9/11 attack the outcome was the same. Both events put in place the superstructure for a Police State. In regard to 9/11 one has to ask who benefited more from 9/11 Bin Laden or the shadow government whose intent has long been to bring the U.S. down.

World Trade Center:

9th Question: What caused the Twin Towers and building #7 to collapse?

Erick: According to what I was taught in school the WTC collapsed as the direct result of the plane crashes. Are you suggesting that that isn't what happened? I have seen the footage of the two planes flying into the twin towers so what I learned in school certainly sounds like the truth.

Gramps: Erick, there is no question that the towers were struck by two commercial airliners, but there were as many or more inconsistencies regarding the WTC as there were involving the Pentagon and Flight 93. For example there were those who believed that the twin towers were brought down by a controlled demolition and not the result of impact by the planes. Then there is building #7 that collapsed in the same fashion as the towers yet it wasn't hit by a plane at all.

Just as with the Pentagon, the government withheld vital evidence which would have proven conclusively what really happened.

Erick: So Gramps what do you say happened?

Gramps: Well first of all it isn't what I say. It is more a matter of the questions that were raised by observers and investigators. It was just like with the Pentagon. <u>Despite virtually incontrovertible photographic evidence that a 757 had not struck the Pentagon the government never changed their story.</u> When it came to the WTC the government's story was that both the Twin Towers and Building 7 collapsed as the result of the plane crashes and resulting fires. On the surface this sounds totally logical, but upon investigation the government story doesn't seem to hold up.

Let's start with statements made by the structural engineers who designed the Twin Towers. *LES ROBERTSO, Structural Engineer WTC: "We designed the building to take the impact of the Boeing 707 hitting the building at any location." FRANK A. DEMARTINI, Manager WTC Construction: "The building probably could sustain multiple impacts of Jet Liners."* In response to these comments the government responded that it wasn't actually the crash itself which brought down the Twin Towers. They claim that the heat from the fire fueled by the jet fuel melted the steel braces supporting the vertical columns causing one floor to collapse creating a chain reaction where the other floors collapsed one on top of the other creating what they described as a Pancake Effect. Sorry but eyewitness accounts as well as experts disagree with that theory as well!

Let's start with eye witness accounts and then consider the scientific facts. *CNN BREAKING NEWS 9/11, "The way the structure is collapsing this was the result of something that was planted. It was not just accidental that the first tower just happened to collapse then the second tower just happened to collapse in the same way, but how they accomplished this we don't know."* ABC BREAKING NEWS CAST 9/11 ***"Anybody who has ever watched a building being demolished on purpose knows that if you are going to do this you have to get at the under infrastructure of a building to bring it down."***

Now let's consider the scientist facts. It is a scientific fact that in order to melt steel requires temperatures in the range of 2,800 degrees F, but according to Thomas Eagar, professor of Materials Engineering Systems at MIT: *"The maximum possible temperature for an open fire fueled by hydrocarbons* [jet fuel] *would be 1,600-1,700 Degrees F."*

In support of this is the fact that prior to 9/11 no steel framed building had ever collapsed from the heat from a fire and experts say the fire wasn't hot enough to cause the building to collapse. That aside how does the government's explanation account for the fact that building #7 collapsed in exactly the same fashion as the Twin Towers? It wasn't hit by a plane and only had small fires on two floors.

Erick: So if it wasn't the fire that brought the buildings down what was it?

Gramps: Let's start with *C-SPAN American Prospective*, Dr. STERVE JONES, Physics Professor Brigham Young University [BYU]: *"47 huge steel columns going up the core. They are interconnected. How do you get them to fail simultaneously so the core disappears? It looks like the core columns were cut..."* Let's explore that train of thought a little further and as we do let's ask just how they could have been cut?

The New York Times complained that: *"The decision to remove the steel columns, beams and trusses from the WTC [and building #7] in the days immediately following 9/11 means definitive evidence may never be known."* What they were referring to is the fact that there are tests which could have been conducted on the steel which would have conclusively proven if explosives had been used. Specifically the question is: was Termite used to cut the columns? More on this in a second. First the government covered the lawn of the Pentagon with gravel and dirt and now they remove the steel without testing it. Coincidently it just so happened that all the steel was in uniform lengths of approximately 30 foot which is just the right size to fit on a truck without having to be cut. Not only is that convenient, it is further evidence of a controlled demolition.

Getting back to Dr. JONES, he said: *"I began looking at the molten metal. All three buildings, both towers, in the rubble and in the basement areas and building #7 there's these pools of molten metal... So I am looking through the official reports. What do they say about the molten metal? They Say Nothing! Wait a minute this is important evidence. Where did that come from? Termite is so hot that it will just cut through steel structural steel for example like a knife through butter.... The products are molten iron and aluminum oxide which go off primarily as a dust. You know those enormous dust clouds you can imagine when you assemble these chemicals in large scale… Dr. Jones found exact traces of not only "Termite Explosives," but due to the high sulfur content… A patented brand of Termite used in the demolition industry… molten metal under both towers after they collapsed and building #7."* Now building #7 wasn't even hit by a jet!

10th Question: *Why given the overwhelming evidence wouldn't the government just agree that a controlled demolition brought the towers down?*

This in my opinion is the $64,000 question. Erick, I have racked my brain and I can only come up with one plausible answer to that question, and that is "there is no credible way to explain how a group of Arab Terrorist could have possibly gotten access to the WTC buildings to rig them with explosives." Security is just too tight. It had to be an inside job. This begs the question as to whether there was anyone with the requisite access?

It just so happens there was someone with access! GRIFFIN reports that according to Scott Forbs [in a letter published in 2001] he was employed by Fiduciary Trust who occupied floors 94-97 of the south tower. He states: *"On the weekend of September 8-9, 2001, there was a 'Power Down' condition in WTC Tower 2, the South Tower. The power down condition meant there was no electrical supply for approximately 36 hours from floors 50 up. I am aware of this condition since I had to work with many others that weekend to ensure that all systems were cleanly shut down beforehand… The reason given by the WTC for the power down was the cabling in the tower was being upgraded… Of course without power there were no security cameras, no security locks on doors while many, many engineers were coming in and out of the tower."* In an e-mail letter to Griffin June 2, 2004 Forbs added: *"What surprises me… is the fact that no authority will acknowledge that there was a 36 hour power down in the top half of tower 2 over the weekend period 9/8-9/9. I have no hidden agenda other than trying to get the truth acknowledged and investigated."*

GRIFFIN quotes Maggie Burns as reporting that: *"Marvin P. Bush, the President's younger brother was a principle in a company called Securacom from 1993-2000 and that the company was in charge of security for the WTC between 1996 and September 2001."* Griffin also reports Wayne Madison as saying: *"That Wirt D. Walker III a cousin of Marvin P. and George W. Bush is the current Chairman of the Board and was CEO from 1999 until January 2002.* Erick, I am not saying that the Bush family was complicit in the attacks, but it would appear they had opportunity and according to Griffin these connections were not reported nor was the company ever investigated in regards to 9/11. I don't know about you but it makes me wonder why? It kind of reminds me of the pleasant coincidence surrounding Bush's election where the election hinged on a recount in Florida where his brother just happened to be Governor.

Gramps: Erick, help me out here. Contemplate the following questions and see if you conclude there is any way the government's *"Pancake Theory"* could account for the collapse of the WTC buildings. If the fire wasn't hot enough to melt metal where did the molten metal come from if not from Termite and given that building 7 wasn't hit by a plane how do you account for its collapse? If there was no explosion how do you account for everything being pulverized to dust? Floors collapsing onto each other would not have created enough energy to pulverize concrete so where did the dust come from if not an explosion?

9/11 Investigation:

11th Question: Why did the 9/11 Commission ignore the facts?

Gramps: Erick there was one last allegation made against the government. It was made by the families who lost loved ones in 9/11. They claimed that the 9/11 investigation was nothing but a rubber stamp by the Bush Administration. PAUL THOMPSON *Author:* Terror Time Line had this to say*: "There is literally nothing in the 9/11 commission report that the Bush Administration did not approve."* Apparently this opinion was shared by relatives of 9/11 victims who demanded that Philip Zelikow resign as Commission Director 9/11. Quoting *GRIF-FIN: "We have found out that he [Philip Zelikow Commission Director 91])...Served on the transition team of the Bush Administration. That he was a person who wrote a draft memo for the set up of the*

Bush Administration National Security Council. That he was an individual who wrote the preemptive strategy that was eventually used for the war in Iraq. That he is a close friend of Condoleezza Rice...We want him to resign... **We can understand therefore why the commission under Zelikows leadership would ignore all the evidence that would have pointed to the truth that 9/11 was a False Flag Operation intended to authorize the doctrines and funds for a new level of imperial mobilization.**

Summary of Wars For Profit!

Gramps: Erick, in the instance of each crash sight the definitive evidence which would have proved the government's version of the events was withheld. The surveillance cameras at the Pentagon were confiscated and the crash sight was covered with tons of dirt covering up forensics evidence. The steel from the twin towers was removed without being tested to see if there had been an explosion. Individuals at the security company owned by Bush's younger brother were never questioned and there was no inquiry into the molten metal in all three buildings, including building #7 which had not been hit by a plane. And now the flight control transcripts for Flight 93 were withheld. Why the cover up?

Before we leave this subject I want to go back to our earlier conversation where we determined that the Bush Administration wanted 1) strategically positioned military bases around the world. 2) to bring about regime change in countries unfriendly to U.S. policy. 3) to increase military spending by upwards of a Trillion Dollars. 9/11 brought all of these things to pass. And lest we forget it also set the stage for the Predatory Lending Practices which resulted in the massive housing bubble of 2008 which drove the economic system into near collapse.

History will just keep on repeating itself till we wake up and put a stop to the wars for profit. For example in WWII America had experienced the largest National Debt in its history, while munitions manufacturers made vast fortunes producing armaments to fight the war and the Federal Reserve made vast fortunes loaning money to the U.S. and other foreign countries to fund the war. Additionally, through the creation of the World Bank they were now positioned to fund the rebuilding of the very countries their bombs had destroyed! Isn't this exactly what is happening all over again in Iraq? We invade the country, take their oil and then use the proceeds from their oil to rebuild the very country we destroyed; while in the process lining the pockets of companies like Halliburton where, coincidently Chaney had been President prior to becoming V.P. of the U.S. Just think about it, all this wealth being made by the Money Manipulators while the U.S. Tax Payers go broke funding a war that was forced on them.

Even worse 9/11 set the stage for the systematic debasement of U.S. civil liberties and the undermining of the U.S. Constitution. In this regard one has to ask, if the government was so concerned about Homeland Security why did it do virtually everything it could to keep our southern border with Mexico open? Any military strategist would tell you that the first thing you do is protect your borders. Could it be like Aaron Russo said:

"...there was going to be a war on terror which is no real enemy and the whole thing is a giant hoax, but it is a way for the government to take over the American people."

According to Defense Department reports, just before the September 11 2001 attacks, over a quarter of a million U.S. military personnel were deployed overseas, in 153 countries [Johnson 2004: 154ff]. – Johnson, Chalmers; 2004; The sorrows of empire; Verso; London. **Deployment of U.S. troops is in and of itself proof that the government had prior knowledge of the events of 9/11. Troops were deployed and we were ready to go to war. That kind of a massive expenditure of resources is no coincidence.**

PAY CLOSE ATTENTION! So in summary I say that the facts do not support the thesis that Bin Laden was behind the 9/11 attacks. The facts indicate that 9/11 was almost certainly a False Flag Attack perpetrated by factions within the U.S. Government. In other words 9/11 was an excuse for another in a long line of wars for profit! If the government takes exception to my conclusions all they have to do is release the video tapes from the Pentagon, the flight control transcripts from Flight 93 and declassify all material regarding the investigation. But they won't do that because it would prove their guilt.

Gramps: Erick I hope I have made my point, which is that while wars enrich the Moneyed Elite and achieve political objectives for them, they impoverish the public, take the lives of our children and systematically erode our civil liberties.

PERSONAL NOTE: Stepping out of character and time line <u>I want to close this chapter by pointing out just how close we are to where our civil liberties have been eroded to the point where our Constitution is irrelevant and the government has the means to impose a police state pretty much when ever they want</u>. About the only thing they have not yet accomplished is to take away our right to bear arms. Once that is accomplished we can expect them to create a **Crisis** that gives them an excuse to declare Martial Law at which point we will effectively be a Police State. Consider the following quotes.

"Our task of creating a socialist America can only succeed when those who would resist us have been totally disarmed." – Sara Brady Chairman, Handgun Control, to Sen. Howard Metzenbaum, *The National Educator,* January 1994, Page 3

2008 Holder argued before the Supreme Court in DC Gun Ban Case Columbia VS Heller, for the complete disarming of the Americans and that only military should own firearms.

Not only does the government want to disarm us, but then they want to turn around and deploy standing armies on U.S. soil. **Why?**

Obama ordered Department of Defense DOD to Issue Directive 1401.10 establishing a one million man army under his control. HR 645 National Emergency Centers Act: Brings local government and police under Federal control. Pentagon plans to keep 20,000 troops in U.S. to supposedly bolster Domestic security. Contrary to campaign promises Obama refused to rescind George W. Bush's Presidential Directive 51 which effectively allows the President dictatorial powers.

Are the troops to protect us or contain us? Never in our history have we needed this kind of domestic military. Why Now? Why not rescind Directive 51 with its dictatorial powers? It is as Noah Webster said:"

"Before a standing army can rule, the people must be disarmed..."

Once again this reminds me of Hitler and what he did with his Brown Shirts and SS.

The mechanism already exists to establish a dictatorship. It is called The Federal National Emergency Act [FEMA] and it grants the sitting president, at his discretion to declare a national crisis in which event he is granted the authority to implement sweeping powers to enact a series of executive orders. For example *H.R.*5122 amends Posse Comitatus and The Insurrection Act which places limits on domestic military deployment to allow the Federal Government to unilaterally take control of State National Guards and position Federal troops anywhere in the country during a public emergency. The Constitution can be suspended and Martial Law can be implemented, effectively turning over the reigns of government to military commanders to run state and local governments. Under provisions of FEMA laws can be suspended, populations can be forcibly moved, citizens can be arrested and held without trial in any of 800 REX 84 detention camps, property, food supplies, and transportation can be seized, the mechanisms of production, distribution of energy sources, wages, salaries, credit and the flow of money in U.S. financial Institutions can be controlled. Most shocking of all is the fact that FEMA was a product of a Presidential Executive Order and as such represents and end run around our Constitution and Congress. Per Executive order #11921 when a state of emergency is declared by the President, Congress cannot review the action for six months! Six months is ample time to dismantle the government and impose a dictatorship.

I wouldn't be so worried about FEMA and in particular Rex 84 if I felt our Legislators were informed and were in a position to make sure the plan was truly in the best interest of the American people. As was clearly pointed out in a speech made in the U.S. House by Rep. Peter De Fazio [D] Oregon 4th District and broadcast on CPAN [Google FEMA Rex 84] Title of speech is: *Congress Kept Away from Rex 84 FEMA Camp.*

"Most Americans would agree that it would be prudent to have a plan for the continuity of government and the rule of law in case of a devastating terrorist attack or natural disaster, a plan to provide for the coordination and continued functioning of all three branches

of government. The Bush administration tells us that they have such a plan. They introduced a little sketchy public version that is clearly inadequate and doesn't really tell us what they have in mind, but they said don't worry, there is a detailed 'Classified Version' but now they have denied the entire Homeland Security Committee of the United States House of Representatives access to their so called detailed plan to provide for continuity of government. They say 'Trust us' ... Trust us the people who brought us warrantless wire tapping and other excesses eroding our Civil Liberties. Trust us. Maybe the plan just doesn't really exist or maybe there is something there that is outrageous. The American people need their elected representatives to review this plan for the continuity of government. "

Conclusions: If you combine The Real ID Act [which can restrict our ability to travel and our access to money] with HR1195 The Violent Radicalization and Homegrown Terrorism Prevention Act [which restricts our right to protest] and The Military Commission Act [which suspends the ineligible rights of Habeas Corpus] it is entirely possible that in the future anyone who objects to government policies could be labeled a dissident, and an enemy combatant and incarcerated with no legal rights what so ever. Now add in the FEMA detention camps and right of the Federal Government to unilaterally take control of State National Guards and position Federal troops anywhere in the country during a public emergency and the government has the means to effectively quell any type of civil protest which might occur. Finally under provisions of Executive Order 11921 the President can declare a state of emergency and impose Martial Law and Congress cannot review the action for six months. This sounds to me like a perfect recipe to establish a dictatorship. If in the meantime the government has been successful in their efforts to take away our Second Amendment rights to bear arms we will be sheep to the slaughter, completely at the mercy of a potential Totalitarian Government. The parallels of how Hitler set up his police state and what is being set up in America are frightening. History is poised to repeat itself if we don't stop it before it is too late. I hope I have demonstrated the opportunity for abuse of power and just how dangerous it is to our National Security. As Keith Olberman said:

"...We have been afraid of the wrong thing... We now face what our

ancestors faced at other times of exacerbated crises and melodramatic fear mongering A Government More Dangerous To Our Liberty Than The Enemy It Claims To Protect Us From."

— MSNBC: Keith Olberman, The End of America

I will close with the following quote from President John F. Kennedy:

"Those who make peaceful revolution impossible will make violent revolution inevitable."

**Please, don't wait till the only solution is violence.
Peaceful protest is still possible.**

Chapter 8

American Hegemony:
Seizing The World's Natural Resources!

Gramps: Erick yesterday we discussed how the American public was repeatedly duped into going to war on the pretext of defending our country from foreign attackers when in fact we were nothing more than the pawns of the Moneyed Elite who were manipulating events in order to perpetuate their scheme of wars for profit, and to methodically further their goal of achieving a one world government where national sovereignty gives way to an open dictatorship ruled by a financial elite who at their own admission are unrestricted by traditional values.

Erick: Gramps what are we going to discuss today?

Gramps: U.S. Imperialism and Hegemony!

Erick: Gee gramps based on what I was taught in school America was the defender of liberty throughout the free world, so based on what you are saying this ought to be a real eye opening experience.

Gramps: I certainly hope so. We need to understand that America has become oppressors like the British before us and at the same time we have become oppressed. We need to understand our policy of Hegemony so we can take responsibility for our actions and hopefully stop our *policies* of U.S. Imperialism.

The American public was literally brainwashed and utterly clueless about the U.S.'s foreign policies and how oppressive it was to underdeveloped nations around the world. America was not the Lilly White Defender of World Peace that we were portrayed to be.

VITALLY IMPORTANT: In the name of <u>Foreign Aid</u> America in concert with the World Bank, IMF, the U.S. Agency for International Development *[USAID]* were engaged in a worldwide scheme to drive resource rich underdeveloped nations into bankruptcy.

Erick: Why would they want to do that? Why wouldn't we want to help them enter the industrial age so they could modernize and in the process break the cycle of poverty, hunger and disease that has so devastated third world countries for decades?

Gramps: Erick you may find this hard to believe but the last thing the U.S. wanted to do was to end poverty and disease. You see the Puppet Masters believe there is a serious over population problem so to actually help these countries address their hunger and disease problems would be contrary to their agenda. We will discuss this in detail later but for now suffice it to say that we were in these countries to get control of their natural resources and to enslave them economically, not to help them.

Erick: Gramps I find what you are saying disturbing but for now I will take you at your word. After all, most everything else you have told me turned out to be true. So I guess my question now is how did they economically enslave these underdeveloped countries?

Gramps: Well Erick it is like I have said throughout my manuscript the surest way to get control of a Nation and enslave its population is to drive it into DEBT! To this end we loaned them massive amounts of money supposedly to help them modernize and join the industrialized world, but it was all part of a sophisticated scheme to drive them into bankruptcy and in the process get control of the only assets they had which was their natural resources, their oil, lumber and mineral deposits. Here is how it worked. The powerful Western Banking Institutions [The World Bank and IMF controlled largely by the U.S.] would loan money and provide technology to an underdeveloped nation to develop infrastructure projects, such as roads, harbors, hydroelectric dams etc. The ploy was that we always made sure that we loaned them more than they could afford to pay back forcing them into default. When they defaulted we were always there to loan them still more money to finish the projects, but the catch was that **they had to pledge their Natural Resources as collateral.** Through multiple rounds of financing we would eventually get control of their natural resources as well as impose **Free Trade Agreements** which were not in their best interest. Generally the poverty level of the country would end up being worse than before we so graciously offered to help them. U.S. corporations would come in to say develop their oil, or lumber but the lion's share of the proceeds would go to the U.S. corporations and an impoverished population would be forced to work under reprehensible conditions for what amounted to slave wages.

Gramps: Erick we will discuss this process in detail shortly, but first I need to take you back to 1951 in order to show you how the policy of U.S. Hegemony got started.

Erick: Gramps what is significant about 1951?

Gramps: 1951 marked a very dangerous change in U.S. foreign policy and sowed the seed of hatred of the U.S. which has gradually spread to nearly every nation of the world, but particularly to the Middle East and Latin America. In 2009 President Obama said that the American Flag is a symbol of hatred and oppression around the world and he is correct! Unfortunately most Americans have no perception of why this is. To find out, let's revisit 1951 and see what changed that would so tarnish the U.S.'s image as the nation that believed that all people have certain *"unalienable rights that among these are life, liberty, and the pursuit of happiness…"*

VITALLY IMPORTANT: In 1951 the U.S. discovered that its interest, namely those of "Global Empire" could be accomplished by means other than direct military engagement. By this point in our history the U.S. had been subverted and **we were aggressively engaged in pursuing Global Empire** in conjunction with our former enemies the British Colonial Empire otherwise referred to as the Money Manipulators. In decades past the resources of interest were gold, silver, spices, slaves etc. but now in a mechanized society oil had become the resource of greatest value.

According to Stephen Kinser author of <u>All the Shah's Men: American Coup and The Roots of Middle East Terror</u> here is what transpired. In 1951 the Iranians rebelled against a British oil company which was exploiting them. In response the *"democratically elected, popular leader"* of Iran Mahammad Massaden, who I might mention was *Time* Magazine's *"Man of the Year"* nationalized the Iranian oil resources. England seeking to reverse this decision sought the help of the U.S. After careful consideration it was decided that because of Massaden's popularity that military intervention would not be advisable. Instead it was decided to conduct a covert CIA led incursion. The grandson of Theodore Roosevelt, CIA operative Kermit Roosevelt was sent in with instructions to destabilize the government. For a scant few million dollars he bribed people, threatened others and orchestrated a series of demonstrations and riots that made it appear that Massaden was inept and unpopular. He was deposed and spent the rest of his life under house arrest. He was replaced by pro American <u>dictator</u> and <u>tyrant</u> Mahammad Reza Shah, known as the Shah of Iran [The Kink of Kings]. ***"In subsequent years this low profile low budget coup would be refined and serve as the model for future U.S. covert operations and Imperialist endeavors."***

Unfortunately for the U.S. the Iranian people despised the pro-American Shah and in 1979 they revolted and led by religious leader Ayatollah <u>Khomeini</u> overthrew the Shah who fled to the U.S. Hatred for the U.S. spilled out into the streets of Iran and in November 1979 an Islamic mob seized the U.S. Embassy in Tehran and held fifty-two Americans hostage for 444 days. In April of 1980 President Carter attempted a failed military rescue and on this note ended 29 years of U.S. intervention into the affairs of Iran. ***"The seeds of Middle East terrorism had been sown by the U.S. and British exploitation of the Iranian people and their oil resources."*** Unfortunately most Americans were too busy living their lives of luxury to realize what we had done in Iran and elsewhere in the world. To this day few Americans understand why so many nations of the world see the U.S. Flag as a symbol of hatred and oppression. By the time you finish this chapter you will understand and you will have to decide if you want to be complicit in this game of empire, this game of Modern Slavery or are you willing to say that it is the right of all people to enjoy the *"unalienable rights promised by the Declaration of Independence."*

In either event once you know the truth you will no longer be able to claim innocence.

Gramps: Erick I am going to jump forward to 1973 and the **U.S. OIL EMBARGO**, then I will come back and fill in the intervening years. I am discussing this event slightly out of its historical timeline because it, more than any other event, explains what we will discuss the rest of the day. It provides the motive for why the U.S./British controlled World Bank adopted such a tyrannical approach to making sure that wherever and whenever possible they would control the world's oil supply by controlling the oil producing countries, by exploiting them just the way the they had exploited Iran.

In the 1960s a group of oil producing countries had formed OPEC and now in 1973 they were about to flex their muscle in a way that got the U.S.'s attention. A group of International Oil Companies known as the Seven Sisters were collaborating in an effort to hold down gas prices which effected OPEC's profits. This was occurring in the mist of mounting Middle East tensions and on Oct. 6, 1973 Egypt and Syria launch simultaneous attacks on Israel. Ten days later on Oct. 16 Iran and the five Arab countries including Saudi Arabia announced a 70% increase in oil prices. Then three days later Nixon asked Congress for aid for Israel and the next day OPEC retaliated with a total embargo on oil shipments to the U.S. Gas shortages caused long lines at gas stations, but few of us had any idea how dramatically this event would shape future economic and political policy and how it would take the Money Manipulators into a new and more sinister level of international manipulation. Whether the gas shortages were real or contrived makes no difference. The U.S. was in the midst of one of those **crises** that creates opportunities that are just too valuable to waste. Out of this crisis the U.S. understood that oil, not money was the currency of power. As a direct result of the embargo the international banks, the corporations and the U.S. Government circled their wagons around a unified oil and power agenda that endures to this day. Oil had always been a priority but now it became our #1 Imperative! If you understand this imperative you can understand most of the U.S.'s Middle East and Latin America Policies, but the real key to understanding the U.S.'s Oil Policy lies in understanding the special relationship that developed shortly after the October War between the U.S. and Saudi Arabia!

Erick: Gramps I see how important oil is to an industrialized nation like the U.S. but I fail to see how this makes the U.S. an Imperialist Nation guilty of Hegemony.

Gramps: Erick bear with me just a little longer and it will become clear.

Immediately after the war the Saudis and U.S. emissaries began negotiations that resulted in the United States-Saudi Arabian *"Joint Economic Commission"* known an [JECOR]. According to Thomas W. Lippman author of Inside The Mirage: America's Fragile Partnership with Saudi Arabia. The terms of the agreement created a hitherto unseen interdependence between the U.S. and what was essentially an underdeveloped country.

Under the Agreement the U.S. Would Provide the House of Saudi With:

- **All necessary technical assistance:** to bring the entire country into the Twentieth Century. This meant billions in consulting, construction and maintenance contracts to U.S. Government insiders like MAIN, Bechtel, Halliburton, Brown and Roth and many others. It not only created an interdependency between the U.S. and the house of Saudi but of equal importance it furthered the interdependency between the banks, corporations and the U.S. government which now had crucially important mutual interest. The Money Manipulators were *"unified as never before"* and this unification would only grow stronger as they took their new unified globalization policies into countries such as Equator, Panama, Iraq and others which we will discuss shortly.

- **Political and if necessary military protection:** This would assure the long term continuation of The House of Saudi. The Saudis would need U.S. protection because Modernization/Westernization would infuriate its more conservative Muslim neighbors and a technologically advanced Saudi Arabia might threaten Israel and other less developed countries in the region.

Under Terms of the Agreement the Saudis Would Commit To:

- **Guarantee oil supplies and prices acceptable to the U.S. and its allies:** In the event any of the oil producing countries such as Iran, Iraq, or Venezuela etc. should threaten another oil embargo the Saudis would step up production to cover any shortages. With the world's largest oil deposits Saudi Arabia could protect the U.S. from any further fears of an oil shortage like what it experienced in 1973.

- **Cash Disbursement:** In his fascinating best selling book Confessions of an Economic Hit Man, John Perkins says: *"The Saudis agreed to use their petrodollars to Purchase U.S. Securities and in turn the interest earned by these securities would be spent by the U.S. Dept. of the Treasury on modernization projects within Saudi Arabia which were mutually agreeable to by the Saudis and the U.S."* This had far reaching implications. For one it meant that the U.S. and the Saudis could undertake whatever projects they wanted without having to justify them to Congress. It also meant that Saudi Petrodollars would be recycled back into the U.S. economy, what Perkins called *"The Money Laundering Deal."* But far and away the most important thing was that it meant that *"Saudi Arabia was obligated to buy U.S. Treasury Notes or put another way they were obligated to the U.S. Dollar and they were obligated to use their money to pay the U.S. National Debt."* According to Lindsey Williams Author of The Oil Non Crisis, following the U.S. meltdown which started in the fall of 2008 the following countries stopped using the U.S. dollar as their currency of choice: China, Kuwait, Ecuador, South Korea, Argentina, Iran, Russia, Switzerland, Malaysia and Brazil. Additionally the following countries said they would no longer use the dollar for oil purchases: Iran, Venezuela, Nigeria, Bolivia, and Russia, and OPEC said it was diversifying. Why was this important? *"It meant they no longer had to prop up the U.S. Dollar by buying our T Bills in order to cover our national debt!"* It clearly showed lack of confidence in the dollar and since the dollar isn't backed by gold if other countries lost confidence in the dollar it represented a serious threat to the value of the dollar!

Gramps: Erick we are finally getting to the point where you will be able to see exactly how U.S. Imperialism and Hegemony are executed against unsuspecting underdeveloped resource rich nations around the world.

Birth of The Economic Hit Man (EHM)

Out of the events of the 1951 Iranian coup evolved a subtler less risky plan for future covert operations. The problem with the Iranian model was that Kermit Roosevelt was a card caring CIA operative. If he had been caught, the U.S. would have no deniability; they would have been caught orchestrating a coup of a popular democratically elected leader of a sovereign nation. The answer to this problem was to enlist the services of a group of men that would come to be known as the Economic Hit Men [EHM] of which John Perkins was one. He recounts his life as a CIA surrogate and explains he never received any money from the CIA, NSA or any other government agency. He was hired as a consultant by the private sector so that if ever exposed his activities would appear to be the result of corporate greed rather than government complicity. He recounts that in addition *"the corporations that hired him, although paid by government agencies and their multinational banking counterparts [*with taxpayer money*], would be insulated from congressional oversight and public scrutiny, shielded by a growing body of legal initiatives, including trademark, international trade, and freedom of information laws."*

In the preface to his book Perkins defines exactly what an (EHM) is. He says:

"Economic Hit Men [EHM] are highly paid professionals who cheat countries around the world out of trillions of dollars. They funnel money from the World Bank, the U.S. Agency for International Development [USAID], and other foreign 'aid' organizations into coffers of huge corporations and the pockets of a few wealthy families who control the planet's natural resources. Their tools include fraudulent financial reports, rigged elections, payoffs, extortion, sex and murder. They play a game as old as empires, but it has taken on new and terrifying dimensions during this time of globalization. I should know I am an EHM."

Perkins coined a name for the confluence of the International Banks, International Corporations and World Governments. He calls them collectively the *"Corporatacracy"* which is just another name for what I call the Money Manipulators. He goes on to say that the Corporatacracy's use of debt, bribery, and political overthrow is what he defines as *"Globalization."* Erick as we continue our discussion it will become clear as to how U.S. policies lead to Imperial Aggression and Global Hegemony.

Political Destabilization Strategies of The Economic Hit Men!

The Money Manipulators have political destabilization down to a science. What follows explains exactly how they/we are able to destabilize Oil Rich/Resource Rich Nations and in the process gain control of their resources.

<u>**Step 1**</u>: **Economic Destabilization:** *[Through Loans and Unmanageable Debt]* According to Perkins, the EHM approach the leader of a country and offer to loan him huge sums of money to develop infrastructure projects [hydro electric dams, harbors, roads, factories etc.] which will supposedly help his country out of poverty and then either through fiscal ineptitude or by corrupting the leader(s) force the country into a situation where they cannot pay the debt. They are then forced to renegotiate the loan, but this time there are unfavorable conditions added which most often take the form of:

- <u>**Trade Liberalization/The British Free Trade System**</u>: invariably places the targeted **Nation State** in unfair competition with **Global Corporations,** resulting in the Nation State losing jobs and experiencing trade deficits which weaken their economy and drive them into additional debt causing currency devaluation. According to Perkins this is what happened in Jamaica where local farmers lost their most valuable cash crops because they were unable to compete with the prices of the multinationals.

  Ironically the very policies which the U.S. used in conjunction with the World Bank and The World Trade Organization to destabilize underdeveloped nations have also been instrumental in the economic destabilization of the U.S. as well. In regards to the U.S. NAFTA and similar agreements with China and WTO have gutted the U.S. manufacturing sector and created a trade deficit that has virtually decimated the U.S. economy. On the subject of unfair trade Lindsey Williams Author of The Oil Non Crisis, had this to say in a speech in December of 2008: *"American companies spent $59.2 billion in China on outsourcing in the last twelve months. The U.S. has lost seven million textile jobs and three million manufacturing jobs to free trade and outsourcing. 152,000 companies have left the U.S. and moved abroad. The U.S. goes into debt to other nations to the tune of one trillion dollars per year."* **The Money Manipulators have the U.S. just where they want us.**

- **Currency Devaluation:** Through *"inflation and debt a nation's currency is devalued"* and when this happens all of the country's resources are correspondingly devalued allowing them to be bought for pennies on the dollar, by the very entities which caused the devaluation in the first place! Sound familiar?

Ironically that is what happened to the U.S.? After all their agenda for the U.S. is no different than for any other country. Matter of fact they are on record as saying that the U.S. must fall in order to achieve their plans for a one world government. Erick tomorrow we will discuss how the Money Manipulators bankrupt the U.S. and then bought our most valuable assets for pennies on the dollar. For example the State of California was forced to have a giant garage sale to raise money for the general revenue fund and Chicago was forced to lease the Chicago Skyway to an international consortium. How pathetic! As a result of financial trickery a vast array of U.S. assets have been sold and are for sale for pennies on the dollar. The list includes such things as U.S. financial institutions, auto makers, real estate of all sorts, highways, utilities, factories and vast arrays of other assets. [More on this tomorrow]. If you don't think the dollar has been devalued consider the following: [An item that cost $1.00 in 1913 when the Federal Reserve was established cost $21.82 as of 2009.] Inflation Calculator: http://www.usinflationcalculator.com/) A couple of examples of what inflation means to you; a postage stamp in 1950 was $0.03 now it's $0.42, the average Medicare monthly payment in 1970 was $5.30 now it's $93.00 etc. For most Americans their salaries have not gone up anywhere near as much as the cost of goods so they have had a serious loss in buying power. Now think about your retirement fund. In the financial collapse of 2007 many Americans saw a 50% or more reduction in the value of their retirement plans. Now factor in an 83% reduction in the value of the dollar from 1950 to 2008 and continued devolution in the future and ask yourself what your retirement plan might be worth when you retire? <u>For many hard working Americans retirement will be impossible!</u> America is for sale! It's the buy of the century!

- **Major Cuts in Social Programs:** What happens is that so much of the target Country's budget goes to repay the debt to the World Bank [or in the instance of the U.S. the Fed and our National Debt] that there is inadequate funding for schools and healthcare and other social services. In underdeveloped countries this results in a level of poverty that makes the people vulnerable to exploitation by foreign companies who come in and set up sweat shops because desperate people will work for whatever they can get no matter how unfair it is. Here in the U.S. the minimum payment on the National Debt costs more than Health Care, Education and Homeland Security combined. One way or the other the **U.S. can expect massive reductions in entitlement programs** over the next several years. What the government giveth it can and will take away! For example our social security fund has been plundered and as a result either our children will be burdened with unmanageable taxes or the elderly will at some point be denied Social Security benefits even though they paid into Social Security their entire adult lives. How can we conclude other than the Money Manipulators have enslaved America and the world?

- **Privatization of Publicly Owned Infrastructure:** This means that public entities can be purchased by private or international investors and operated for profit. For Example, according to Perkins, in Bolivia the World Bank forced the sale of the water company of the country's third largest city to be sold to a subsidiary of U.S. owned Bechtel. Finally after civil unrest broke out the contract was rescinded. Make no mistake <u>if the U.S. is foolish enough</u>

to allow the sale of our infrastructure we can expect the same thing to happen to us! By the way former Secretary of Defense Casper Weinberger was a former Bechtel V.P. and General Council. George Schultz who was Secretary of the Treasury and Chairman of the Council on Economic Policy under Nixon, and ultimately Secretary of State under Reagan was also a former President of Bechtel. Do you begin to see just how deep the connections go? The Money Manipulators place their men in key positions and then like a master Puppeteer pull their strings. For example until recently it was illegal to sell U.S. infrastructure to private or international investors, but never mind if you know the right people, anything is possible! Enter George H. Bush and Executive Order #12803 and magically what was illegal is now legal. America is for sale and our highest ranking politicians and corporate leaders are in charge of the sale. America we have to put a stop to this type of un-American activity by our leaders.

Step 2: CONTROL OR OVERTHROW: [Trough, Bribery, Corruption, Coup, Political Destabilization, assassination or Military Invasion!] According to Perkins if the EHM fail then CIA sanctioned jackals are called in and the leader is either overthrown or assassinated and if the jackals fail then the government creates a reason to invade the country.

- **Latin America:** According to Perkins the U.S. led Corporatacracy has for decades sought to control governments in Latin America because of the vast amount of oil and other resources they have, but following the 1973 oil embargo it became an imperative! As you will shortly see the strategy has been to drive these countries into unmanageable debt, extort their resources, pollute and destroy their rain forest, enslave their inhabitants in sweat shops and drive the population into intolerable poverty.

I call this Modern Slavery, but no matter what you call it, it's still slavery and it's immoral and inhumane and it is why the U.S. is hated by those who suffer under this oppression.

- **Panama**: Is the most strategically important country in the southern hemisphere and for that reason the U.S. has been more blatant in its domination of Panama than any other country in the region.

Our actions in Panama leave no doubt that no matter how democratic or humanitarian the U.S. is domestically its foreign policy
is anything but! The U.S. has maintained an iron grip on Panama
since it was torn away from Columbia over 100 years ago. Panama clearly demonstrates why the American flag has become a
symbol of hatred, tyranny and oppression! It is going to take some
time to unravel over 100 years of Panamanian history so please
bear with me. I promise you it is important for you to understand
U.S. policy in Panama.

It's 1903 and the French effort to build the Panama Canal has ended in
financial ruin, but U.S. President Roosevelt had designs on the canal.
Roosevelt demanded that Columbia sign a treaty turning control of
the canal over to a U.S. Consortium and when Columbia refused
Roosevelt sent in the U.S. War Ship Nashville seized the canal and
declared Panama an Independent Nation. The treaty that was subsequently signed was signed by the U.S. Secretary of State and a French
Engineer, but *"it was not signed by a single Panamanian."* The U.S.
set up a puppet government which ruled the country under Washington's control for approximately the next fifty years.

It's July 31, 1981 and headlines in the U.S. read:

PANAMANIAN LEADER GENERAL TORRIJOS
DIES IN PLANE CRASH

But in Panama and elsewhere around the world the headlines suggest a:

CIA ASSASSINATION!

What really happened? During the Carter Administration democratic
leader Omar Torrijos renegotiated the Panama Canal Treaty, but now
Reagan was in office and like Roosevelt before him he demanded the
treaty be renegotiated. Torrijos refused and a few weeks later he died in
a plane crash. People around the world mourned the death of the man
they called the defender of the poor and defenseless and the people of
Panama pushed for Washington to investigate CIA involvement.

From the Panamanians' viewpoint there were ample reasons to sus-
pect that the CIA was behind the assassination of Torrijos. In addition
to refusing to renegotiate the canal treaty Torrijos wanted the School

of The Americas and the Southern Command Tropical Training Center closed because they were known for teaching repressive regimes interrogation and covert operations skills. He was also talking with Japan about a new Japanese funded sea level canal.

He was *"Not a U.S. Puppet"* but neither was he anti-American. He was pro Panamanian and all he wanted was fair deals with international corporations for his country's oil and other resources. Latin America was watching him. If he could stand up to the U.S. maybe they could too. He believed his country had rights as divinely inspired as those of the United States. Supporters say that, that belief and his refusal to be corrupted made him dangerous!

Torrijos was replaced by Manuel Noriega who developed a reputation for corruption and drug dealing but there were certainly a lot of leaders who were worse than him. Yet on Dec. 20, 1989 the U.S. invaded Panama which represented no threat to the U.S. Proponents of U.S. involvement contend that the U.S. could have had Noriega assassinated as Torrijos before him but they didn't. Why? It has been suggested that the U.S. wanted to send a message to Latin America *"get in line or else!"* In any event, *"America sent troops into Panama to get one man"* and in the process killed an untold number of innocent civilians and left thousands homeless. David Harris editor at the *New York Times* and Author of Shooting the Moon says:

"Of all the thousands of rulers, potentates, strongmen, juntas and warlords the U.S. has dealt with in all corners of the world, General Manuel Noriega is the only one the Americans came after like this. Just once in 225 years of formal national existence has the United States ever invaded another country and carried its ruler back to the United States to face trial and imprisonment for violations of American law committed on the ruler's own native foreign turf."

According to Peter Eisner author of The Memoirs of Manuel Noriega, Noriega had this to say regarding the invasion:

"I want to make it very clear: the destabilization campaign launched by the United States in 1986, ending with the 1989 Panama invasion, was a result of the U.S. rejection of any scenario in which future control of the Panama Canal might be in the hands of an independent

sovereign Panama-supported by Japan...Schultz and Weinberger, meanwhile, masquerading as officials operating in the public interest and basking in popular ignorance about the powerful economic interest they represent, were building a propaganda campaign to shoot me down."

At the end of the day Noriega was in a U.S. prison and control of Panama was turned over to the Arias Family who had been the U.S.'s puppets up till Torrijos was elected so the issue of the canal treaty was mute.

Erick: Gramps I had no idea the U.S. was this kind of international bully. It amazes me that the U.S. could do all these things and the American public could be utterly clueless.

Gramps: It is exactly because of these kind of escapades that the Financial Elite have to own and control the media, so they can keep the American public in the dark as to the kind of horrible things that are being done by U.S. Surrogates.

■   **Ecuador:** According to an article by Abby Ellin in the *New York Times* May 8, 2003, *"A group of American lawyers representing more than 30,000 Ecuadorian people filed a $1 billion lawsuit against Chevron Texaco Corp. The suit exerts that between 1971 and 1992 the oil giant dumped into open holes and rivers over four million gallons per day of toxic waste water contaminated with oil, heavy metals and carcinogens and that the company left behind neatly 350 uncovered waste pits that continue to kill both people and animals."*

According to Perkins: *"Equator is typical of countries around the world that EHM have brought into the economic-political fold. For every $100 of crude oil taken out of the Ecuadorian rain forest, the oil companies receive $75. Of the remaining $25 75% must go to pay off the foreign debt. Most of the remaining covers military and other government expenses which leaves about $2.50 for health education and programs aimed at helping the poor."*

According to Perkins: *"Since 1970 during the oil boom the official poverty level grew from 50% to 70%, under and unemployment increased* *from 15% to 70% and public debt increased from $40 million to $16 billion and the share of national resources allocated to the poorest segment of the population declined from 20% to 6%."*

On August 10, 1979 the then newly elected President of Ecuador Jamie Roldos wanted to better the lives of the Ecuadorian people and at his Inaugural address he said: *"We must take effective measures to defend the energy resources of the nation. The state must maintain the diversification of its exports and not lose its economic independence... Our decisions will be inspired solely by national interest and in the unrestricted defense of our sovereign rights."*

In 1981 Roldos formally presented the "Hydrocarbon Bill" of which he alluded in his inaugural address to Congress. He like Torrijos stood up to the U.S. and the big oil companies. He like Torrijos represented hope for Latin Americans and on May 24, 1981 he like Torrijos died in a fiery plane crash and as with Torrijos there were allegations of a U.S. sponsored CIA ASSASSINATION!

Gramps: If these kinds of actions don't constitute Imperial Aggression and Hegemony I don't what would.

■ **Brazil:** Situated in the vast Amazon *River Basin,* Brazil has arguably the vastest storehouse of natural resources on the planet. Its natural resources include, oil, timber, hydropower, phosphates, nickel gold, bauxite, uranium, tin, platinum and manganese. Funded largely by loans from the World Bank Brazil's crown jewel Capital City Brasilia had its inaugural in 1960 and by the late 1980s Brazil had become the largest of the third world debtors and had more than once defaulted on loan payments resulting in much of the wealth of the Amazon River Basin being transferred to the World Bank.

Gramps: Erick it is like I have said repeatedly throughout our conversation. The Money Manipulators are committed to controlling the world's resources through any means necessary, whether it be by debt, political overthrow or assassination or even as we are about to see invasion and occupation.

Erick: Gramps do you believe the citizens of these various countries see the U.S. as being in some way behind the oppression in their countries?

Gramps: Absolutely. That is why we are called ugly Americans!

■ **Iraq***:* As Panama is the key to Latin America, Iraq is the key to the Middle East. It is estimated to have oil deposits as large as or larger than those in Saudi Arabia. It is positioned between the Tigress and Euphrates and as such controls critical water supplies. It has access to the Persian Gulf and from a military standpoint it is in easy missile range to both Israel and Russia. Additionally; according to Perkins the U.S. had visions of Iraq being the second Saudi Arabia. The U.S. hoped to make a deal with Saddam similar to what it had made with the house of Saud; Iraq's petrodollars in exchange for modernization, armaments, whatever he wanted. It didn't matter to the U.S. that Saddam was a mass murder and a tyrant. All that mattered was that he cooperate with the U.S. but he didn't and so he had to go. In 1990 Saddam invaded Kuwait, which had once been a part of Iraq, and that gave George H. Bush the excuse he needed to take Saddam out. There was some talk that Saddam had discussed the invasion with the U.S. and been told we would remain neutral, but that could not be confirmed. In any event Bush denounced Saddam for violating international law and a multi national force of 500,000 men were sent in to root out Saddam. But as always in the game of power politics there was a double standard being applied here, because let us not forget that less than a year prior Bush and the U.S. had violated that same international law by invading Panama. But when the U.S. is the one violating the law no retaliation occurs because we are too powerful, not because we are in the right. As they say might makes right!

■ **Afghanistan:** Officially the war in Afghanistan [Enduring Freedom] Oct. 7, 2001 was in direct response to the 9/11 attack on the U.S., [allegedly orchestrated by Osama bin Laden.] However there is evidence that the war was planned months earlier and that 9/11 was just the justification. NBC News reported May 2002 that a formal National Security Presidential Directive *"submitted two days before the 9/11 attacks"* had outlined essentially the same war plan that the White House, the CIA and the Pentagon put into action.

The BBC News reported on September 18, 2001, exactly one week after the September 11 attacks that <u>Niaz Niak a former Pakistani Foreign Secretary, had been told by senior American officials in *mid-July* that a military action against Afghanistan would proceed by the middle of October at the latest.</u> The message was conveyed during a meeting between senior U.S. Russian, Iranian and Pakistani diplomats.

Why did the U.S. have plans to attack Afghanistan two months before the 9/11 attacks? Erick don't forget that we discussed earlier that large numbers of U.S. troops were deployed to bases around the world prior to 9/11.

According to NBC: On Oct. 14, 2001 seven days into the U.S./British bombing campaign the <u>Taliban offered to surrender Osama bin Laden</u> to a third country for trial, if bombing was halted and they were shown evidence of his involvement in September 11 terrorist attacks. This was their second offer to surrender Osama and it was also refused by U.S. President Bush who declared: *"There's no need to discuss innocence or guilt. We know he did it."* I am sorry Mr. Bush but there is always a need to discuss innocence or guilt. Ask yourself why in the world President Bush would refuse to have Osama surrendered for trial? Could it be that there was no evidence? Could it be that *"Osama was more valuable to Bush alive as the face of terror than he could ever be in a jail?"* As is always the case with the Money Manipulators there is always a hidden agenda.

Gramps: I finally understand why America was so hated by so many nations of the world. We were intent on being The World's Largest Most Powerful Superpower.

PERSONAL NOTE: Stepping out of character and timeline I want to speak in the present tense about the dangers facing the U.S. and about our role as an Imperialist Nation who is guilty of Hegemony and oppression of nations around the world.

The End Game Revealed!

The Puppet Masters are individually comprised of international bankers, international corporations, and government leaders drawn together by greed, lust for power and mutual benefit. Collectively they are comprised of Money Manipulators who use debt, bribery, and political overthrow in a process of Globalization intended to culminate in a One World Government whereby they control the world's resources and have indebted the world's population to the point that we are all reduced to being their slaves. It is the culmination of the European Plan of Empire where the slave masters have freed themselves from the burden of caring for labors because wages control the labors. This is *"Modern Slavery"* and it is what awaits us all if we don't wake up and take back, as the Declaration of Independence says: *"Our unalienable rights of life, liberty and the pursuit of happiness..."* We need to remember that our Declaration of Independence says that: *"When any form of government becomes destructive to these ends, it is the right of the people to alter or to abolish it, and to institute new government, laying its foundation on such principles and organizing its power in such form, as to them shall seem most likely to effect their safety and happiness."*

I hope that the last two chapters have made it abundantly clear that the U.S. has been complicit in oppressing nations around the world in order to expand our empire and in the process we have controlled other countries, stolen their resources and oppressed their populations. Hopefully the truth about the U.S.'s policies of Imperialism and Hegemony will become common knowledge and I sincerely hope that if and when that happens that we will put a stop to such oppressive policies.

Given our economic plight we can no longer afford to maintain military bases around the world and continue to spend more on military than any other nation in the world. If we stopped being the planet's number one arms dealer and stopped interfering in the affairs of Sovereign Nations as though they had no rights we would not have to be worried about spending so much on defense. America is an aggressor and we need to stop our aggression, pure and simple.

Let's put our supposed humanitarian efforts in perspective. According to John Robbins author of <u>Diet For A New America</u> and <u>The Food Revolution</u> the U.S. spends over $87 billion on the war in Iraq while the United Nations estimates that for less than half that amount we could provide clean water, adequate diets, sanitation services, and basic education to every person on the planet. I guarantee that if the U.S. did that, the American Flag would no longer be a symbol of hatred and oppression. But let us not forget that our foreign aid does not go to these kinds of truly humanitarian efforts. Our Foreign aid goes instead to impoverish nations, to ravage habitats, to enslave people and to make the U.S. a symbol of hatred and oppression

We can no longer financially afford to maintain our global empire and besides our policies of hegemony are immoral and are the principal reason that nations around the world hate America and why we are targets of terrorism!

Chapter 9

America Is For Sale:

Betrayed By Our Leaders And Sold
To The Highest Bidder!

Erick: So Gramps what are we going to talk about today?

Gramps: I want to expand on one of the topics we just touched on briefly yesterday, namely privatization of publicly owned infrastructure!

Erick: Dad has told me a little about how there used to be public utilities. But now of course they are all owned by private corporations, but I really never gave it much thought till we started our discussions.

PAY CLOSE ATTENTION! Gramps: The entire U.S. infrastructure was originally built and maintained by tax payer money which is why they were referred to as public utilities or public works projects. But as part of the planned bankruptcy of the country, U.S. infrastructure was intentionally allowed to go into disrepair and then the State and Local Governments, which were themselves broke, were forced to sell public assets to private international investors which up till that point had been **illegal.** So part of what we are going to discuss today is how the Federal Government stepped in and led the way for the states to change their laws so assets paid for with tax payer money could legally be sold to foreign investors, who of course ran them at a profit. So for example what used to be free highways were turned into toll roads.

Ironically it is one of the strategies which the U.S. through [The World Bank, IMF and the U.S. Agency for International Development *[USAID]* had used for decades as one of their chief means of driving developing nations into bankruptcy and abject poverty. So in an ironic twist of fate America found itself being systematically dismantled by the very mechanism which through our policy of U.S. Hegemony we had inflicted on so many other countries. As they say what goes around comes around.

Gramps: Erick the sale of U.S. infrastructure was tied to an even more devious plan. The Security and Prosperity Partnership [SPP] entered into by former President Bush, without any input from the American people or Congress was intended to bypass the normal treaty process and use bureaucrats to create trade agreements designed to undermine the U.S., Constitution and drive us into a North American Union consisting of Mexico, Canada and the U.S. This is exactly the same mechanism which was used to create the European Union which had preceded it. For example, *NAFTA Chapter 11 Tribunals* **override U.S. law even the Supreme Court making U.S. laws subject to integration and harmonization with laws from Mexico and Canada.** Erick the following quote is from the 2006 U.S. Senate Debate by Stan Jones U.S. Senate Candidate for the Libertarian Party. [CSPN Debate]

"I risk sounding like a conspiracy theorist, but it is no longer a theory. What I am about to say is fact. The secret organizations of the world power elite are no longer secret... They have planned and are now leading us into the One World Communist Government. This combining of National governments began with the European Union. That union started with trade agreements, then a common currency the Euro and now a European Parliament that is feverishly passing laws. A constitution was drafted but was rejected by a few of those nations, but never mind they implemented it anyway. Now it is North America's Turn. Building on the 'North American Free Trade Agreement' the NAFTA section of the Commerce Department is busy drafting laws and regulations for a North American Union, a union of Canada, America and Mexico. The President [Former President Bush] has attended secret meetings and signed at least two agreements under the 'Security and Prosperity Partnership Program.' Information leaked

out about the meetings and now it is in the open. No treaty has been signed so Congress has not become involved; however money from our treasury is now being spent for this effort. We will have a new currency the Amero. We will have a new constitution modeled on the Soviet Union's Constitution.

> **VITALLY IMPORTANT:** *Our rights will not be 'Enailable' but they will be granted by the government which can also take them away.*

One Sign that this is our future is the plan for a super highway across Southern Mexico through America and into Canada. These plans are not secret any longer. Huge amounts of public property will be taken in the name of free trade, peace and security. You will have a 'National ID Card' with a radio frequency chip in it. This is terrorism of the most worst kind brought on you by our own Government. ***The strongest freest nation in the history of mankind will be averaged into world Communism."***

This chapter will provide facts to back Mr. Jones allegations from debate night.

As I have said before in order to achieve a Communist take over America had to be driven into bankruptcy. The process of bankrupting an Economic Super Power like the U.S. is, as you can imagine, more complex and takes longer than bankrupting an Under Developed Nation. Debt is still the key ingredient to bankrupt any nation but with an economic Super Power it is a very involved process to burden it with enough debt to take it down. So Erick in this context I would ask the question how do you eat an elephant?

Erick: Everybody knows that, one bite at a time.

Gramps: Exactly! And in the context of bankrupting the U.S. it is a process whereby step by tiny imperceptible step the nation is driven into unmanageable debt. A number of mechanisms including unfunded entitlement programs are employed, but for purposes of our conversation today we will be focusing mainly on how they dismantled the U.S. manufacturing base and then enacted unfavorable Free Trade Agreements which created an unfavorable balance of trade which eventually siphoned off the nation's wealth leaving it economically incapable of sustaining itself. At that point the Moneyed Elite stepped in and through their Puppets in the government they bought the country's assets, including its infrastructure for pennies on the dollar.

America's Manufacturing Gutted – Its Middle Class Destroyed

Gramps: Erick have you ever asked yourself how, in the span of a few short decades, the once wealthiest nation in the world could boast the largest trade deficit in the world and be the world's number one debtor nation? When I learned what I am about to disclose I got so mad I could have bitten sixteen penny nails in half. All of the sudden I had irrefutable evidence that the American people have been sold-out!

U.S. Is The Only Major Industrialized Nation With No Trade Protection

According to Auggie Tantillo, Executive Director at the American Manufacturing Trade Action Coalition [AMTAC]: **"Of 138 major manufacturing nations the U.S. is the only nation that does not take advantage of a "Value-Added Tax" [VAT] in order to protect its manufacturing base and maintain a favorable balance of trade."** The VAT was created by a French Economist Maurice Laure in the 1950's. At each stage of production the manufacturer adds a *"Value-Added Tax"* which is assessed by the government as a percentage of the final value of the good or service and is passed on to the consumer as an indirect tax much like sales tax. Though the VAT varies from country to country the average is 15%. When a product is sold domestically the government retains the VAT, however if the same product is exported the government rebates the VAT to the manufacturer as a [government subsidy]. Since the U.S. imposes no VAT its products incur on average a 15% export penalty when competing with "Free Trade Countries" which subsidize their manufacturers by rebating the VAT. It gets worse! U.S. imports into VAT countries are hit with the VAT a second time, this time in the form of a [Tariff]. <u>Since the U.S. Government neither subsidizes exports nor charges a tariff at the border on imports U.S. products incur on average a 30% tax disadvantage.</u> This is not by accident. It is by design and as far as I am concerned it is nothing short of criminal. It is no accident that the U.S. has the largest trade deficit in the world?

Erick: Gramps I am not quite sure I follow you.

Gramps: Erick, it is somewhat complicated so let me see if an example won't clear up your confusion.

- **U.S. Domestic Sale:** Say a car is manufactured in the U.S. and sells domestically, taxes included, for <u>$25,000</u>.

- **U.S. Export to VAT Country:** When that same car is exported to a VAT participating country they add on average 15% VAT **[Import Tariff]** to the $25,000 price which means the U.S. manufactured car now sells on the foreign market for <u>$28,750.</u>

- **Import to U.S. from VAT Country:** Conversely, assume a car was produced in a VAT Country for the same $25,000, and it is exported to the U.S. having received a 15% VAT rebate **[government Subsidy]** of $3,750 **and incurring <u>no</u> VAT [Import Tariff]** upon entering the U.S. that car would sell in the U.S. for <u>$21,250.</u>

The net result is that domestically the U.S. manufactured car sells for $25,000 while the foreign import is able to be sold for $21,250 or $3,750 less. As an export the U.S. car sells overseas for $28,750 while an identical foreign car sells here in America for $21,250 or some $7,500 less. Is it any wonder we have the world's largest trade imbalance? From the get go the deck is stacked against us.

> **VITALLY IMPORTANT**: NAFTA and other Free Trade agreements the U.S. is engaged in are one sided agreements which create an imbalance of trade and siphon off the wealth of the U.S. and give it to the 137 nations who assess a VAT.

Gramps: Erick it is as we discussed earlier; the Free Trade policy is exactly the opposite of the American System of Economics which imposed high tariffs against Free Trade Countries in order to protect U.S. domestic markets.

PAY CLOSE ATTENTION! It was the <u>American System</u> which was responsible for America's rise to the status of Economic Super Power, so one has to ask why we would want to do the opposite of what had been proven to be the basis of our economic success? History had already shown us that Free Trade is a recipe for economic enslavement so to embrace it can only be construed as an intentional effort to bankrupt our economy.

As Tantillo, explains:

"... the VAT differential is a core driving aspect as to why U.S. companies find themselves continually at a disadvantage. If you extrapolate to the next step the VAT differential is a core reason for why we see the escalating growth in the U.S. trade deficit on an annual Basis."

Unlike Tantillo I would not describe the U.S. companies as being at a disadvantage. I would describe them as making a conscious decision to sell out the American people. The market the globalists want to target is America.

> **VITALLY IMPORTANT**: By not imposing a Value-Added Tax like other countries *the U.S. Government has in fact encouraged and enabled U.S. corporations to have their products produced abroad and then imported back into the U.S.* This allows them to make obscene profits. They can seek out the cheapest labor on the planet [china and India] avoid EPA standards, avoid paying health benefits, and pensions and as importers into the U.S. they can even take advantage of the Value-Added Tax as importers.

PAY CLOSE ATTENTION! There is a cost to doing business this way and the government and the corporations are fully aware of that cost. Obscene profits were made by gutting America's manufacturing base and the ongoing trade deficit has siphoned off our wealth but this was not due to structural trade disadvantages, it was due to conscious decisions to maximize short term profits no matter what the long term cost to our nation. America's Multinational Corporations, by in large, have no allegiance to any nation, not even America. Their rational is that they provide the jobs which create the wealth which is the base of the taxation and revenue which individual *"Nation States"* depend on so they have the right to do as they please regardless of the impact on any given nation or group of nations. This is the driving force behind the movement toward globalization. They see to it that those politicians who support their agenda have plenty of money to run their campaigns and stay in office. Everybody wins except the American people.

According to Congressman Duncan Hunter [R-CA] in an interview with *Human Events,* Dec. 4, 2006:

"We practiced what I call 'Losing trade' – deliberately losing trade- over the last 50 years. Today, other countries around the world employ what they call a value-added tax, in which foreign governments refund to their corporations that are exporting goods to the United States the full amount of their value-added taxes that that particular company pays in marketing a product...When American products hit their shores, they charge a value-added tax in the same amount. So they enact a double hit against American exporters. One is that they subsidize their own imports going out, and the second is that they tax us going in. The United States doesn't do this."

PERSONAL NOTE: I want to step out of character and state emphatically that to me there can be absolutely no question that the U.S. Government willfully bankrupt the United States of America in order to facilitate the agenda of the Financial Elite to establish a hybrid Communist/Capitalist One World Government!

Gramps: Erick the U.S. government knowingly engaged in a number of policies that systematically destroyed the U.S. middle class. The things that were done to bring the U.S. down were not done out of ignorance, but instead they represent a carefully conceived plan to bankrupt the U.S. by:

1) **Budget Deficits:** Intentionally running enormous budget deficits year after year with no regard for the debt burden being placed on future generations.

2) **Entitlement Programs:** They repeatedly passed extraordinarily costly unfunded entitlement programs without any concern for how we were going to pay for them. In certain instances such as the Health Care Program passed under Obama they actually rammed unwanted entitlement programs down our throats. Surprise, surprise; after the fact we discovered that the cost estimates for Obama's Healthcare Program omitted key cost components which made it much more costly than represented. Ill-regardless of the fact that the majority of the American People were against Obama's health care program it was inflicted on us as a means to seize control of 1/6 of the U.S. economy and to control our access to medical care.

3) **Open Border Policies:** We can build fences and hire Border Guards to stem the tide of illegal aliens or if we actually want to solve the problem we can refuse social services to anyone without a valid visa or proof of citizenship. This means that the citizenship status of anyone attempting to enroll in a public school, obtain a drivers license or auto insurance, employment, purchase real estate or purchase health insurance or receive medical care at an emergency room would be verified and if they turn out to be in the U.S. illegally they will be deported. It couldn't be simpler.

4) **Legalized Sale of U.S. Assets And Infrastructure:** The Federal Government allowed our infrastructure to fall into a *state of disrepair* so severe that it posed a serious threat to the safety of millions of Americans and was estimated to cost $2.2 trillion dollars just to repair. But President Bush had a solution. EO #12803 expressly *allowed privatization of U.S. infrastructure*. Thanks to Mr. Bush international investors were allowed to buy U.S. infrastructure **[which had up till that point been illegal]** paid for by American Tax payers and then turn around and charge us to use infrastructure that was previously public property.

5) **Dismantling of U.S. Corporations:** During the Carter Administration the U.S. opened trade with China resulting in the formation of the World Trade Organization [WTO]. It just so happened that at the same time the U.S. experienced a period of **corporate raiding** which saw many U.S. corporations purchased, only to have their pension funds raided and or to be dismantled and sold off division by division. The net effect of this policy was to facilitate the dismantling of key U.S. corporations facilitating encroachment by free trade from China.

6) **Engaging In Intentionally Losing Free Trade Agreements:** The U.S. trade deficit which virtually bankrupt America was simply impossible short of the intentionally losing trade policies of the U.S. Government. As we discussed a second ago of 138 major industrialized nations the U.S. is the only nation not to impose the combination of a [VAT] and Tariffs in order to protect their domestic markets. As if that wasn't bad enough we did everything we could to provide further advantages to countries like China by streamlining customs procedures and building deep water ports so they could cut their shipping cost through economies of scale. Lastly we allowed U.S. Corporations to gut the American manufacturing sector by allowing them to incorporate abroad, take their manufacturing overseas and then after abandoning the American worker they were allowed to take advantage of [VAT] and Tariff protections as importers. Our legislators are not so dumb as to not understand what I have just outlined. No, they are guilty of nothing less than treason.

Gramps: Erick the outcome of these policies resulted in the intentional demise of the U.S. middle class resulting in America becoming a two class society comprised of the very poor and the financial elite which rule over us and oppress us.

Erick: Gramps you never said how it was that our public infrastructure became privatized.

Gramps: I guess I skipped that. I will start with our transportation system.

U.S. Transportation System Redesigned To Optimize Trade With China!

PERSONAL NOTE: Stepping out of character the events I am about to discuss are current events so we still have a chance to influence their outcome if we stand up and **Say No To Federal Government!**

<u>Trans Texas Corridor 35</u> **[TTC-35]:** In order to further secure its economic strangle hold on North America, Red China is endeavoring to influence the redesign of the North American transportation infrastructure <u>to optimize international trade as opposed to domestic trade.</u> How you may ask could Red China influence the design of the U.S.'s transportation system? I will discuss this issue in detail later in this chapter, but first I need to establish exactly what [TTC-35] is.

PAY CLOSE ATTENTION! It is vitally important that we realize that China's plan to dominate North American trade is impossible without the cooperation of the U.S. Government. As we will discuss shortly we have it within our power to stop China's plans cold in their tracks.

Plans to build a super-transportation corridor have been cloaked in secrecy and have been referred to as an urban myth, but it is not a myth. The Bush administration through the [FHWA] Federal Highway Administration has pushed to build a NAFTA Super-highway from the Mexican border at Laredo, Texas through the heartland of the U.S. to the Canadian border north of Duluth, Minnesota. The first Trans Texas Corridor [TTC] segment of the NAFTA Super-highway is already under construction. Plans for the TTC-35 Project are available on www.keeptexasmoving.org which is an official Texas Department of Transportation [TX DOT] website.

The super highway will include separate lanes for cars, truck and trains as well as a utility corridor for gas and oil pipelines and utility lines. It is designed to tie together Mexico, the U.S. and Canada, <u>but strategically its importance is that it provides the backbone for containers from the Far East and China to penetrate U.S. markets through Mexico.</u> The *"Free Trade"* slavery and semi-slavery system of Red China has cut production cost to bare bones, circumvented pollution regulations, health care benefits and pensions. <u>All that remains is to cut transportation cost and bypass expensive U.S. union labor.</u> With the help of our Federal Government they are poised to do just that. I well tell you how momentarily. We need to wake up and realize that while China economically benefits from *"Free Trade"* with the U.S., America is systematically impoverished and as I will establish our national security is jeopardized!

Federal Government Intimidation Tactics: As I have researched this book it has become increasingly apparent that virtually every time Local or State Governments or for that matter our Congress attempts to protect the interest of the American people <u>the Federal Government, most frequently through the office of the President, steps in and blocks their efforts.</u> The TTC-35 Project parallel to I-35 is no exception!

When the Texas Legislature proposed a two year moratorium on construction of the TTC-35 the Federal government stepped in and applied pressure. According to Jerome Corsi author of <u>The Late Great USA</u>:

"The chief council for the [FHWA] sent a letter to the executive director of the Texas Department of Transportation [TX DOT] ***threatening a loss of federal highway funds should the legislature approve the memorandum.****"*

I don't know about you but where I come from this is called extortion and the people who do the extorting are called mobsters. Has our Federal Government degraded to being extortionist?

Deep Water Ports In Mexico: In addition to redesigned super-highways Red China's plans to dominate North American Trade requires that they invest in deepwater ports in order to accommodate unprecedented volumes of containers from China. Corsi sites company websites: "Hutchison Ports Holdings [HPH] a wholly owned subsidiary of China's giant Hutchison Whampon Limited [HWL] is investing millions to expand the deep-water ports of Mexico's Pacific Coast at Lazaro Cardenas and Manzanillo."
www.hutchison-whampoa.com/eng/about/overview.htm
http://www.hph.com.hk/business/ports/america/mexico/let.htm

So why is this important to Americans? Having deepwater sea ports which can accommodate larger ships allows China to lower the cost of ocean transport. Bringing their cargo in through Mexican ports then allows them to circumvent the expensive U.S. Longshoreman's Union and utilize cheaper Mexican workers. Then, thanks once again to cooperation from the U.S. Federal Government they are able to load their cargo on Mexican Trucks and use the emerging super-transportation corridor to move their goods throughout North America effectively cutting out the U.S. Teamsters Union. In Red China we are dealing with a country that is willing to exploit and enslave their own people in order to undercut the world labor market. Are we naive enough to think they will treat us any better. We need to wake up and realize that we are dealing with a ruthless country in Red China and that despite what may look like Capitalist leanings they are still a Communist Country with a Communist Agenda. Consider the following quotes:

"Passivity is fatal to us. Our goal is to make the enemy passive."
– Mao Tse-Tung

"Communism possesses a language which every people can understand – its elements are hunger, envy, and death."
– Heinrich Heine, German Poet

"Communism is not love. Communism is a hammer we use to crush the enemy."
– Mao Tse-Tung

"Communism is the death of the soul. It is the organization of total conformity – in short, a tyranny – and it is committed to making tyranny Universal."
– Adlai E. Stevenson, Ambassador to United Nations

"Every Communist must grasp the truth; Political power grows out of the barrel of a gun."
– Mao Tse-Tung

"Free Trade is the scourge of the world and if we do not wake up and see it for what it is, it will engulf America, strip away our freedom, transcend into socialism and finally digress into Communism."
– Larry Ballard, Author of <u>Modern Slavery</u>

Electronic Sensor Inspection and Tracking System: According to Coris: Lockheed Martin and the North American Super Corridor

Coalition, Inc. [NASCO] are building an electronic tracking system to track all cargo approaching and within the U.S. I should note that Hutchison Port Holdings, a Chinese owned company, owns 49% of the Lockheed Martin subsidiary which was involved in implementing the corridor technology project with NASCO. OOPS! Despite what the government tells us the focus is on the profit margins of international corporations not security! By relying on electronic inspection and tracking technology containers can cross our borders and move throughout the country without ever being inspected by a human being. This means international cargo entering the U.S. through Mexican seaports can be loaded onto Mexican trucks which can be designated as "Trusted Traders" and enter the U.S. without manual inspection using electronics technology similar to the I-Pass technology used on U.S. Toll Roads. To make matters even worse the first customs stop in the U.S., located in Kansas City, will be a Mexican Customs Office, built with $3 million of U.S. taxpayer money. Quoting Coris: *"Internal emails obtained under Missouri Sunshine Law request shows that the Kansas City Smart Port officials have been told that the facility will most likely be considered Mexican Soil though it is located in the heartland of the U.S."*

So if I sum things up, the U.S. in the name of "Security and Prosperity" **[Ha Ha]** has opened our borders to illegal aliens, drug smuggling and terrorism. Our government understands this yet they do it anyway. **WHY!**

HCR 40 & 22: On 1/22/2007 Congressman Virgil Goode [R-VA] introduced House Concurrent Resolution 40 [HCR 40] to express the sense of Congress that the United States should not engage in the construction of a super corridor system or enter into a North American Union with Mexico and Canada. [HCR 40] charges that: *"The actions taken by the Security and Prosperity Partnership [SPP] to coordinate border security by eliminating obstacles between Mexico and the U.S. actually makes the U.S.-Mexico border less secure because Mexico is the primary source of Illegal immigration into the U.S."* The resolution expresses that:

"The U.S. should not engage in the NAFTA North American Free Trade Superhighway. Should not allow the SPP to implement additional

regulations that could result in a North American Union with Mexico and Canada. The President should oppose any proposals that threaten the sovereignty of the U.S. "

On 1/10/2007 Congressman Goode also introduced [HCR 22] co-sponsored by Congressman Walter Jones [R-NC] expressing the position of Congress that the U.S. should withdrawal from NAFTA. Additionally the legislatures of Oregon, Arizona, South Carolina, Utah, Virginia and Washington also introduced bills opposing The North American Union and NAFTA. So why are we still in NAFTA? Why are we still going forward with the TTC-35 superhighway? Because despite the best efforts of our Congressmen and State Legislatures there are forces operating through the Federal Government that take their orders from other than the American people and their elected officials. I have said it before; **the office of the president has been compromised by the agenda of the Moneyed Elite who want a One World Government at any cost.**

In light of 9/11 how could our government ever expose the U.S. to such a security risk? So given our ludicrous open borders policy what exactly is the Patriot Act protecting us from? We have left the door wide open and invited the terrorist in! I can look into the future and envision that an enemy could use our open border's electronic transportation system [built by a company with ties to Red China] to launch a lethal attack that would make 9/11 look like child's play. It is a Monday morning and people are on the way to work just like any other day, unaware of the horror which is about to be unleashed. A fleet of trucks moves through every major city in the U.S. They are loaded with cargo which originated somewhere in the Middle East, crossed our borders in Mexican trucks, passed through customs at a Mexican owned customs office in the U.S. In those trucks are containers filled with nerve gas. At the appointed time an electronic signal is sent. The canisters explode releasing deadly nerve gas into the streets of every major city in the country. People drop like flies. 75% of the population is killed within minutes. All our real estate is in tact and we are primed for an invasion and occupation. I certainly hope noting like this ever happens, but the question is why would our government ever put us in such a vulnerable position?

Erick: Gramps you still haven't answered my question as to how most of our public utilities ended up in the hands of foreign investors. You discussed the TTC-35 highway project and the North American Union both of which more relate to Free Trade Policies than the sale of U.S. infrastructure. I have a handle on that, but I am still confused as to how U.S. infrastructure fell into the hands of foreign investors.

Gramps: Erick I guess you are right, but that is because the entire process started with the TTC-35 project and expanded from there. Let me explain.

Government Leaders Sell Out America To Private Investors!

Everywhere I turn I keep finding footprints in the sand. Footprints left by those who stand to profit from selling out America. The privatization of TTC-35 could never have happened had it not been for yet another of President George Bush's Executive Orders. This time it was EO #12803 which expressly allows privatization of U.S. infrastructure. If a husband and wife want to sell their house both parties have to agree to the sale and sign off on the paperwork, but the government affords the American people no such rights when it comes to American infrastructure bought and paid for with tax payer money. No discussion occurred before the People or Congress, just the decision of one man who stands to benefit from his decision. According to World Net ARTICLE_ID=51113 http://www.worldnetdaily.com/news/article.asp? our highways are not the only thing for sale. Former President Bush made it very clear that the U.S. government has no objection to foreign investors buying U.S. Corporations, including Airports. How could he even think of doing such a thing? Didn't he ever hear of 9/11?

According to Corsi who sites *The Guardian*, President George W. Bush gave speeches and advised on various Carlyle Group projects for which he received substantial compensation. Why is this important? When you know who the Carlyle Group is Bush's actions look like **influence peddling of the worst kind**. As stated previously according to author Dan Briody in his book The Iron Triangle: Inside the Secret World of the Carlyle Group former Secretary of Defense Frank

Carlucci and former President Ronald Reagan created the Carlyle Group in 1987. The intent was to bring together former military and government officials to form a Capital Investment Group that would, use their contacts in order to leverage investments in Defense Industry Projects. Who says war isn't profitable and who says government officials don't profit from their positions?

According to Corsi in March 2006 the Carlyle Group website announced that: The Carlyle Group, by now a global private investment equity firm headquartered in Washington DC, was forming an eight man investment team. Their stated objective was, to raise a multi-billion dollar fund the purpose of which was to purchase U.S. Infrastructure Projects, including U.S. highways which would become toll roads. The Team was headed by Robert W. Dove formerly of Bechtel Enterprise and Barry Gold former Managing Director of The Structured Finance Group of Citi-Corp., Salomon Smith Barney. These companies just keep popping up.

Euromoney Seminar

"You are cordially invited to dinner.
The fatted calf has been slaughtered,
the table is set, the meal prepared.
Come feast on the remains of The Late Great U.S.A.,
compliments of the Moneyed Elite and their puppets.
The cuisine is excellent and all who attend
will be afforded great riches!"

Per Corsi the website of Euromoney Seminary posted a brochure announcing that on September 19 & 20, 2006 Euromoney Seminars, a division of the London based international investor PLC was hosting a PPP conference in New York at The Waldorf Astoria Hotel. The conference brought together an elite group of investors including Lehman Brothers, Goldman Sachs, The Royal Bank of Scotland, HSBC, J.P. Morgan Assets Management Group and The Carlyle Group together with State and Federal Highway officials, tax attorneys, accountants and municipalities to discuss details of how to invest in U.S. infrastructure and how to expand on the TTC model developed in Texas.

Government representatives included attendees from U.S. Department of Transportation [DOT] and the Government of Mexico, in addition to representatives from State Departments of Transportation from the states of Virginia, Wisconsin, Louisiana, Florida, Oregon, Alaska, Indiana and Texas. The FHWA website encourages the use of PPP's to build transportation infrastructure and went so far as to show administrators and legislators which laws they needed to change in order to allow PPP investment. The Euromoney Conference Brochure noted that given that it takes $90 billion per year just to maintain U.S. infrastructure that virtually all U.S. infrastructures were up for grabs, that includes highways, schools, water departments, hospitals, seaports, airports, municipal buildings etc. What is going to be left for Americans? It would appear not much! We paid for and have maintained these infrastructure projects, doesn't it seem only fair we have a say in what happens to them?

Necessary Steps To Restoring Our Economy and Our Manufacturing Base!

If America hopes to stop the flow of money and jobs out of the country we have to drive *"Free Trade"* products off the continent and rebuild our manufacturing base. This means we must go back to the *"American System"* of Protective Tariffs which underpinned the source of America's rise to the status as an Economic Superpower.

End Free Trade: We will have to end our dependency on cheap [slave labor and near slave labor] goods from China and in the process we should take a stand for human rights by imbedding human rights clauses in future trade agreements.

Renegotiate NAFTA: We need to force the renegotiation of NAFTA and all such free trade agreements so they are *"Fair Trade Agreements."*

Impose VAT: In order to establish a healthy balance of trade it is essential that the U.S. impose a VAT and limit imports through tariff restrictions. This should not be just added to our existing income tax. Our current income tax must be done away with and a new fairer flat tax implemented.

Withdraw From SPP and End Our Open Borders Policy: By facilitating open borders with Mexico we jeopardize national security, put downward pressure on U.S. wages, invite the continued gutting of our manufacturing base and enable the Free Trade System to destroy our economy. We therefore need to withdraw from the SPP and oppose any efforts to form a North American Union, not allow a Mexican customs office on U.S. soil, not allow electronic tracking of cargo, restrict access of Mexican truck drivers, and it is crucially important that we stop efforts by the federal government to build TTC-35 and other such highways designed to facilitate **international trade** and instead expand the capacity of our existing highways [**designed for transcontinental traffic**] to prevent the gridlock caused by under capacity issues.

Rescind EO #12803: Which allows privatization of U.S. infrastructure.

We can expect opposition from the multinational corporations and from the government which by in large sees to it that their agenda is implemented. <u>The multinational corporations feel that they have a right to run things because they feel that they are the base on which the Nation builds its wealth.</u> It is time we stood up and showed them that without the cooperation of the American people their power base is not nearly as strong as they think. They need us as much as we need them. It is time the masses flexed our muscle and take back our country.

Must Take Stand Against The Sale of U.S. Infrastructure

We cannot let our Government sell off our infrastructure. If we do we will regret it in the long run. If for example we allow international investors to buy rights to future highway projects they will not only charge us to use them, they will design them, in which event they will be designed to facilitate international [Free Trade] not [Domestic] transcontinental traffic. Incidentally projects like TTC-35 will not help the gridlock problems developing in most of our major urban areas because the intent is to facilitate North/South movement of commerce from Mexico through the U.S. into Canada. <u>If we allow our</u>

infrastructure to be sold we will pay for perpetuity to use an asset which we originally built and paid for with tax payer money. This is just another way for the Moneyed Elite to control the masses and drive us into economic servitude. We cannot allow them to do this to us. Do you really want you water systems, schools, airports, seaports etc. owned by International Corporations? Think about the loss of control and the National Security issues. Pleas take a stand before it is too late.

"What is being sold to the American people today as Americanism, if you peel off the label you find so much similarity to what we were fighting against when we were fighting Communism, Nazism and Fascism... The media controls the information a person gets. In various ways can make sure that the average American watching the tube, reading the newspaper is going to come out with a certain mind set. This is good. That is bad."
– G. Edward Griffin Author, <u>Creature from Jekyll Island</u>

I hope I have made the case that policies of the U.S. Federal Government have intentionally driven the U.S. into unmanageable debt. It has to stop!!!!

Chapter 10

The Global Warming Hoax:

The Government's Secret Agenda!

"In this present crisis government is not the solution to the problem, Government is the problem."
                                                    – President Ronald Reagan

President Reagan also held the position that man made CO2 emissions is not the cause of Global Warming and we should not rush to that conclusion:

"Approximately 80% of our air pollution stems from hydrocarbon released by vegetation, so let's not go overboard in setting and enforcing tough emission standards from man made sources."

On the other hand former Vice President Al Gore [self appointed expert and government shill] talks about Global Warming in his documentary *"An Inconvenient Truth"* and presumptuously says *"the debate is over, the facts are in;"* Global Warming is real and the solution is implementation of Cap and Trade Legislation which [feloniously] promises to reduce CO2 emissions to target levels set by the government by 2050. In reality, as I will prove, Cap and Trade is just a smoke screen for implementation of the largest tax increase ever imposed on the American Tax Payer and offers no viable means of preventing Global Warming!

For those of you who may not know exactly what Cap and Trade is I will explain. It calls for the government to set a cap on total CO2 emissions. Companies would be issued certificates entitling them to emit a specified amount of CO2 per year in the operation of their business. Each year through 2050 the cap [or ceiling] would be reduced. Those companies which can operate below the set limits would sell their excess certificates on the open market to those who need extra certificates. Each year as the limits go down there would be fewer and fewer certificates available for sale which would of course drive up the sale price of the certificates. Eventually those companies which could not operate within the set limits would either be forced to go abroad or go out of business. In the meantime the cost of the certificates would be passed on to the consumer in the form of an excise tax on virtually everything from electricity to food to consumer goods of all types. It would be the largest tax increase ever imposed on the American public and as we shall discuss shortly it will have virtually no effect on reducing Global Warming which is of course the supposed reason for the program in the first place. Lastly for those of you who remember the Enron energy deregulation debacle, Cap and Trade offers the same type of opportunity for speculation except with much greater consequences.

If real, Global Warming is the biggest threat mankind has ever faced, but unfortunately our political leaders have as usual played politics and made it difficult to determine if it is real or not, and if it is real just how critical the problem really is.

VITALLY IMPORTANT: <u>Global Warming as a Trojan Horse</u>: Before this chapter is over I will dispel the lies and give you the scientific facts as well as exposing the political agenda which is driving the government propaganda. I will expose Global Warming as a Trojan Horse for **1) Global Governance 2) Redistribution of Wealth 3) Population Control and 4) Forced Limitations On Resource Consumption**. **NOTE:** The term Global Warming does not adequately describe the scope of the situation so throughout the rest of the chapter, where appropriate I will be substituting Global Warming with **"Climate Change"** which is a much broader more embracive term.

The Government Propaganda Machine: As a proud American I would like to be able to trust my government to tell me the truth about something as important as Climate Change but as you shall shortly see the government is less concerned about the truth and more concerned about advancing its political agenda. Consider the following quotes:

"We've got to ride the global warming issue. Even if the theory of global warming is wrong...."
                                – Timothy Wirth, former U.S. Senator [D-Colorado]

"A global climate treaty must be implemented even if there is no scientific evidence to back the greenhouse effect."
                                – Richard Benedict, State Dept. employee
                    working on assignment from the Conservation Foundation

Climategate Scandal: It turns out that a hacker breaks into E-mails of East Anglia Univ. Climate Unit in the U.K. and uncovered literally thousands of E-mails intended to do such things as:

■ **Control Access to Peer Review Journals:** the very sources which Gore pointed to in order to support his thesis of Global Warming.

*"I can't see either of these papers being in the next IPCC report... Kevin and I will keep them out somehow...**Even if we have to redefine what the peer-review literature is**..." From: Phil Jones To: Michael Man - July 8, 2004*

*"Our only choice was to **ignore this paper**. They already achieved what they wanted..." From: Michael Mann To: Phil Jones - March 11, 2003*

■ **Delete/Suppress Data:**

"Mike can you delete any Emails you have had with Kevin Re: AR4? Kevin will do likewise. He is not in at the moment, family crisis..." From: Phil Jones To: Michael Mann – May 29, 2008

"We need to cover our behinds on what was done here, lest we be vulnerable to the snipes..." Source Eastangliaemails.com

It is obvious from what you have just read that the government has an agenda which it is promoting and that the truth is secondary to that agenda. Unfortunately they deal in ½ truths because they can be sold better than an out and out lie.

- **The truth is that:** *"Planet Earth is facing its sixth mass extinction and man made causes are a factor."*

- **The lie is that:** *"The cause is rising temperatures caused by man made CO2 emissions and that Cap and Trade is the Solution."*

In other words we have a real problem which needs to be addressed, but the government is not telling us the truth about the cause of the problem or their intended solution. Before you finish this chapter you will know the truth and then you will have to decide what you intend to do about it!

The Scientific Debate:
In Search of the Truth About Climate Change!

The Two Opposing Scientific Views: Al Gore and the U.N. tell us that in the last 650,000 years CO2 [the supposed chief culprit in global warming] has never gone above 300 parts per million in the atmosphere, and then all the sudden it went from 280 parts per million in the early 1800s [start of industrial revolution] to 380 parts per million at the turn of the century and is still climbing. They therefore contend that Global Warming is caused by adding CO2 and other green house gasses from burning fossil fuels into the atmosphere in large enough quantity that the gasses collect in the upper atmosphere and trap infrared energy in the earth's atmosphere resulting in Global Warming. The measurement of CO2 in the atmosphere is, I am sure an accurate account of what is happening as a result of industrialization, [a ½ truth as I like to say] but the theory becomes pseudoscience unless they can also show measurements which correlate the increased presence of CO2 in the atmosphere with an increase in temperature. They have developed theoretical models complete with scientific looking charts to support their theory, but this is where their theory starts to fall apart. They are not based on actual measured data like their rising CO2 numbers. Science does not allow you to make such correlations unless they are backed by actual empirical data.

> **VITALLY IMPORTANT:** Gore's theory gets in real trouble when you realize that recently there has been a reversal in the trend of rising temperatures and temperatures have actually been dropping. This flies in the face of Gore's claim that rising temperatures were caused by man made increases in CO2 levels in the atmosphere. **The recent drop in temperature virtually debunks the government's theory.**

Enter Professor Richard Lindson of MIT a man some repute to be the world's foremost meteorologist. Interestingly enough Lindson has spent the last twenty years collecting actual data. The measured data, the real science proves that Gore's and the U.N.'s theory is bunk. His data shows that as temperature increases the amount of radiation going out into space also increases. In other words **Professor Lindson's data proves that there is no correlation between the rise in CO2 and temperature and therefore Gore and the U.N. are wrong. As Gore would say "Case Closed."**

Sun Spots and Temperature: Lest you still have any doubts consider these Inconvenient Truths. What I am about to present is not scientific evidence but I do believe it represents an alternate more plausible theory for Global Warming than the flawed theory postulated by Gore and the U.N.

About 1,100-1,200BC there was a period called the Mid-evil Warm Period which corresponds to a period of maximal sun spot activity and then about 1,600-1,650BC there was an ice age in northern Europe which corresponded to a period of minimal sun spots.

It so happens that our current warming period also relates to a period of maximal sunspot activity. This alone could be just coincidental, but it takes on more credibility when we learn that the earth is not the only planet in our solar system which is experiencing an increase in temperature. This gives increased credibility to the theory that **sun spot activity** not CO2 levels is the cause of Global Warming. I will come back to this theory momentarily but first consider this:

PAY CLOSE ATTENTION!
Experts Say CO2 Is Cause of "Global Cooling": There was a fall in temperatures around 1945-1970 and experts were saying we were

heading for global cooling and an ice age. [The Cooling World, *News Week* April 28, 1975] Wait a minute. This is another Inconvenient Truth. In order for an agent like CO_2 to be a causative factor, in this instance the cause of Global Warming it must exhibit a consistent not inconsistent pattern of behavior. Given this fact I wonder how Gore and the U.N. can explain that during a period of increased CO_2 there was a marked decline in temperature for approximately a twenty five year period. A decline that was in fact so severe as to create <u>concern about a coming ice age.</u> Don't you just hate it when the truth bites you in the butt? It just so happens that John Holdren, Obama's science Czar was saying at the time [1975] that *"there is going to be so much ice accumulation in Antarctica because of the extreme cold that is coming because of our activities that the ice will fall over into the ocean and cause the largest tidal wave in human history."* <u>Now isn't that interesting? Accumulation of CO_2 in the atmosphere seems to simultaneously be the cause of Global Warming and Global Cooling.</u> **That is impossible!** You have to pick one or the other so which one is it guys? Or what is much more likely is that it isn't the cause of either warming or cooling.

I want to go back to the sun spot theory. As it turns out the Bible, Egyptian's, Inca's, Maya's, Hopi and people like Nostradamus, Edgar Casey and others have all predicted a time when our climate would go haywire causing biblical proportion floods, droughts, hurricanes, tornados and cataclysmic earth changes. Ironically all these events seem to converge in and around a specific time period 2012 [give or take 10-15 years on either side]. As it turns out there is an astrological event occurring in 2012 that gives credence to these predictions. The earth is completing a 28,000 thousand year cycle that has been referred to as the *"End of the Age"* and which has been associated with catastrophic natural disasters in the past. In 2012 when the end of the age cycle is complete the earth is aligned with the center of the galaxy and <u>in the center of the galaxy there is a black hole.</u> Alignment with the black hole and the increased gravitational forces it exerts could well provide a unifying theory which ties together all the Climate Changes we have been seeing. The increased gravitational pull from the black hole would predictably cause increased sunspot activity, resulting in warmer temperatures both on earth and other planets in the solar system and erratic weather patterns with both floods and droughts and generally more severe storms. The increased gravitational pull could also explain the increase in both frequency and severity of both earth-quakes and volcanic events. Having said this don't expect to wake up on the day of the alignment in 2012 and expect it to be any different than any other day. We have been experiencing the effects of proximity to the black hole for at least the last 10-15 years and we can expect to continue to experience them for the next 10-15 years.

Even though I believe sunspot activity, not CO_2, to be the cause of Global Warming and more pervasively Climate Change that does not let us off the hook. CO_2 does cause acid rain which has been proven to kill plants and animals on land as well as lakes and it may well be affecting the oceans. We will discuss this later. That is just the tip of the iceberg as they say. There is all the toxic waste which pollutes our rivers lakes and oceans. The deforestation of crucially important life giving equatorial rain forest through intentional burning [talk about CO_2 pollution] and destructive logging practices. There is the loss of habitat and associated species extension associated with the overex-ploitation of resources caused by over consumption and over popu-lation. And last but not least there is the danger to our food supply caused by genetic engineering. Interestingly none of these environ-mental issues [other than potentially acid rain] would be addressed by Cap and Trade. I wonder why? **Could it be because Cap and Trade is a tax policy masquerading as an environmental policy?**

Climate Change:
The Political End Game Revealed!

Experts Say If U.S. Passes Cap and Trade It Will Ruin U.S. Econ-omy and Not Save The Climate: Al Gore says: The debate on Global Warming is over, arrogantly inferring that Cap and Trade is a foregone conclusion. Let us not forget that he is positioned to take advantage of Cap and Trade to add considerably to his already sizeable fortune. I wonder if he cares what his fellow Climate Change Nobel Prize Win-ner Dr. Steve Running from the University of Montana had to say about Cap and Trade. I quote:

"If the U.S. passed a Cap and Trade and other countries did not it wouldn't work. It would ruin the U.S. economy and it wouldn't save the climate either." – Hannity Nov. 1, 2009

Based on everything I have read the chances of China and India agreeing to anything like Cap and Trade are virtually non existent. China is building coal power plants right and left and the last time I checked coal power plants were not exactly CO2 friendly.

And then there is Lord Christopher Monckton former advisor to British Prime Minister Margaret Thatcher and climate change expert who has disputed Gore's findings and challenged him to a public debate on climate change. Gore has been uncharacteristically silent regarding the challenge which has been outstanding for a considerable amount of time. Oh, I forgot according to Gore the debate on climate change is over.

Even Global Limits on CO2 Emissions Won't Work: Lord Monckton goes even further than Steve Running and says that even a global initiative wouldn't work. He sites the proposed <u>Framework Convention on Climate Change</u> which is a treaty which is expected to be signed by potentially as many as 190 nations. As discussed above he disputes the science behind the U.N.'s data but he goes on to say, let's assume for a second that the U.N. is right, which they aren't, it wouldn't work anyway. Based on the U.N.'s data he says that the temperature is expected to increase by 7 degrees Fahrenheit over the next century but to forego a single degree of temperature increase would require total abstinence of human caused CO2 for 33 years so we cannot make a meaningful impact on Global Warming no matter what we do. Here is how he arrived at his conclusions:

Step 1: He says the annual world wide output of CO2 is 30 billion tons which equals 2 parts per million per year in the atmosphere. He explains that you have to reduce that number to 1 part per million per year in the atmosphere which is done by dividing 30 billion tons by 2 which equals 15 tons of CO2 per part per million in the atmosphere.

Step 2: The U.N. says we are going to increase the amount of CO2 in the atmosphere by 468 parts per million in the next century. He explains that, that means that over the next century total worldwide CO2 emissions will be 7 trillion tons which is [15 Billion X 468]. Additionally the U.N. says that 7 trillion tons of CO2 will increase the temperature by 7 degrees Fahrenheit over the next century.

Step 3: That means that in order to prevent 1 degree Fahrenheit increase in temperature we must forego the emission of 1 trillion tons of CO2 [1 degree per trillion tons of CO2].

Step 4: The final step is to determine how many years it would take to forgo 1 trillion tons of CO2 in the atmosphere. That number is derived by dividing 1 trillion by our original 30 billions tons of CO2 which equals 33 years.

I hope I explained that adequately. But for clarity's sake the bottom line is that it takes 33 years of total abstinence of human caused CO2 to forgo 1 degree of temperature increase and 1 degree is not environmentally significant.

VITALLY IMPORTANT: So based on the U.N.'s own data no matter what they do, the Framework Convention on Climate Change Treaty <u>cannot work</u>. It is nothing more than a scheme to redistribute wealth and the primary target of the wealth redistribution is the U.S.

Remember I said at the onset of this chapter that I would expose Global Warming as a Trojan Horse for global governance, redistribution of wealth, population control, and forced limitations on resource consumption. Here is your proof.

1) <u>Global Governance and</u>

2) <u>Redistribution of Wealth</u>: Consider the following quotes and the facts that follow.

French President Chirac: said in a speech at the Hague that the UN's Kyoto Protocol [an earlier environmental agreement] represented *"the first component of authentic global governance. For the first time, humanity is instituting a genuine instrument of global governance."*

Al Gore: *"Climate bill will help bring about global governance... But it is the awareness itself that will drive the change and one of the ways it will drive the change is through global governance and global agreements."*

Monckton goes on to say that the real intent of the treaty [The Framework Convention on Climate Change] is to Transfer Wealth from rich countries like the U.S. to poorer countries **[Redistribution of Wealth]** and to create the framework for a one world government **[Global Governance]**. Gee that sounds eerily like Obama's agenda. I wonder if they are working for the same handlers. You know those pesky bankers who say things like:

"The super national sovereignty of an intellectual elite and world bankers is surely preferable to the National Auto-determination practiced in past centuries." – David Rockefeller Council Foreign Relations

"We shall have a One World Government whether or not we like it. The only question is whether world government will be achieved by conquest or consent." – Paul Warburg Council Foreign Relations Architect of The Federal Reserve System

Appearing on the Glen Beck show 10/31/2009 Lord Monckton explained that he was here in the U.S. to warn Americans to oppose this treaty and any other like it because if we don't we risk losing our Democracy and our Constitution like Britain has. Specifically he said:

*"...the danger here that we have seen time and again in negotiations in Europe is treaties by which Britain's Democracy has all but gone. **90% of our laws are now made by Commissars who we do not elect and cannot remove**...There made [referring to the laws] in secret and then our Parliament is made to pass them. It has no option but to do so. We have lost our Democracy through exactly this kind of carelessness...all the sudden another slice of our freedom is gone. Do not relax. Do not take a risk with your Constitution."*

Once again this sounds familiar. Our non elected [revolutionary, wealth transferring Czars] are influencing policy while key legislation like the Stimulus is being written by scandal ridden special interest groups like Acorn and the President is not even giving legislators the opportunity to read the bills. It's like Lord Monckton said we better wake up before we lose our Democracy and our

Constitution the way Britain did. Hind sight is 20/20. Let's not miss an opportunity to learn from it.

Lord Monckton goes on to provide details about the Framework Convention on Climate Change Treaty and why it is particularly harmful to the U.S. He Says:

"I have negotiated international treaties ...in fact I have written them. Never before have I seen the word government put in a treaty in this capacity, with enormous powers. **They are going to take down the free market... They are going to have take powers in that treaty to operate in interference of and control of all financial markets world wide....** *They are going to take a tax of 2% of every financial transaction into an Annex 1 country. That's a rich country like America. Now if you take a 2% levy on financial transactions where the margins are absolutely tiny you can destroy the financial system of New York, Wall Street, the Chicago Exchange, close it all down. That is the power that will be transferred to this new government entity...***I think we are heading for what could be a global government....they have given this body powers which I have never seen transferred to any transnational entity by any treaty ever...this whole treaty is targeted at America."**

The idea behind the treaty is that the U.S. and other rich countries have been burning CO2 and damaging the climate so now we have to pay reparations in the form of a Climate Debt Tax to nonpolluting 3rd world countries. According to Lord Monckton there isn't any scientific or economic cause for any of this.

Also appearing on Glen Beck former Ambassador to the U.N. John Bolton agreed with Lord Monckton saying: *"... this is not about climate debt. The same people who were arguing for this redistribution of wealth to the underdeveloped world from the developed world were arguing for it 60 years ago... Back then they were calling it a debt of the colonist to pay a debt to the newly independent colonies, then it was our responsibility to pay because the terms of trade disadvantaged suppliers of basic commodities and now there is the environment."*

More recently John Holderin President Obama's Science Czar put it this way:

*"There has been a strain of what many people call U.S. Exceptionalism in the United States...I think roughly that the rate of growth of material consumption is going to have to come down and **there's going to have to be a degree of redistribution of how much we consume in terms of energy and material resources** in order to leave room for people who are poor to become more prosperous... Instead of increasing the business as usual path forward-by the way, if we keep doing what we are doing we will double those emissions over the next fifty years – and what we need to do instead is have those emissions declining over the next fifty years."*

John Holderin is definitely talking about the notion of social justice when he exposes this redistribution process, but Van Jones Former Green Czar Under Obama and self acclaimed Communist finally tells it like it is. When you read what he says you can only describe it as a Revolutionary Transformation of the Republic for which America Stands:

"This movement is deeper than solar panels, deeper than solar panels, don't stop there. We're going to change the whole system. We're going to change the whole thing. We're not going to put a broken battery in a broken system. We want a new system, a new system... So the green economy will start off as a small subset and, uh, we're going to push it, uh, until it becomes the <u>engine for transforming the whole society.</u>"

3) **Population Control:** It took 10,000 generations, until approximately 1945, for the world's population to reach 2 billion, then in the span of a single generation [1945-2005] it reached 6.5 billion and by the end of the 21st century it is projected to be 8-9 billion. <u>Experts say this population explosion is severely stressing the natural resources of the planet and threatening to disrupt the planets natural balance!</u> The Obama administration has a czar who is on record saying he is in favor of putting sterilitants in the public water system. The following quotes give us an idea of just how far the government is willing to go in order to control population.

Jacques Cousteau: UNESCO Courier, November 1991. *"The United Nation's goal is to reduce population selectively by encouraging abortion, forced sterilization, and control of human reproduction, and regards two-thirds of the human population as excess baggage, with 350,000 people to be eliminated per day."*

Professor Maurice King: Said *"Global Sustainability requires the deliberate quest of poverty... reduced resource consumption... and set levels of mortality control."*

Psychologist Barbara Marx Hubbard: member and futurist/strategist of Task Force Delta; a United States Army think tank said ***"One-fourth of humanity must be eliminated** from the social body. We are in charge of God's selection process for planet earth. He selects, we destroy. We are the riders of the pale horse, Death."*

4) <u>**Forced Limitations On Resource Consumption**</u>: In a previous chapter we discussed the fact that the U.S.'s Hegemony Policy has been targeted at: [Getting Control of the Natural Resources of Third World Countries].

The U.S. Government and their Puppet Masters, the Globalist Money Manipulators consider the world's resources to belong to them and they intend to do what ever is required to conserve them. The reason our government is not concerned about the fact that Cap and Trade is a non-workable solution to Global Warming is because it is a tax masquerading as an environmental solution! <u>The U.S., UN and the Globalist plan to force reductions in resource consumption through bogus usage taxes imposed under Cap and Trade, and if necessary commit genocide in order to bring population in line with desired levels of resource consumption</u>. In this context though Cap and Trade will not impact Global Warming it will reduce resource consumption by placing such high taxes on such things as beef and other items with large carbon footprints as to make them simply unaffordable except by the elite. **These policies must be opposed!**

Consider the following quotes.

Appearing on PBS on <u>Bill Moyers Journal</u> political analyst Kevin Philip said, *"America has become little more than an energy protection force doing anything to gain access to expensive fuel **without regard to the lives of others or the earth itself.***"

"Protecting the environment is a RUSE. The goal is the political and economic subjugation of most men by the few under the guise of preserving nature." –J.H. Robbins

The Stimulus is another Trojan Horse. People like Al Gore stand to make billions from Cap and Trade and the Stimulus. In the chapter on "Wars For Profit" we learned how politically connected companies like Rockefeller's Standard Oil and Bechtel with affiliations to former V.P. Chaney make billions from government contracts to either supply munitions or rebuild infrastructure destroyed by U.S. bombardments. In this instance energy companies like GE with their Smart Grid and other politically connected **Green Companies** will be funneled sweetheart contracts which will make them billions. Additionally these same companies will benefit by reduced competition as smaller less advantaged companies are driven overseas or out of business all of which will severely damage the U.S. economy.

Oil is essential in a modern society, and that gives oil companies tremendous clout. Combine that with the fact that oil is the biggest business on the planet, generating 4-5 trillion dollars revenue per year and it is not hard to envision that the oil companies control the very government which is supposed to control them. Add to this the fact that <u>since the 1978 oil embargo oil has been the number one National Security issue of our government</u>. This has forged an inseparable mutual interest alliance between the U.S. Government and the oil companies.

<u>Cap and Trade Is Irrelevant:</u> As we shall see in the next chapter the oil companies meter out oil to us while all the while denying us access to truly revolutionary clean, cheap energy solutions which are capable of dramatically reducing man made CO_2 emissions. These inventions, if made available, would make the entire concept of Cap and Trade irrelevant.

But you can rest assured that short of a mass revolt where we stand up and demand such technology be made available it will never see the light of day. Instead the government and the oil companies will be in control of determining when and how we transition to clean energy alternatives. **The one thing you can be confident in, is that whatever solutions they allow us to have will not be cheap because by design they will generate reoccurring revenues equivalent to the oil companies lost revenues.**

In this context please reflect on the following quote.

"Giving society cheap, abundant energy... would be the equivalent of giving an idiot child a machine gun."
                                    – Paul Ehrlich, Stanford University

The following quote pretty much sums up what the government has in store for us.

"The Environmentalists Dream is an Egalitarian Society based on: rejection of economic growth, a smaller population, eating lower on the food chain, consuming a lot less, and sharing a much lower level of resources much more equally." – Aaron Wildavsky

By definition such a society could not be based on Capitalism. Unless we stand up and fight the globalist take over we can expect in the not too distant future to have an Open Global Communist Dictatorship!

The Truth, The Whole Truth and Nothing But The Truth, So Help Me God!

It is time for the unabridged truth. The government's strategy is to use ½ truths to misinform and confuse the public so we cannot reach a consensus as to the validity of Global Warming [or for that matter any important issues facing our nation] and in this instance to deny us the facts which would lead us to the undeniable conclusion that their solution of Cap and Trade is nothing more than a tax masquerading as an energy policy. As we just discussed they don't want us to realize that Cap and Trade and the Stimulus are Trojan Horses for global governance, redistribution of wealth, population control, and forced limitations on resource consumption. But now you know the truth so you are empowered to fight their tyranny.

Global Warming is arguably the most important issue the world may ever faced, because the fate of the human race and the planet hang in the balance. As I said at the start of this chapter:

- **The truth is that:** *"Planet Earth is facing its sixth mass extinction and man made causes are a factor."*

- **The lie is that:** *"The cause is rising temperatures caused by man made CO2 emissions and that Cap and Trade is the Solution."*

I want to make it perfectly clear that if the temperature rises sufficiently it will have devastating effects on life on earth, but I do not believe for a second that, should that occur it will be as Al Gore postulates because of man made CO2 emissions. Hopefully I have proven his theses to be bogus. As I stated earlier I believe the more likely cause of recent temperature increases is due to a period of **maximum sun spot activity** which we did not cause and cannot control. If it turns out that the recent temperature increases are also related to gravitational effects from the black hole at the center of the Galaxy then I fear we could well be in for another 10-15 years of sever climatic disruption.

ACTION STEPS: 18) Oppose Passage of any Federal Energy Bill till such time as the government comes clean and tells us the truth. This includes Cap and Trade and The Framework Convention On Climate Change, which is even more harmful to the U.S. Economy than Cap and Trade." Climate Change is a real problem and it needs to be addressed, but we cannot let the government use it as an excuse to impose the largest tax increase in history especially not when the scientific facts simply don't support their position. As I said earlier Cap and Trade is nothing but a tax masquerading as an energy policy. The fact is that Cap and Trade is not capable of making an environmentally relevant impact on temperature and is therefore a non solution and the Framework Convention On Climate Change is nothing more than a means to impose Global Governance, Redistribution of Wealth, Population Control and Forced Limitations on Resource Consumption. Fortunately there are clean energy alternatives available which I will discuss in the next chapter.

> **VITALLY IMPORTANT:** In any event we need to recognize that Global Warming is not the only factor threatening the planet. For example we need to consider the effects of: Deforestation, as thousands of acres of timber land in the tropics are intentionally burnt in order to clear the land for cattle ranching and many thousands more are logged. Then there is destruction of the food chain in rivers, lakes and the oceans due to agricultural and industrial pollution, over fishing, inappropriate recreational use and as we now know the dangers of oil spills. There is also loss of habitat due to encroachment by man, overexploitation of resources due to over population, depletion and contamination of aquifers because of excess human usage, decertification caused by human activity and the threat to the food supply posed by genetic tampering. **If we hope to live in harmony with planet earth all of these issues need to be addressed, but the most serious problem we are facing is "overpopulation" and either we voluntarily address the problem or the government will do it for us and I can guarantee you, you won't like their solution.** For a detailed plan see the last chapter.

What follows is a description of the Ecological/Planetary mess we could leave to our children if we don't face the gravity of Climate Change and take the appropriate actions! I want to be very clear. That does not mean being stampeded into Cap and Trade. It is a non-solution.

Effects of Climate Change: Assuming temperature continues to rise, **[which is a big if]** we can expect polar and glacial ice to continue melting, oceans will rise and worldwide weather patterns will be affected. Storms fed by moist warm air become more energetic and violent and some regions will experience floods while others will experience drought and famine, severely effecting agricultural production and causing widespread famine. Disease and plagues can be expected to become more prevalent as harmful infectious agents are able to expand into regions where they are not indigenous and plants, animals and humans stressed by drought, famine and sever heat succumb to disease at a rate not seen in modern times. As oceans rise they flood coastal regions displacing millions, fresh water aquifers are contaminated, storms batter coastal areas destroying property and battering reefs already weakened by temperature induced bleaching, pollution and numerous diseases. The combination of heat, pollution and acid rail foul the oceans killing plankton and algae disrupting the marine food chain causing a mass extinction of marine life. With algae and plankton production severely reduced, the ocean is not able to clean the air by absorbing CO_2 so levels of greenhouse gasses explode. At the same time oxygen production worldwide is severely diminished because of the reduced populations of plankton and algae which produce up to 75% of the earth's oxygen. The earth slowly suffocates and dies and the earth's sixth mass extinction has nearly run its course. All that remains is for the ocean conveyor belt which circulates ocean water and determines weather patterns to shut down plunging the world into an ice age. With planet and animal populations [including humans] dramatically reduced the planet can begin the centuries long process of rejuvenation and revitalization.

Effects of Earth Changes: Assuming temperature continues to rise **[which is a big if]** we can expect melting ice at the poles to unlock trapped tectonic plates which have been pinned down for hundreds of thousands of years by the weight of the ice. At the same time melt run off increases the sea level in turn increasing the weight on the ocean floor unbalancing the underlying tectonic plates in all the oceans of the world. The result is that global seismic activity on earth is now five times more energetic than it was 20 years ago. As the ice caps continue to melt, turning off the planet's AC System, temperature and stored seismic energy can be expected to rise at an accelerated rate. The outcome will be more frequent and powerful earthquakes and volcanic eruptions worldwide. Volcanoes are the most devastating forces in nature because they can erupt with the force of thousands of atomic bombs going off at once and they can expel so much material into the atmosphere that it can affect photosynthesis killing the plant life, disrupting the food chain and causing mass extinctions. This is why Australian Scientist Dr. Tom Chalko who analyzed data from U.S. Geologic Survey of over 386,000 earthquakes which occurred between 1973 and 2007 said:

"The most serious environmental danger we face may not be climate change, but rapid and systematic increasing seismic, tectonic, and volcanic activity."

This fear seems to be echoed by Michael Mandeville, Systems Scientists who warns that Torrid Zone activity and worldwide volcanic activity has increased in the range of 500% in the last 50 years. [History Channel Documentary <u>Decoding The Past</u>, 8/3/06] The bible warns of end time earthquakes and volcanic eruptions as never seen before. It even warns of the earths axis shifting. Could it be possible that melting ice caps could affect the wobble of the earth's axis and could that imbalance triggered by massive earthquakes and volcanic eruptions be the cause of the catastrophic life altering pole shift predicted by the Bible, the Maya, and Hopi Indians. Science doesn't have that answer but it has been foretold for centuries. I would like to think that the end time revelations are a warning to a greedy, materialistic world and that if we change and turn to God and become good stewards of the planet he gave us dominion over that the worst of what is predicted could be avoided. But it won't just happen, we have to take responsibility for our actions and change. If you think what you just read is bad, wait it gets worse.

Planet's Sixth Mass Extension Threatens Plants, Animals and Humans!

Scientists tell us we are in the midst of the planet's sixth mass extinction. The human race is not immune. We live in a delicate balance with nature. If we destroy the food chain we will suffer extinction just as easily as the rest of the plants and animals on the planet!

*"Planet earth is facing a mass extension that equals **or exceeds any in the geologic record** and human activities have brought the planet to the brink of this crisis."* – Dr. Peter Raven, Director of the Missouri Botanical Garden and adjunct professor at the University of Missouri, St. Louis University, and Washington University.

An international study published in the science journal *Nature* predicted that, *"climate change could drive more than a million species towards extinction by the year 2050."*

"By perpetuating the world's sixth mass extension mankind may compromise our own ability to survive. We need to steer this nation and lead the world toward a sustainable path." – David Wilcove, Professor

of ecology and evolutionary biology and public affairs at Princeton University.

Oceans Could Become Barren Deserts: This heading echoes an end time biblical prophecy that most of the life in the oceans will die. Is this possible? Sadly it appears very plausible. Microscopic plankton which come in plant and animal forms, provide the base of the ocean's food chain and phytoplankton [the plant variety] account for about 50-75% the earths photosynthesis. **Destroy the plankton and all the animals above them in the food chain become extinct,** and additionally there is a secondary effect. The phytoplankton serves as a natural *"Carbon Sinks"* by absorbing vast amounts of carbon dioxide which is dissolved from the atmosphere into the oceans. The phytoplankton converts the carbon dioxide into organic carbon stored in their bodies and shells. When they die their bodies sink to the ocean's floor where the organic carbon can remain undisturbed for thousands of years. Without the phytoplankton to absorb greenhouse gasses global warming could run rampant. **[That is if Gore's postulations are correct, which they aren't].**

So just exactly how do rising ocean temperatures threaten plankton production in the world's oceans? Plankton constantly circulates from the depths of the ocean where they absorb vital nutrients such as nitrogen, phosphorous and iron, and then they return to the surface where photosynthesis takes place. When the oceans become warmer there is a stratification effect which occurs where by warmer less dense water on the surface does not mix as effectively with the colder denser water below and the plankton are denied the nutrients they need and they die. When the plankton die the food chain is disrupted turning the oceans into under water deserts and threatening all life on the planet.

Warning Signs: *"The critical base of the ocean food chain is shrinking, new NASA satellite data shows. The discovery has scientists worried about how much food will grow in the future for the world's marine life. The data shows a significant link between warmer water and reduced production of phytoplankton of the world's oceans."* –According to a study in the journal *Nature."* By Seth Borenstein, AP Science Writer.

The Blue Whale, the planet's largest animal weighing up to 200 tons is in danger of extinction. Not too many years ago there were 300,000 Blue Whales roaming the oceans of the world, and now fewer than

9,000 remain. The Blue Whale feeds almost exclusively on Krill [a tiny shrimp like crustacean] and the Krill in turn feeds on Plankton. One Blue Whale can eat up to four million Krill per day. Such gargantuan harvest depend on fertile oceans, but rising ocean temperatures threaten the massive plums of plankton which are at the base of the marine food chain. As plankton production diminishes all the animals which depend on them will be put in peril. – The History Channel, <u>The Seven Signs of Apocalypse</u> 1/05/09

Coral Reefs Face Extension: According to BBC News, Richard Black, Environmental Correspondent: *"With approximately two thirds of all reefs considered to be deteriorating they are one of the planets most threatened ecosystems, and certainly one of the most important. Coral reefs represent the planet's most biologically diverse marine ecosystems. Though they account for less than ¼ of 1% of the marine ecosystem, they account for ¼ of all known fish species."* Should we lose the biodiversity of the reefs and the plankton that form the base of the marine food chain it could threaten most marine life on the planet! Reefs are rivaled only by the tropical rain forest for their species diversity. The world's oceans and rain forest are critical to the carbon dioxide absorption and oxygen generation which is essential to life on planet earth. **Whether we realize it or not perpetuation of the human species is irreparably tied into a delicate balance which depends on the survival of the planet's rain forest, reefs and oceans.**

Coral grows very slowly, and like the ice caps are measured in geologic time spans. Present day reefs have been in existence for about 200,000 million years and reached their present level of diversity approximately 50 million years ago. So if we humans, who have walked this planet for far less time than the reefs have existed, allow them to be destroyed we will be upsetting the ecological balance of the planet for potentially millions of years to come!

Corals grow only in warm tropical waters ideally between 70-85 degrees Fahrenheit. They are extremely sensitive to temperature, so as ocean temperatures go up reefs worldwide are stressed and can experience a phenomenon known as *"bleaching."* Bleaching occurs when coral is exposed to excessive temperatures over a prolonged time. When this happens they expel the symbiotic algae which give the coral its color and which the coral depend on for survival. When this occurs the white skeletal system of the coral is exposed thus the term "bleaching." If the water temperature returns to normal soon enough the algae return and the coral can recover. Additionally, when stressed by increased temperature the coral become more susceptible to a number of diseases. **Coral has survived for millions of years, but now temperature changes, climate change and human activities threatens to cause changes that will prove lethal.**

Though rising temperatures are arguably the most important threat to coral reefs around the world there are other human caused threats that we must also be aware of if we hope to save the reefs and indeed the oceans for future generations. These threats include pollutants such as sewage and fertilizers, sediment from coastal development, over fishing, damage from recreational activities such as boating and diving, and more intense hurricanes fueled by global warming.

 Warning Signs: According to a report from the Intergovernmental Panel on Climate Change [IPCC] *"Australia's Great Barrier Reef could be dead within decades because of the effects of climate change."*

According to a resent study by NASA: *"Over the past 500,000 years Elkhorn and Staghorn coral have been the dominant reef builders in the Caribbean and in Florida. However, since the 1980s the area has seen a startling 97% reduction in Elkhorn and Staghorn coral due to rising temperatures, disease, hurricanes, and human damage. In May 2006, both Elkhorn and Staghorn coral were listed as threatened under the Endangered Species Act."*

"By and large, reefs have collapsed catastrophically just in the three decades that I've been studying them," said Nancy Knowlton, a marine biology professor at the Scripps Institution of Oceanography in La Jolla, California.

Predictions of Famine of Biblical Proportion: Paradoxically rising temperatures can simultaneously cause both flood and drought conditions. Warmer temperatures mean the oceans send more water into clouds, but that frequently means heaver rains which can cause flooding. Correspondingly hotter temperatures evaporate water from the soil leaving it parched and dry so that rain water has a tendency to run off instead of being absorbed into the soil. Also warmer temperatures can result in altered weather patterns resulting in some areas receiving more than normal amounts of rain while others areas are drought ridden. Additionally increased demand for water in drought stricken areas can deplete underground aquifers while rising sea levels can contaminate others.

Warning Signs: Agricultural yields are expected to drop in most tropical and subtropical regions and in temperate regions too. If the temperature increase is more than a few degrees centigrade, drying of continental interiors, such as Central Asia, the African Shale and the Great Plains of the U.S. is also forecast. Given that these areas represent the major grain belts of the world the outcome could be famine on a biblical scale.

According to Mark Lynas author of High Tide: *"We're talking about 30% of the world's surface becoming virtually uninhabitable in terms of agricultural production in the span of a few decades...these are parts of the world where hundreds of millions of people will no longer be able to feed themselves."*

A study conducted at the United Nations University by over 200 experts from 25 countries suggests that: *"Climate change is making decertification the greatest environmental challenge of our times. If action is not taken the report warns that some 50 million people could be displaced within the next 10 years."*

Rising oceans will contaminate both surface water and underground aquifers, resulting in increasing fresh-water shortage. Aquifers in Thailand, Israel, China and Vietnam are already experiencing salt-water contamination.

If Greenland and Antarctic ice caps melt entirely, sea levels could increase by as much as 30 feet by the end of the century. Fresh water supplies would be fouled for billions of people. [That is assuming temperatures continue to rise which at least for now they are not.]

We Can Make A Difference!

VITALLY IMPORTANT: The Government and oil companies want to keep us confused and complacent because if they
can they have won. They will simply stall on any meaningful
solutions to Climate Change till such time that they have a solution that assures the government of retention of its Geopolitical
Power Base and the oil companies of replacing their lost oil revenues. In the meantime the government will place enormous tax
burdens on us through their bogus Cap and Trade legislation and
environmental treaties. That is unless America and other countries around the world unite and demand immediate action. **If we
stand united we will be unstoppable**. What we need is a viable
technology solution around which to rally. There are such technologies available and we will discuss them in the next chapter.

The problem with the government's half truths is that they focuses us on
a single issue [Global Warming] which we have no control over while
ignoring the real problem which is that we are in fact in the middle of the
planet's sixth mass extinction which we can and must do something to
address. The real danger to the earth is overpopulation which threatens the
delicate balance of the planet's echo systems. If we destroy the oceans and
the rain forest we destroy the base of the food chain as well as the planet's
ability to produce oxygen and all life is threatened including man. This
crisis is serious and must be addressed. We are polluting the environment
and overexploiting natural resources, but reducing human caused CO_2 is
not the answer to our problems. We must voluntarily reduce population [or
the government will do it for us and we will not like their methods] which
will automatically reduce pollution, overexploitation of resources, loss of
wildlife habitat and most of the man made causes of Climate Change! This
issue is the biggest issue facing planet earth and we must come together
to solve it, but we cannot afford to allow our government to turn it into a
political issue which they are doing. The government's strategy will not
reduce CO_2 emissions enough to make any difference. In addition to population reduction we need access to the revolutionary, truly clean, truly
renewable energy solutions which our government and corporations are
withholding from us because to give us access to them threatens the geopolitical balance of power and threatens the revenue stream of the energy
companies. In order to maintain control they are willing to take us to the
brink of destruction. As you will see in the next chapter the technology we
need is available and we must get access to it at all costs.

Chapter 11

Revolutionary Energy Inventions:

Being Suppressed by the Government!

No Need to be Dependent on Fossil Fuels! Clean, Cheap, Renewable Energy is Available?

As we shall shortly see there is no reason other than human greed that we have to be dependent on fossil fuels. Clean, cheap, renewable technology exists. The problem is getting the government and corporations to give us access to it. They do not want any solution that does not perpetuate the existing corporate and political power structure. If we want clean energy we are going to have to come together as a united force and demand it. Ultimately all wealth comes from the earth's natural resources, and the only way man can coexist with the rest of the planet is if we are willing to put self serving interest aside and adopt clean renewable energy sources that allow us to live in harmony with the planet that sustains our very life!

Any government that denies society access to cheap, clean, renewable energy is a <u>Rogue Government</u> and it must by necessity of the benefit of society be replaced.

What follows is a brief discussion of the pros and cons of the most frequently proposed government energy solutions followed by a discussion of the technological breakthroughs the government doesn't want you to know about. As you shall shortly see there are options which are much better than those being put forward by the government.

Government's Most Frequently Proposed Energy Solutions!

Nuclear: While the current administration is proposing renewable energy solutions which include such options as solar, wind, geothermal, and biomass <u>there is also an effort being made to get nuclear energy categorized as a renewable energy source. If this happens it will take the focus off of the other truly clean, renewable, inexpensive solutions which are available.</u> The only advantage to Nuclear is that it keeps us on the grid and keeps revenues flowing to the powers that be. At one point in my carrier I worked for Atomic Energy of Canada and I have seen the safety precautions which are necessary when dealing with radioactive material. If we allow nuclear power plants to proliferate we will one day regret it! Think of what would happen to a planet which has proliferated nuclear power plants if the biblical end times earth changes predicted in the Bible occur. Nuclear is anything but a clean safe energy source. <u>We need to stand up and let our politicians know that we do not want more nuclear power plants.</u> There are much better alternative available.

Biomass Fuels: Biomass material refers to organic material i.e. agricultural crops such as sugarcane, corn, soybeans or other fast growing grasses, shrubs and trees which can be used as energy sources. They can be burnt to produce electricity or chemically broken down to produce Biofuel i.e. [Ethanol]. Proponents of Biomass claim it is CO_2 neutral because when the plants grow they absorb CO_2 which compensates for the CO_2 released when burnt. This claim is incorrect, because it does not take into account the energy required during the planting, maintaining, harvesting, transporting and refining of the biomass.

Ethanol: According to the Renewable Fuels Association as of Oct. 30, 2007 there were 131 grain ethanol refineries in production with another, 72 construction projects under way. Though Ethanol is a renewable energy source it is neither a cost efficient or clean energy source, when compared to wind, solar and other available solutions, yet it is being aggressively pursued. The only advantage to ethanol is that it reduces our dependency on foreign oil, but the real solution is to end our dependency on oil period. Ethanol is made primarily from sugarcane, corn and soybeans which has resulted in substantial amounts of agricultural land being taken out of food production. <u>Given the effects of Climate Change on global food production and given that over 100 nations depend on the U.S. to prevent starvation this hardly seems like a socially responsible or sustainable energy solution.</u>

Hydrogen: Is virtually an inexhaustible resource. However according to George Sverdrup, a government researcher there are three major obstacles to producing hydrogen. They are: **1) How to produce hydrogen** at a cost of $2 to $3 per equivalent gallon of gasoline. **2) How to store enough hydrogen** on board a vehicle to economically allow a 300-mile [483-kilometer] driving range; and **3) How to design cost competitive, reliable fuel cells** that can compete with gasoline engines. Sverdrup is technology manager for the U.S. Department of Energy [DOE] National Renewable Energy Laboratory's [NREL] Hydrogen, Fuel Cells And Infrastructure Technologies Program. 3/04/08 – Environment: Protecting our Natural resources Staff Writer, Cheryl Pellerin.
http://www.america.gov/st/env-english/2008/March/2008030417560 3lcnirellep0.4716761.html

The National Hydrogen Association says to expect hydrogen vehicles to be available by 2020, but some manufactures say it could be as soon as 2012. As you shall shortly see the government is once again lying to us. Those obstacles only exist because the government wants to force us to buy hydrogen at a gas station so they can meter it out to us like they currently do oil, and remember hydrogen is highly explosive so they have to deal with the hazard they create when we drive around in hydrogen bombs masquerading as cars.

As you shall shortly see Technology exists to deliver cheap on demand hydrogen without any of the government's bogus obstacles.

Geothermal Energy: Geothermal power generation is clean but with current technology its potential is limited to only a few sites where geothermal activity is at or near the surface, so for purposes of this discussion it is not a viable option. **http://www.energy-consumers-edge.com/pros_and_cons_of_geothermal_energy.html**

Wind Energy: Wind energy has been criticized as being a weak impractical alternative because of its location and weather dependency. However in 2007 The Department of Energy admitted, *"If wind was fully harvested in just 3 of Americas 50 states it could power the entire nation.* – Industrial Designer and Social Engineer, the Venus Project"* http://www.thevenusproject.com/

Solar Energy: It has been estimated that solar energy has the potential of one day being able to provide 100% of our energy needs. That day may not be far away. See revolutionary energy solutions below.

What do all of the government supported technologies have in common? With the exception of some solar applications they keep us either on the electrical grid dependent on the Utility Companies for electricity or taking our cars to a fueling station where we are dependent on the oil companies. Whether it is conventional gasoline, ethanol or compressed hydrogen we are buying we are still dependent on the oil companies. Indications are that better solutions are available. Read on and find out what they are.

End of Dependency on Fossil Fuels!
Scientific Breakthroughs Promise
Clean, Cheap, Renewable Energy!

"Our great industrial nation is controlled by its system of credit. Our system of credit is privately centered. The growth of the nation, therefore, and all our activities are in the hands of a few men...Who...chill and check and destroy genuine economic freedom."
                         – Woodrow Wilson 28th U.S. President, 1913-1921

The simple truth is that the men of which Woodrow Wilson speaks have consistently suppressed technological breakthroughs if those breakthroughs in any way threatened their existing revenue streams. Patents have been acquired and shelved and those who stood in their way have died. **We cannot let them withhold clean energy. Our very existence as a species depends on us winning this fight!**

<u>Garbage Recycling:</u> Ancient alchemy supposedly turned led into gold but this new technology is no myth. Brian Appel Chairman and CEO of CWT has developed the technology to turn any organic material, [that is anything containing carbon, which is almost everything on the planet] into oil, gas or charcoal. This gives alchemy new meaning. There are 12 billion tons of solid wastes produced each year in the U.S. alone. Appel says, *"We can conservatively convert all the agricultural waste, in the U.S. which is 6 billion tons into over 4 billion barrels of light oil a year. That is the same number we import."* The process is called Thermal-depolymerzation. The process mimics Mother Nature. Here is how it works. Solid material is ground up and mixed with water, then heat and pressure is applied to break the material down at the macular level, then solids, gasses and liquids are separated. The oil is processed into gasoline and the water is recycled. Appel's company recently built a $20 million dollar plant in Carthage Missouri to process 200 tons per day of turkey processing waste and there are plans for new plants in Nevada, Alabama, Colorado and Italy. Report by Tonya Hutchins. http://www.youtube.com/watch?v=CWf9 nYbm3ac&feature=related

I want to elaborate further on this technology so that its full potential can be appreciated. Imagine all the agricultural waste recycled and turned into oil, gas or charcoal. That's just the start. The sludge from water treatment plants can be recycled as well as our garbage. Think of it! Most of our garbage would be recycled. With this kind of revolutionary technology available why in the world is the government pushing Biomass [Ethanol] which is not CO_2 neutral and converts agricultural land from food production to fuel production. That is neither sustainable nor prudent. With Appel's solution there is nothing to plant or harvest and existing garbage trucks could take trash to recycling plants instead of dumps. This technology solves ecological problems on several levels. One would think that rather than building 72 new Ethanol Plants we would be building 72 new Thermal-depolymerzation plants and solving the planet's waste problems at the same time we address our energy needs. **Remember this technology is capable of eliminating our dependency on foreign oil as well.**

Why isn't this front page news?

<u>Solar Energy Breakthrough</u>:   Source CBS News the National. According to CBS's Peter Armstrong Israeli professor David Thamer has invented a new solar energy cell that is 1,500 times more efficient than previous technology and allows solar to compete with conventional electric sources and given its low operating cost is actually cheaper than coal powered electric plants. <u>Solar energy once a bit player is now a realistic alternative to conventional energy sources, that is if the politicians will allow its large scale development.</u> I ask you why did Acorn [a corrupt community organizing organization] get $8.5 billion of you tax money and breakthrough technology like this got $0, Nada. For my money I would much rather see us take advantage of a breakthrough in solar than build more nuclear plants. See http://www.youtube.com/watch?v=pXyJrFKwjrc Solar Energy Technology Breakthrough.

Compressed Air Engine: Yet another revolutionary technology comes from France where inventor and head of MDI, Motor Development International, Guy Negra has designed a car that runs on compressed air. Negra is a former formula 1 race car designer. Since the car runs on compressed air the only emission is clean air. It can be filled at a service station in about 3 minutes or plugged into an electrical outlet and filled by an onboard compressor in about four hours at a cost of about two dollars. The top speed is 110 Kilometers [68.35 miles per hour] and driving distance is 200 kilometers [124.28 miles.] There are also plans for a hybrid that can drive from LA to NY on a single tank of gas. Thanks to funding from an Indian company the car is expected to be on the market in Europe and India in approximately one year at a starting price of $15,000. <u>If President Obama is as concerned about CO_2 emissions as he claims, then why is this car not being made available in the U.S.? It is 100% nonpolluting. The only emission is clean air.</u> I will tell you why. Under his Cap and Trade Plan this car would cost him tax revenue. Don't let him fool you it is all about the money. – Beyond Tomorrow Gram Phillips Reporting, Nice France http://www.youtube.com/watch?v=jjSOvbsE460 also see CNN news cast @ http://www.youtube.com/watch?v=f4w6aJMNXSk

Revolutionary Inventions Being Withheld: The Three technologies I have just discussed are absolutely real and they are practical. The technologies I am going to discuss next challenge our current precepts of science and because of just how truly revolutionary they are there will be some who will dismiss them out of hand, but I would encourage you to keep an open mind. I have included links to a number of quite convincing news clips which appear to show that the technology is real and commercially viable. If so then the bounds of science as we have perceived them have just been broken and a new paradigm must be embraced. I would add that if the news clips are true they also give compelling evidence that the government has known about these technological breakthroughs for a considerable length of time and have not disclosed them. In that case it is further evidence that Cap and Trade is nothing but an attempt to enslave us. The technologies I am about to discuss all share several very important attributes. They are cheap, renewable, nonpolluting and they would end our dependency on the utility companies and the oil companies and they would end the government's geopolitical strangle hold on natural resources!

Think of it, a world where nonpolluting energy was available to all. The economic and geopolitical balance of world power would be forever changed. In the early 19th century a scientist by the name of Tesla was reported to have discover a universal source of renewable energy and when his benefactor J.P. Morgan found out just how truly revolutionary it was he is quoted as saying: *"One universal energy source could never be allowed."* In any event it is a fact that Morgan cut off funding and had the prototype destroyed. Why would we expect anything different from our government?

Water Engine: Denny Cline originally stumbled on his invention when looking for an alternative to volatile acetylene in the welding industry. His invention actually produces a flame as hot as the sun. I am not a scientist but with the atomic power of hydrogen at our disposal I immediately think of the possibility of cost effective clean electric plants and water desalination plants. **It certainly appears that virtually free, clean, renewable energy is available if only we can get access to it!** Inventor Denny Cline of Hydrogen Technologies has patented his revolutionary electrolysis process which converts tap water H_2O into HHO producing a gas that combines the atomic power of hydrogen with the stability of water. As the gas burns the by-product is water. **Government Cover Up!** According to Fox

News 26: *"The inventor is already in negotiations with one U.S. auto maker and talks are in process with the U.S. Government to develop a Hummer that can burn both water and gas. His prototype has passed all performance safety inspections and members of congress recently invited Denny Cline to Washington to demonstrate his invention."* Watch out something is up. This should have been headline news, but since it isn't it may well be one more revolutionary patent destined to be shelved by auto makers and the government. I urge you to view this news cast and see for yourself. Fox News 26, Craig Patrick reporting entitled Engine Runs on Water. http://www.youtube.com/watch?v=KZOsOB3z3IE&NR=1. I also urge you to watch this clip entitled HHO On Demand Water Powered Vehicle The Energy Lie. http://www.youtube.com/watch?v=XWhHCGlv9r8. It shows a car developed by Japanese auto maker Genepax. It also uses a fuel cell to convert water into hydrogen on demand.

Salt Water Generator: According to Channel 3 News, Mike O'Mara: While looking for a cure for cancer inventor John Kanzius has stumbled on a way to burn salt water as a fuel. He uses radio waves to break the salt water into its chemical components of oxygen and hydrogen and burn it as a fuel. At the AVP Company in Akron top engineers who checked out his invention were amazed. Engineer John White says, ***"We saw the temperature go up to 1,500 degrees centigrade. That's incredible."*** Imagine salt water, the most abundant element in the world available as a cheap, clean energy source! It could be used to power electrical generators or to fuel your car. No more expensive, polluting oil, only cheap clean energy. – Channel Three News, Erie Pennsylvania, Mike O'Mara reporting. http://www.youtube.com/watch?v=JiKa4nOkHLw

THE GOVERNMENT IS LYING TO US!

The water cars discussed above share one thing in common. They use fuel cells which **convert water into hydrogen** on demand, unlike U.S. auto makers who are developing hydrogen cars that require you to go to a gas station and fill up a hydrogen fuel tank at a cost of $3-4 dollars per gallon. I encourage you to view the news clip @ http://www.youtube.com/watch?v=AgWTU54SJbs&feature=related. This is a clip of a gorgeous GM car of the future; the only catch is it requires that you buy compressed Hydrogen at a gas station. Again the government wants to keep us dependent on expensive energy solutions when cheap, virtually free solutions are available. **We have to demand access to the technology which could potentially save the planet!**

<u>**Zero Point Magnetic Energy**</u>: Inventor John Cristie has invented an electric motor that is based on the attraction and repulsion force of the positive and negative poles of magnets. The motor is expected to sell for approximately $5,000 and is capable of supplying the entire electrical requirements of a home, allowing home owners to get completely off the utility grid. Cristie says his invention *"could also be used in cars and could replace the internal combustion engine."* Once started with a battery the motor will run till the magnets are depleted [approximately 400 years]. This technology is called zero point energy and represents what physicists have long theorized was the most efficient energy source in the universe. Steve Brassington an independent electrical engineer has evaluated the invention and says, *"It's revolutionary. These guys have thought outside the box."* Says Cristie, *"I think there is an opportunity here to share an invention with the world that goes beyond anything we have ever contemplated before."* – Chris Alan reports Sky News, Australia. http://www.youtube.com/watch?v=qI5jtx0IFgQ. See also Michael Nugents 300 horse power "Cyclone" magnetic engine @ http://www.youtube.com/watch?v=zu8LaVH-pn0. See also inventor Troy Reed and his magnetic powered electric hybrid car @ http://www.youtube.com/watch?v=Syc2Z9I_C8A   For you skeptics and I suspect there are many of you out there, I suggest you look at this newscast from Asia Brief Kean Wang reporting. Japanese based Axle Corporation just unveiled a new hybrid magnetic motor bike that it says is seven times more cost effective than conventional gasoline bikes. http://www.youtube.com/watch?v=ADd3Pp6GZP4

Government Suppresses Scientific Inventions Which Could End Dependency On Oil!

The history of science is the history of suppressed genius! In the Dark Ages scientists were branded as heretics, and persecuted and even killed if their scientific discoveries challenged prevailing religious beliefs. Unfortunately little has changed. The only difference is that today it is not the church doing the persecution and killing. It is our banking institutions, corporations and our own government.

In the present instance the heretics whom they seek to punish are those who have the audacity to try to give the world cheap, nonpolluting, renewable energy! And what could possibly be wrong with that? <u>In a modern society money is a source of power, but in a technology driven society energy is even more important than money</u>. That is why political analyst Kevin Philip said, *"America has become little more than an energy protection force doing anything to gain access to expensive fuel without regard to the lives of others or the earth itself."*

VITALLY IMPORTANT! <u>Why Withhold Energy Technology</u>? There are several reasons the oil companies, banks, and the U.S. Government want to withhold energy technology.

<u>Limit Access To Energy</u>: From the perspective of the oil companies there is of course the $4-5 trillion per year in **lost oil revenue.** Equally important is the fact that The Modern Slavery System of The Money Manipulators depends on **limited resources metered out by those in power.**

<u>Strangle Hold On Power</u>: From the prospective of the U.S. government, if they lose control of the oil their **geopolitical strangle hold** on the rest of the world will be lost forever. The Money Manipulators would cease being the all powerful overlords. All the sudden the World Bank and IMF would be much less able to stifle the development of other countries of the world. Ultimately all wealth comes from Nature so if we let their greed destroy the ecological balance of the planet there won't be any wealth for any of us.

<u>End Poverty and War</u>: As crazy as it sounds the government is also against cheap renewable energy because it *holds the possibility of ending world poverty and war.* War is nearly as profitable as oil and it yields a second currency which is power. As long as we have a serious gap between the haves and the have-nots, and as long as we have one group controlling the resources of the planet at the expense of those it is suppressing there will be war. Though war makes a few elite people extremely wealthy it impoverishes those paying for the war, which in this instance is the U.S. tax payer. If the money we spend on war could be diverted to social programs or to end world hunger society would be far better off.

Given that we are in the midst of a planetary mass extinction that could take the lives of billions of people, countless species of plants and animals and possibly even threaten the ability of the planet to sustain life, mankind cannot tolerate any power structure that suppress and withholds the technology which could save the planet.

According to the Declaration of Independence any government that supports such actions is not a government of the people by the people for the people. **It is a self-serving Rogue Government and the people have the right to alter or abolish it.**

Government Suppressed Technologies!

<u>1917 Nicola Tesla The Forgotten Genius</u>: Were it not for the suppression of technology by Banking Mogul J.P. Morgan it is entirely possible that the world could have had limitless, nonpolluting free energy as long ago as 1917, and that the global warming crisis which we now face could have been completely avoided! Most of us instantly recognize the names of scientist and inventors such as Albert Einstein, Sir Isaac Newton and Thomas Edison, yet few people know who Nikola Tesla was. Yet his contributions to science are as far reaching or more so than any of them. He held over 700 patents including such technology as alternating electric current, wireless technology, radar, laser technology, X-Rays, neon, robotics, remote control, cellular and radio [No Marconi did not invent Radio]. The U.S. Supreme court declared that Marconi stole his work from Tesla. The reason we have not heard of Tesla is because J.P. Morgan blackballed him and drove him into obscurity. Morgan was interested in being able to send transatlantic wireless signals and knowing Tesla's reputation as a visionary genius he approached him to develop the technology. Tesla built a communication tower called the Wardenclyffe Tower in order to send his wireless signal. Though Tesla's invention did what Morgan wanted it did something else that Morgan hadn't bargained for. It was capable of electrifying the stratosphere and transmitting an electrical current around the world. This meant that wireless electrical energy was available to anyone anywhere in the world simply by putting up an antenna.

When Morgan found out that Tesla's invention would provide a single source of free energy, he severed relations with Tesla, had the tower torn down and saw to it that Tesla could not get other backers. Tesla died at 86 in poverty, his dream of free, nonpolluting energy for the world having been obstructed by Morgan. Immediately following his death J. Edger Hover had Tesla's files confiscated. If you want to know more check out the videos below. http://www.youtube.com/watch?v=jImdQtZdktY Free Energy Destroyed http://www.youtube.com/watch?v=GJxzza_dKWg Nicola Tesla

1968 Daniel Dingel's Water Car: Dingel's water car invented in 1968 utilizes the same basic technology as Denny Cline's discussed above. Both convert water into hydrogen. Neither of them have as yet gotten their inventions on the market despite the fact that they absolutely work and despite the fact that they represent absolutely breakthrough technology which could provide the world with a clean unlimited energy source that could end our dependency on oil. How could that be? Dingel, a Philippine citizen; says *"he took his water car to the President of the Philippines who was initially very excited, but later came back and said, 'The government couldn't pursue the project.'* Dingel explains: **"That under agreement with the IMF and World Bank the Philippines are obligated not to produce anything that will compete with their products."** *[Referring to oil]* To do so would jeopardize the country's 40% oil tax and there would go the revenue for the country."* This is how the U.S. helps underdeveloped countries by lending them money and then applying conditions that keep them poor. http://www.youtube.com/watch?v=T35bgYqKZGE Pilipino Water Car

This is an unabridged example of abuse of power. Remember the U.S. Government is virtually in control of the World Bank so you cannot tell me they were not complicit in this suppression of technology!

1977 Bruce De Palma's N Machine: Is a zero point magnetic engine capable of producing five times the energy it consumes. According to De Palma shortly after inventing the N machine he met former astronaut Michael J. Michel who at the time was operating an institute in California which was supposedly set up to develop alternate energy sources by attracting inventors from around the country. De Palma says, *"Michel offered to buy the N Machine"* and when he refused, *"Michel told him that if he ever tried anything on his own in California he would get his head blown off."* De Palma also said **_"The CIA operates through innocent fronts to find out what people are inventing."_** The link below tells the story of how and why the oil companies have kept free energy from the world. http://www.youtube.com/ watch?v=jImdQtZdktY Free Energy destroyed.

1988 Stan Meyer's Water Car: According to Ralf Robinson of Action 6 News, Meyer's invention utilizes a hydrogen fuel cell that produces hydrogen on demand so unlike the approach of the auto makers there is no hydrogen fuel tank. The car runs on fresh or salt water. Meyer says, *"he was offered a billion dollars for his invention by oil producing companies, but he turned them down."* Leonard Holihan, from the Advanced Research Institute of Great Britain says, *"We recently took a delegation to evaluate Stan's work and we came away saying this was one of the most important inventions of the century."* Meyer says his fuel cell can be manufactured for $1,500 and there is no maintenance. In 1998 Meyers signed a contract with the Department of Defense to develop a $30 million research facility. The next day he was reportedly poisoned. Stan's invention produces Hydrogen on demand so unlike the government's solution there is no fuel to buy or store. All you need is water. At a cost of $1,500 with no maintenance it overcomes the cost and reliability concerns of the government's solution. I encourage you to view the news clip entitled Inventor Killed: http://www. youtube.com/watch?v=GDHT0hBgVOw&feature=related

My question is what happened to Meyer's water car? Don't forget about Cline's water car. It is reported to have passed all performance safety inspections and members of Congress supposedly invited Cline to Washington to demonstrate his invention, so where is it?

Cap and Trade Is A Ruse!
Clean, Cheap, Renewable Energy Is Available!

Cap and Trade Revisited: As discussed earlier under the governments proposed Cap and Trade System the government sets a cap [limit] on the total amount of CO2 that can be emitted nationally. Companies then buy certificates [on the open market] to emit CO2. The limits would be gradually reduced allowing less and less pollution, until by 2050 the proposed CO2 levels would theoretically be meet.

The Government's True Energy Agenda! As we discussed earlier there is zero chance Cap and Trade will generate any meaningful reductions in CO2 emissions, but there is every assurance it will put us under an onerous tax burdens which will ultimately reduce resource consumption by driving food and energy cost through the roof. As emission limits are lowered the cost of certificates will raise dramatically not only increasing taxes, but even worse it will create an opportunity for speculation. Remember the Enron debacle? If this gets out of hand it could make Enron look like Child's play. Lastly as emission levels are ratcheted down and companies are unable to comply they will either be forced out of business or forced to produce their products out of the country and ship them back into the U.S. **Any way you look at it Cap and Trade enslaves us and drives the country ever closer to bankruptcy! If you agree with what I have told you them the only responsible thing to do is to vigorously oppose this legislation!**

We have the technological wherewithal to have inexpensive, nonpolluting, renewable energy. The technology has existed for decades, but the oil companies and the government have suppressed it because renewable energy ends the public's dependency on the oil companies and threatens the Governments Geopolitical Power Base. I used the following quote before, but it warrants repeating.

"Giving society cheap, abundant energy...would be the equivalent of giving an idiot child a machine gun."
                                              –Paul Ehrlich, Stanford University

Clean Energy Is Available: Brian Appel's Thermal-depolymerzation which converts garbage into oil, gas and charcoal is a working technology that could end our dependency on foreign fuel and it makes much more sense than Ethanol but we are busy building ethanol plants and diverting agriculture land from food production to fuel production when it is unnecessary and unsustainable. Why? Why isn't the Israeli solar breakthrough that promises cost effective solar energy getting pushed? Why is the air car not licensed for production in the U.S.? It would appear that both the magnet motor and the water engine are capable of replacing the internal combustion engine and ending our dependency on oil and the oil companies. In terms of electricity for our homes the Australian inventor of the magnetic motor says: *"For $5,000 he can produce a version of his invention capable of supplying 100% of a homes electric needs."* Put another way, for $5,000 per household we could all be off the electric grid and never have another electric bill! Additionally if we can tap hydrogen and solar power, as new technologies promise, the options are limitless. **We can have clean energy and we can have it before the government's target date of 2050 and we can do it without Cap and Trade; that is if we are willing to fight for clean energy alternatives. Our survival as a species depends on us winning this fight.**

One added comment. Any hope we have of actually getting the revolutionary technologies I have discussed depends on public awareness. I encourage you to watch the clips I have referenced and send the links to everyone you know. It is precisely to block information such as this that the government wants to sensor the internet and that is why we have to fight to protect it.

Closing Comments

I hope I have provided enough facts to convince you that climate Change is a serious problem. The problem is the Money Manipulators own most of the newspapers and TV Networks and just like the tobacco companies they are not about to tell us the truth, so though we know we have a problem it is much less clear as to what the cause is. Make no mistake the oil companies, banks and government are in this together and all they are concerned about is maintaining the status quo. It is their money and power that they are protecting and that is all they care about. Remember the oil companies stand to lose $4-5 trillion per year and the government stands to lose its political leverage.

Like I have said several times before, if we want clean energy and if we want to break the hold of the Money Manipulators we are going to have to fight for our rights. I hate to think what this world will be like in a few decades if we lose this battle.

"One ought never turn one's back on a threatened danger and try to run away from it. If you do that, you will double the danger. But if

you meet it promptly and without flinching, you reduce the danger by half...Victory at all costs, victory in spite of all terror, victory however long and hard the road may be; without victory there is no survival."
                                                    – Sir Winston Churchill

United We Stand and United We Will Prevail!

Remember when we discussed the *"American System,"* an economic system which:

"Sought to Elevate While Equalizing the Condition of Man"

Well that system, *"The American System"* was at the heart of the American Industrial Revolution and America's rise to prominence as an Economic Super Power.

If we can force access to and development of the revolutionary technologies discussed a moment ago, particularly [The Thermal-Depolymerzation/Garbage Recycling, Solar Cell, Water Engine, and Magnetic Motor] **America could truly start a <u>Green Technology Revolution</u> that would replace our lost manufacturing jobs and create a technology revolution that could change the world.** The beauty of these technologies is that they have nowhere near the infrastructure requirements of conventional technology like Nuclear or Coal Plants for example. Imagine the impact on the economy and the environment if every car in America could be retrofitted with a Hydrogen fuel cell for $1,500 and from that point on would not have any fuel cost, not to mention the immediate and dramatic impact on the environment. Imagine having a $5,000 magnetic generator that could supply your home's entire electric needs for your entire life span. Imagine converting garbage into fuel and cleaning up the planet at the same time. Imagine getting the cost of these technologies down and making them available to third world countries. I tell you the world would be a better place, a more peaceful place. Americans could once again hold our heads up in pride as we:

"Elevate While Equalizing the Condition of Man Throughout the World"

The U.S. Government Is A Rogue Government!

<u>Demand Access to Technology</u>: Patents were intended to motivate people to invest in technology They were never intended to be a vehicle to deny technology crucial to society. For this reason **I believe that the American public is well within our rights to demand access to clean energy technology patents or no patents.** If the government can take our land to benefit corporations and foreign investors we can likewise take patents which are being wrongfully withheld in order to benefit society at large! More on this in the next chapter.

Any government that withholds technology capable of saving our economy and saving the planet is a self-serving Rogue Government and the people have the right to alter or abolish it!

In the next chapter I will detail exactly how we can take back control of our Government and regain our dignity and our liberty!

Chapter 12

The American Restoration Platform:

The Plan To Return Government To The People!

"Remember that a government big enough to give you everything you want is big enough to take everything you have."
— U.S. Senator Barry Goldwater

Introduction: I promised that by the time you finished this book you would know what needs to be done to save our freedom, our liberty, our government and the American way of life. I will shortly reveal the plan of which I have alluded, **[The American Restoration Platform]** but first we need to refresh our memories as to exactly what got us in this mess and take a look at Obama's agenda and see where it is taking us. Then with these events fresh in our minds we will be in a better position to know what we need to do to fix things and save our freedom, our liberty our government, and our way of life.

<u>Collapse of The U.S. House of Cards</u>! [A Review]

As our forefathers had predicted the collapse of the U.S. economy was brought about from within when a group of Moneyed Elite got control of creation of our currency [with the inception of the Federal Reserve] and were able to systematically, over decades, debase our currency, steal our wealth through multiple orchestrated financial crises, control our corporations, and corrupt our political leaders. And all the while the citizenry was oblivious to what was going on having been blinded by what at the time seemed like the good life. We were oblivious to the fact that the government was influencing our opinions and controlling them in scuttle and yet powerful ways by their insidious encroachment into virtually every aspect of our lives. The government run schools determined what future generations thought. We were being conditioned to believe that Capitalism was somehow fundamentally unfair, that it oppressed one segment of society at the expense of another. In the name of the greater good the government began introducing social welfare programs [entitlement programs], and the citizen's naively went along with them not realizing that they were intentionally driving the country into unmanageable debt so they could bankrupt it and transition America into a Socialist/Communist Order. At the same time our moral value system was debased by an unrelenting attack on Christian values. The entertainment industry distracted us from the reality of what was happening in society while they subtlety debased our perception of morality. As our financial system began to break down Mothers were forced into the job market and thus began the gradual breakdown of our family values. Increasingly the value system of our children was controlled by outside forces and the family structure began to fracture. Meanwhile media sound bites were used to feed us ½ truths and steer public opinion relentlessly toward the agenda of the power brokers who controlled both the media and the public. The stage was at long last set for execution of the end game as a financially weakened America was forced to face the economic reality of decades of fiscal mismanagement. All that was needed was a crisis of sufficient magnitude. Then came 9/11 and the process of establishing a police state began. We were told that The Patriot Act and other such laws were for Homeland Security, but in reality they were intended to control the population should we wake up and revolt against what was being done to us. It was at long last time to take what little wealth the American people had left, bankrupt the country and force it into the New World Order that had for so long been envisioned. So the Sub-prime collapse of 2008 was orchestrated by Bush and then Obama pushed Healthcare reform in order to get control of

1/6 of the GDP and control our access to healthcare and who lives and who dies.

Obama then immediately turned his attention to Cap and Trade [his energy initiative] in order to impose onerous tax increases on us and control our access to food and energy and right on queue there is another one of those oh so convenient crises! It just turns out that we have our first ever oil rig blow out and the granddaddy of all oil spills. There is absolutely no evidence that the government or BP caused the accident, but boy do those crises keep coming on queue. Regardless of what caused the spill there is no question in my mind that the government is making sure that they get every bit of political mileage out of it they can, regardless of the harm it does to the environment or the economy. I am writing this in 2010 in the midst of the oil spill in the Gulf of Mexico and I just came back from a trip to the region. Housing prices in the region have already had a 40-50% drop from their peak prior to the 2008 real estate collapse. Faced with the threat of the loss of the fishing and tourism industry in the entire Gulf and possibly even a substantial portion of the East Coast I predict that the housing market could be looking at losing another 40-50% of their remaining values which would mean a total drop in value from the peak of 60-75%. All in all, the crisis is large enough to cause a double dip recession which will affect the entire U.S. economy.

So faced with this crisis what does Obama do? He threatens a six month moratorium on drilling in the Gulf despite outcries from citizens that it will seriously harm their economy. Additionally we can expect that such action will cause a dramatic spike in oil prices which will further hurt an already fragile economy. He threatens to Nationalize BP and threatens criminal charges, none of which helps the residents of the region. But it does seem to fit with his agenda. After all he nationalized the banks and auto industry so why not BP? He is doing just about everything he can except stop the oil from washing up on the beaches causing a devastating collapse of the entire Gulf Coast economy.

Given what happened with the Super Tanker the Valdez several years ago the government and the oil companies were certainly aware of just how devastating a major oil spill can be and yet we are to believe they had **no plan in place** for such a catastrophic event. As events unfolded and I saw how the Federal Government obstructed efforts of State and Local Governments to address the crisis, sighting all kinds of environmental regulations which prevented action, I became certain that this was going to be used to further drive the nation into bankruptcy.

VITALLY IMPORTANT! Then I got furious when I watched a program on Fox where former Governor Huckabee had guests which demonstrated several products which would absorb the oil and were biodegradable which meant they required no clean up and had no harmful environmental impacts. I thought there was hope! Then I listened as one after another the person demonstrating these products was asked if their products were being used and the answer was always no. Then I heard that 75% of the Pelicans in the region had been killed and I realized that it had been totally preventable because one of the products that was demonstrated: **1) absorbs the oil 2) is biodegradable, and 3) prevents oil from adhering to plants and animals, so if for example a Pelican came in contact with the material it would not be harmed!** When the representative was asked about availability of the product he responded that they had millions of tons of the material available for immediate use. Neither BP nor the Government is taking advantage of this technology to save wildlife, the environment or the Gulf Coast Economy. WHY? No my friends this goes beyond ineptitude. This is the government driving us ever closer to collapse and take over! We better wake up and take a stand before it is too late.

Getting back to our review, the control mechanisms are in place and the government is poised to execute their take over. All that remains is to determine if the American people will, like our forefathers rise up and say give me liberty or give me death or will we just surrender without a fight. I certainly hope we will defend our great nation!

The Planned Bankruptcy of America!

When all is said and done history will record that there were seven key political and financial actions which the Money Manipulators took in order to bankrupt the U.S. and transition it into the New World Order.

They are as follows:

1) **Formation of The Federal Reserve:** Which allowed our currency to be printed by private banking interest and therefore gave then the power to manipulate the U.S. currency and ultimately bankrupt the Nation!

2) **Perpetual Budget Deficits/National Debt:** Caused by irresponsible spending, especially on maintaining our Global Empire and massive unfunded entitlement programs.

3) **Excessive Trade Deficits:** Caused by Free Trade Agreements such as NAFTA and the WTO and the Governments policy of allowing the U.S. to practice intentionally losing trade by being the only major industrialized nation not to impose a VAT or Tariff to protect its trade and manufacturing.

4) **Savings Deficit/Credit Card Debt:** Caused by imposition of Usury Predatory Credit Card Rates which kept people in perpetual debt.

5) **Sub-Prime Collapse:** The economic house of cards finally began to unravel in 2007-2008 when the Sub-prime Real Estate Collapse was inflicted on an unsuspecting public when then President Bush blocked efforts by all 50 Governors to ban Predatory Lending Practices which could have prevented the collapse!

6) **Leadership Deficit:** The American people wanted to believe in our government so it was hard for us to see that as our Founding Fathers had predicted our government had been hijacked by the Moneyed Elite who had corrupted our political leaders in Washington.

7) **Denial of Civil Liberties/Imposition of A Police State:** 9/11 was used as an excuse to pass The Patriot Act and other legislation which gave the government the legal means to implement a police state if and when the American people realized what was being done to them and rose up in protest.

Then Came Obama!

Lastly, we need to look at Obama's agenda and see it for what it really is; **A plan to transition America into open Communism!**

1) **The Stimulus:** Put the government in the banking business, opened the door to private sector salary control, and funneled billions to special interest groups supportive of Obama's agenda? [i.e. Corrupt banks and community organizations like ACORN], but most importantly it; Made Americans Slaves To The National Debt!

2) **Obama Care:** Professes humanitarian goals when in reality it will result in limited access and rationing of healthcare coupled with increased cost and lower quality of care, but, it will achieve its goal of giving the government control of 1/6 of the GDP!

3) **Cap and Trade:** Is a tax bill masquerading as an environmental program. It is nothing more than a means to impose Global Governance, Redistribute Wealth, Control the Population and Limit Resource Consumption!

4) **Imposition of a Police State:** Obama refused to rescind G.W. Bush's Presidential Directive 51 which effectively allows the President Dictatorial Powers. He has plans for a Million Man Standing Army reporting directly to him while doing everything he can to deny Americans the right to bear arms as a means of self defense. The stage is set for imposition of Martial Law. All we need is the right crisis!

What is happening to America is what I refer to as **"Incrementalism"** which expresses the fact that if an agenda is executed over years or decades the public is not able to connect the dots and figure out what is being done to them, therefore some very radical programs can be pushed through. This is exactly what is being done to us and we have to put a stop to it. **All we need is a National Emergency of any kind [real or imposed] and America is poised for a take over!** We have to regain control of the government and see to it that it once again becomes: *"A government of the people by the people for the people.*

Before I outline the American Restoration Platform there is one last thing I want to review. Throughout the book I have listed a number of Actions Steps which were presented in sequential order. I want to list them again, but this time I want to categorize and prioritize them so we get a sense of the most pressing issues we need to address in order to save our Republic.

Key Action Steps

PHASE ONE:
<u>In Order to Regain Control of the Political System We Must</u>:

1) **Vote out all incumbents, both Republicans and Democrats:** Because with very few exceptions our elected officials in Washington have demonstrated that they place their vested interest and those of special interest groups ahead of those of the Public. Simply speaking we don't know who to trust so they all have to go.

2) **Implement election reform:** Limit ability of legislators to put their interest ahead of those of the public by: Imposing Term Limits, Limits on Contributions and Banning of Gerrymandering.

3) **Ban lobbyists:** As a means of limiting influence peddling.

4) **Call for removal of all government appointees who belong to the TC, CFR and BG:** And prohibit secret meetings with any non-elected officials.

5) **Force our Government to close our borders:** The government's open borders policy poses a National Security threat, causes social strife, particularly in Border States, puts downward pressure on salaries and places economic strain on our economy at a time when we can ill afford it.

6) **Require candidates to Sign a Pledge**: Supporting an Election Plank designed to take power from the special interest groups and return it to the public.

PHASE TWO:
In Order To Regain Control of The Economy
We Must:

7) **Withdraw from or renegotiate all Free Trade Agreements such as NAFTA & WTO:** This is essential if we hope to end the devastating trade deficits these agreements impose on the U.S.

8) **Oppose the [SSP] and North American Union:** Because they threaten U.S. Sovereignty and threaten to further damage our trade balance by flooding the U.S. with Free Trade Goods.

9) **Oppose passage of any energy bill including participation in The Framework Convention On Climate Change:** Because it is nothing more than a means to impose Global Governance, Redistribution of Wealth, Population Control and Forced Limitations on Resource Consumption. **Also support repeal of Obama Care:** Because it was forced on us for political reasons and will not solve the problems with the healthcare system.

10) **Reform the welfare system and cut entitlement programs:** Because they ultimately lead to economic collapse and besides what most people really want is a job not a hand out. They want the government to stop taxing us into poverty so we can regain our self-reliance.

11) **Replace The Fed with A National Bank:** By getting rid of the Fed we will stop private bankers from manipulating the economy through control of the money supply and interest rates causing boom bust cycles at their discretion. We will also be able to reduce the National Debt.

12) **Repeal the Illegal Federal Income Tax:** Since our Federal Income Tax goes to pay interest charges to the Fed for issuing our currency it will know longer be necessary if the Fed is eliminated.

13) **Boycott the nation's largest banks:** Most of them are affiliated with the Fed and besides any bank too large to fail is a Monopoly and needs to be broken up in the best interest of the public.

14) **Support passage of national usury law:** In order to end predatory lending practices of banks where by they charge usury rates and target those least able to pay.

15) **Encourage business growth and rebuild the manufacturing sector by:** Supporting low interest rates for infrastructure projects and private sector capital investment projects.

16) **Establish an international development fund to:** Develop Global Infrastructure Projects as the basis of Global economic prosperity.

17) **Reestablish The American System of Economics with tariff protection and fair trade not free trade agreements:** Puts focus on development of sovereign nations as opposed to Globalization. World peace will only be possible when: the nations of the world join together to equalize and elevate all of mankind, not just a select few. We can no longer allow one group to oppress another.

PHASE THREE:
Accept Personal Responsibility
and Change Accordingly:

18) **Become informed and politically involved:** So the government can no longer lie to you and deceive you with their half truths. Learn the truth and then stand up for what is right, just and moral not just for a few but for all people of the world. In order to regain our Republic we must once again Become A Moral Society, willing to abide by The Law [The Constitution] not majority rule which invariably leads to social breakdown as the least productive members of society vote to give themselves hand outs.

19) **Accept responsibility for our greed:** Face up to the U.S. Government's policy of Imperialism and Hegemony and support spending cuts of U.S. military adventurism. We need to protect our domestic borders not occupy foreign nations for their natural resources. Beside we can no longer afford to spend more on military than any other nation in the world. Also if we want to

end Free Trade and reverse our trade deficit we are going to have to <u>stop buying Chinese Free Trade Goods produced by people working in sweat shops</u>.

20) **Surrender to God:** Whether or not we want to admit it <u>America has failed to be Good Stewards</u> of the vast wealth which God bestowed on our nation. If we hope to save our country we are going to have to stop raping the rest of the world and become the stewards which God intended. Lastly we are going to have to <u>reestablish our family and Christian values</u> in order to end the system of greed which rules America.

What follows is the American Restoration Platform which is a comprehensive political and economic agenda for America's restoration. It contains many of the initiatives which were just highlighted, but it goes into more detail and proposes several very simple common sense solutions to problems which the government tells us are too complicated for us to grasp. As it turns out they are not complicated at all. For example the only reason we need a 2,000 page healthcare bill is to make sure the government regulates absolutely everything and rewards the special interest groups to the detriment of the American people. <u>I think you will be amazed at how truly simple the solutions to our social, political and economic woes actually are</u>, that is if we can get rid of our big Federal Government which is actually the source of virtually all of our problems.

Taking Back America!
The American Restoration Platform!

With the government's strategy fully exposed and fresh in our minds we are finally in a position to look to the future and determine what we must do to *"Save Our Nation!"* The plan which I am about to present systematically addresses the route causes of our economic collapse and endeavors to reinstate many of the safeguards which have been systematically stripped away [removal of which allowed the banks to drive us into bankruptcy.]

I urge you to take this platform to your legislators at the upcoming mid term elections and ask them if they will support it, if not then do not support them. Our legislators are on record as saying that, *"It is a shame to waste a crisis,"* so let's not waste this one. **This is probably the first time in 200 years that Non Washington Insiders have a chance of being elected. Let's use the Tea Party to put in legislators sworn to uphold the Constitution and restore our rights!**

U.S. Senator Barry Goldwater got it right when he said: *"I have little interest in streamlining government or making it more efficient, for I mean to reduce its size. I do not undertake to promote welfare, for I propose to extend freedom. My aim is not to pass laws, but to cancel old ones that do violence to the constitution or that have failed their purpose, or that impose on the people unwarranted financial burdens. I will not attempt to discover whether legislation 'is needed' before I have first determined if it is constitutionally permissible. And if I should be attacked for neglecting my constituents' 'interest' I shall reply I was informed that their main interest is liberty and that in that cause I am doing the best I can."* **America it is time to stand up and tell our government:**

Enough is Enough!

"We are taking back our country and reinstating the principles upon which it was founded!"

American Restoration Mission Statement: America needs to get back control of its currency and take back the seat of power from the Money Manipulators and their puppet figure heads. We need secure borders, good paying jobs [including jobs in the manufacturing sector], protection from unfair foreign competition, abolishment of usury interest rates and predatory lending practices, and restoration of our civil liberties. In short we need to go back to the small government engendered by our founding fathers, a government of the people by the people for the people, a government based on Christian Morality and the rule of law [The Constitution], directed by a morally informed, socially, responsible citizenry who are willing to fight for those things which are for the betterment of all of society. America is facing some very real problems, but we need to refuse to allow a power thirsty big government directed by special interest groups to stampede us into making hasty decisions which we will regret for generations to come.

This is a time for calm resolve. This is a time for informed decision making. This is a time for visionary thinking. This is a time for mutual respect and solidarity. This is a time for Americans from all walks of life to come together, put aside their differences and take advantage of our mutual hardships in order to forge a stronger America, an America our children can be proud of, an America the world can once again look to in wonder and Ah! To this end we resolve to support an **American Restoration Platform** consisting of the following initiatives:

<u>Key Reform Initiatives:</u>	<u>Legend to Action Steps:</u>
1) Banking Reform	Top Priority = Immediate Action
2) Trade Reform	Level 1 Priority = 2010 Platform Issue
3) Election Reform	Level 2 Priority = 2012 Platform Issue
4) Energy Reform	Level 3 Priority = Implement Post 2012
5) Healthcare Reform	
6) Reinstate Liberties	
7) Education Reform	

Comprehensive Reform Initiatives:

1) Banking Reform:

Balanced Budget Amendment to the U.S. Constitution:

[Top Priority] We support Congressman Ron Paul's call for a public roll call vote in the Congress calling for a Balanced Budget Amendment to the U.S. Constitution. If passed The Balanced Budget Amendment would: Require a two-thirds Congressional majority to raise taxes. Limit any increase in Federal spending to no more than population growth plus inflation Allow for exceptions only under an official Congressional Declaration of War, so Congress and the President aren't able to involve the U.S. in never ending military conflicts. Force Congress to return any budget surplus to the American people in the form of tax cuts. If you are interested in finding out more about this proposed legislation you can contact: John F. Tate, President, Campaign for Liberty, Lake Jackson, TX 77566

Anyone who votes against the amendment is voting against responsible government and for continued reckless spending and needs to be voted out of office **[no exceptions.]**

The key to fixing the economy is to understand where we went wrong and to put into place legislation which will prevent those same mistakes from occurring again in the future. A mandatory balanced budget will prevent the out of control spending which has resulted in America becoming the worlds #1 debtor with a national debt of approximately $117 trillion if unfunded entitlement programs are included as they should be. We cannot afford any more Entitlement Programs. By acting as though our Republic was in fact a Democracy we have brought on ourselves the inevitable outcome suffered by all Democracies. They invariably morph into socialism and self-destruct, most frequently ending up as Dictatorships. What happens is that burdened with debt and with productivity falling the less-productive majority **[the mobocracy]** comes to realize that it can vote itself hand outs **[entitlements]** from the more productive minority by electing political leaders based on who promises the most benefits from the public treasury. In order to keep their positions these politicians find themselves in the position where they have to keep the entitlements coming resulting in ever increasing spending funded by higher taxes and deficits. As taxes become onerous the incentive to produce decreases causing many of the once productive to join the ranks of the non-productive. **[This is socialism]** When there are no longer enough productive members of society to fund the essential functions of government it collapses into bankruptcy, social disorder results and most often a Dictatorship arises. This is what is happening in America today. America was founded on rugged self reliance and we must return to those principles or perish!

Impose National Usury Law:

[Level 1 Priority] We call for a National Usury Law which caps interest rates at 9% and establishes guidelines for Hardship with interest rates as low as 2-4% and Debt Restructuring/Settlement in lieu of bankruptcy.

There is no need for a 2,000 page Finance Reform Bill. Predatory Lending **[related to credit card debt]** can be virtually eliminated by removing the loopholes which have allowed banks to incorporate in states that have no usury laws, effectively allowing them to block state initiatives to limit interest rates on credit cards. Additionally we are calling for provisions for documented financial hardship i.e. health problems or loss of job. Under predefined conditions a borrower would be immediately put on a hardship program where his interest rate is automatically dropped to 2-4% based on extent of hardship as defined by a predetermined debt to income ratio. There would be no need to negotiate the rate with the credit card company and no need to pay a credit scavenger to negotiate the rate. The rate would be set by law. Lastly under dire circumstances there would be provision to **[restructure or settle the debt]** without having to go through bankruptcy proceedings by paying a percentage of the loan balance based on predetermined debt to income ratios. **These measures would make banks lend responsibly.**

The American tax payer bailed out the banking industry and now it is time to change the laws that caused the problem. Personal debt is through the roof, with the average American owing $10,000 in credit card debt. Given the high interest rates credit card companies can charge they have no incentive to issue credit based on credit worthiness. Their best customer is the one least able to pay, the one that will make the minimum payment and incur late fees and over limit fees. <u>By lowering the legal interest rate credit card companies will no longer have an incentive to target those least able to pay and predatory lending related to credit cards will cease to be a problem.</u> Additionally bankruptcies would go down and savings rates should go up which translates into funding for capital development which creates jobs. We can no longer allow the greed of the bankers to negatively impact the entire economy as it has in the past.

Establish Two-tier Mortgage Option:

[Level 1 Priority] In order to allow the public to pay off their mortgages and save for retirement we call for enactment of a Two-tier Mortgage Program. Under the proposed *Two-tier Mortgage Option* when a person moves or refinances instead of being forced to get a completely new mortgage they would have the option of staying with their current lender and going on a two-tier mortgage where their current mortgage balance would be carried over to the new loan at the same interest rate and with no adjustment made to the amortization table. **[The loan goes with the person not the property]**. Any amount above the current mortgage balance would be treated as a new 2nd loan subject to current interest rates and starting at month one on the amortization table. Standard closing costs would apply.

It is time that the interest of the banking concerns stopped being put ahead of those of the public. Current banking practices are designed to make it difficult for the average person to ever pay off their mortgage. The problem is that the average American moves or refinances every 5-7 years and every time they move or refinance they are forced to get a new mortgage which is subject to current rates and their amortization table starts over at month one. The chart below explains how and why this makes it extremely difficult for people to pay off their mortgages.

Terms 30 Year Mortgage

Mortgage Amount	$200,000
Interest Rate	6 percent
Remaining Term	360
Interest Payment	$1,000.00
Principal Payment	$199.10
Escrow Amount	$415.00
Total Payments	$1,614.10

Debt Amortization Years 1-5 of Mortgage

Year	1st Mortgage Balance	Total Debt Paid	Total Interest
1	$197,541.99	$ 2,458.01	$11,933.19
2	$194,936.50	$ 5,063.50	$23,714.90
3	$192,168.20	$ 7,831.80	$35,335.80
4	$189,229.13	$10,770.87	$46,785.93
5	$186,108.80	$13,891.20	$58,054.80

Paid one third of original loan amount and have only $13,891.20 in equity!
Over five years 80 percent of mortgage payments go to interest!

This chart highlights the fact that after five years, payments total $71,946.08. **[$58,054.80 interest payments PLUS $13,891.20 debt reduction]** The original loan was $200,000 so approximately 1/3 of the original loan amount has been paid yet only $13,982.00 went toward equity which means that over 80% the payments went to interest. When we move or refinance it cost us much more then we realize and in a mobile society such as our current banking policies guarantee that a substantial segment of society will never be able to pay off their homes.

This legislation will allow people to pay off their homes sooner and save for retirement, which means people will be financially prepared for retirement so we will not have to be dependent on the government. Additionally increased personal savings means money will be available for capital investment to fund business growth.

Get Rid of Federal Reserve Per EO #11110 Signed By JFK:

[**Level 2 Priority**] and return control of issuance of U.S. Currency to the Treasury Department where it belongs thus ending the unscrupulous policy of having private bankers provide U.S. Currency to the Government @ *Interest!*

Though getting grid of the Fed is ultimately even more important than the Balanced Budget Roll Call Amendment political reality is that our current Congress will not touch this issue. It will have to wait till after the 2012 elections when we have voted out all of the incumbents in Washington and can start with a clean slate. There are a couple of exceptions such as Ron Paul who deserve to stay in office.

Repeal of the Federal Reserve is essential because it will return issuance of U.S. Currency to the Treasury of the U.S. where it belongs. It will also end the interest charges which we are charged for the issuance by the Fed of worthless paper currency which is created out of thin air with the stroke of a computer key. If we are to prevent private bankers from manipulating interest rates and money supply causing currency devaluation coupled with orchestrated cycles of economic expansion followed by recession/depression, then the Fed must go! The strangle hold on the U.S. economy will never end and our National Sovereignty will never be safe as long as the Fed exist! The Fed Must Go!

I am not an economist so in this instance I am relying on guidance from those who are far more knowledgeable than me. There is precedence for this however. Andrew Jackson successfully got rid of the Federal Reserve Bank that preceded the current Federal Reserve System and then proceeded to pay off the entire national debt. And if Kennedy had not felt this was doable he would never have signed EO# 11110 which was intended to dismantle the Fed. What follows is a basic outline of an economic plan formulated in part by Economist Milton Freedman. The trick is to dismantle the Fed without triggering run away inflation. I would add however that given the rate of decay of the U.S. dollar run away inflation may be inevitable even if we keep the Federal Reserve System. After all there is a limit to how much debt even the U.S. can carry.

The basic idea of the Monetary Reform Act is that: **1)** We pay off debt with debt free U.S. Notes which amounts to substitution for one type of government obligation for another. **2)** As the Treasury buys bonds on the open market with U.S. notes the reserve requirements of all banks and financial institutions would be proportionally raised so the amount of money in circulation would remain constant. As those holding bonds are paid off in U.S. Notes the money will be deposited thus making available the currency needed by the banks to increase their reserves. **3)** Once all U.S. Bonds are replaced with U.S. Notes banks will be at 100% reserve banking instead of the fractional reserve system currently in place. **4)** At this point we repeal The Federal Reserve banking Act of 1913 and National Banking Act of 1864 which delegated money powers to a private banking monopoly. **5)** From this point on the former Fed building would only be needed as a central clearing house for checks and as vaults for Notes. There would be no further creation or contraction of money by banks. At this point we could abolish the Fed without inflation, bankruptcy or any serious economic crisis. **6)** Having successfully dismantled the Fed we would then withdrawal from the International Monetary Fund [IMF], Bank Of International Settlement [BIS] and World Bank finally returning control of the U.S. Monetary System to the Treasury Department of the United States of America instead of private banking monopolies.

Repeal Federal Income Tax and Reform The Tax Code:

[Level 2 Priority] We call for repeal of Federal Income Tax on the following grounds **1)** It is illegal. The Supreme Court ruled in six separate cases that the 16th Amendment inferred no new power of taxation thus Federal Income tax is Illegal and the government cannot produce a law that requires individuals to pay Federal Income Tax. **2)** None of the taxes go to pay for public services, but instead they go directly to a private banking cartel [The Fed] to pay interest charges for issuance of U.S. Currency which is the right and responsibility of the Treasury. **3)** Because the Federal Tax Code is used to reward or punish based on alignment with political agendas of those in power. **Note:** We can't get rid of Federal Income Tax, even though the Supreme Court says it is illegal, until and unless we get rid of the Fed because it is our Federal Income Tax which is used to pay the Fed their interest payments for issuing our currency. At the same time we repeal the Federal Income Tax we need sweeping tax reform and imposition of a <u>Flat Tax</u> in order to stop the government's policy of using the tax code to reward and punish various segments of society.

It is important to remember that none of the money from Federal Income Tax goes to the services tax payers expect from the government. Your Federal Income Tax Check is deposited in a Federal Reserve Bank, not the Treasury. Additionally The Federal Tax Code has come to be a tool of the government to reward those that support their policies and punish those that do not. For example after giving the corrupt banks billions from the Stimulus, Secretary Henry Paulson [Bush Administration] miraculously remembered to *"reverse Section 328 of the tax code which said a corporation couldn't avoid paying taxes simply by purchasing a failing company and magically the banks got an extra $120-140 Billion windfall."*

Establish Two-tier Credit System:

[Level 2 Priority] Per provision of Home Owners Bank Protection Act **[HOBPA]** provide low-interest rates of 1-2% for economic growth/infrastructure projects and a higher rate for conventional consumer loans. Unfortunately this is another initiative that practically speaking cannot be pushed through as long as the Fed is in power.

This Act assures money will be available to fund the types of capital intensive projects which are essential to revitalize our manufacturing sector and stimulate small business so we can get Americans back to work and so we can rebuild our crumbling infrastructure and keep it from being sold to international interest which will charge us usage fees to use infrastructure which was built with tax payer money.

New Bretton Woods System of Fixed Exchange Rates:

[Level 2 Priority] Between U.S., Russia, China and India per provisions of *(HOBPA)* to stop currency speculation and the economic instability which it causes.

This initiative is tied to the Two-tier Credit System discussed above. It is imperative that something be done to stabilize exchange rates. This is essentially reinstatement of legislation that was repealed in order to allow predatory lending practices.

Bankruptcy Legislation:

[Level 3 priority] The intent is to repeal legislation [written by banking concerns] and to put together an impartial panel of experts to write a bill which does not unfairly favor the banks as the current legislation does. Additionally it would be illegal for a bank or any other special interest group to write legislation. This is influence pedaling of the worst kind. Before this legislation can be addressed we need a National Usury Law and other provisions to stop the Predatory Lending Practices which cause the bankruptcies in the first place.

As it turns out the current bankruptcy bill, like so much of our recent legislation, was written by special interest groups. Specifically it was written by NBNA who was at the time the nation's second-largest credit card company and just happened to be President Bush's largest campaign contributor in the 2005 election campaign. A bank has no business writing legislation that benefits themselves? The current legislation can result in situations where a creditor may have to pay the original loan amount and upwards of twice that amount in fees, penalties and legal costs. There needs to be caps set on the amount of money that can be collected and there needs to be provisions for partial payment settlements and actual defaults. The outcome of this legislation would be to create a disincentive for predatory lending practices and a reduction in bankruptcies

Reinstate Dismantled Regulatory Legislation:

[Level 3 Priority] Have an independent panel review dismantled Banking and Energy regulations and evaluate the merits of reinstating such legislation in part or in total.

Our immediate priority must be initiatives which address our current economic crisis, not those which have already occurred.

___**Glass-Steagall Act**___: The 2007 Sub-prime collapse might have been prevented had the Glass-Steagall Act not been dismantled. The Act **[prohibited commercial banks from owning or being owned by full service brokerage firms.]** Had Glass-Steagall been in effect it would have been much more difficult to bundle the Collateralized Debt Obligations [CDOs] which figured so prominently in the sub-prime collapse. **Note:** As you will recall a [CDO] is a bundle of loans that are put together, rated by a rating company and then sold on the stock market to buyers all over the world. A bundle of [CDOs] typically contained some Conventional Loans, but it also contained a large number of high risk Sub-prime Loans.

___**Other New Deal Legislation:**___ Regulations governing Banking, S&L's and Energy have been systematically dismantled in order to allow the predatory lending practices which have figured so prominently in our current financial crisis. All such regulatory legislation needs to be reviewed and appropriate safeguards need to be put in place to prevent abuse of power.

2) Trade Reform/Open Borders Policy:

Support [HCR 40]:

[Top Priority] [HCR 40] charges that: *"The actions taken by the Security and Prosperity Partnership [SPP] to coordinate border security by eliminating obstacles between Mexico and the U.S. actually makes the U.S. Mexico border less secure because Mexico is the primary source of Illegal immigration into the U.S.."* The resolution expresses that: *"The U.S. should not engage in the NAFTA North American Free Trade Superhighway. Should not allow the SPP to implement additional regulations that could result in a North American Union with Mexico and Canada. The President should oppose any proposals that threaten the sovereignty of the U.S."*

This legislation is essential to maintaining the sovereignty of America. The super corridor system which the legislation references is a Super Highway System comprised of separate lanes for trucks, cars, rail and a utility right of way, which in and of itself is not the problem. The problem is that the super corridor is designed as an [International Transportation Corridor] intended to facilitate the flood of [Cheap Free Trade Goods] coming into the U.S. from China. In order for China to under price domestic U.S. manufacturers they depend on cheap labor which we can't do anything about, but they also depend on unfair trade agreements like NAFTA and cheap transportation cost. The super corridor will drop their transportation cost to the bare minimum further placing the U.S. at a disadvantage. The long term economic outcome will be to literally destroy the U.S. economic system by creating an ongoing continuation of the trade deficit policies that have made the U.S. the world's #1 debtor nation and China our creditor.

National Security is also at risk. The easing of border restrictions between Mexico and the U.S. creates a serious National Security risk as it opens the door to drug traffic, illegal aliens and terrorism. The Kansas City Customs office is the first check point for goods entering the U.S. from Mexico. It is planned to be sovereign Mexican property. As such Mexican officials will be responsible for U.S. security. That is just insane. **Given our ludicrous open borders policy what exactly is the Patriot Act protecting us from? We have left the door wide open and invited the terrorist in!**

Lastly there is the issue of U.S. sovereignty. The Security and Prosperity Partnership [SPP] entered into by former President Bush, **[without any input from the American people or Congress]**, threatens to lead us into The North American Union and see our constitutional rights taken away through merger with Mexico and Canada. For example, *"NAFTA Chapter 11 Tribunals"* override U.S. law even the Supreme Court making U.S. laws subject to integration and harmonization with laws from Mexico and Canada. Could the U.S. Bill of Rights eventually be in question?

Support [HCR 22]:

[Top Priority] (HCR 22) expresses the position of Congress that the U.S. should withdrawal from NAFTA.

If we don't renegotiate NAFTA and other Free Trade Agreements the U.S. will continue to run the trade deficits which have contributed so heavily to our current economic crisis! The legislatures of Oregon, Arizona, South Carolina, Utah, Virginia and Washington have all introduced bills opposing The North American Union and NAFTA. So why are we still in NAFTA? Why are we still going forward with the TTC-35 super highway? Because despite the best efforts of our Congressmen and State Legislatures there are forces operating through the Federal Government that take their orders from other than the American people and their elected officials. I have said it before: *"The office of the President has been compromised by the agenda of the Moneyed Elite who want a One World Government at any cost."* **We simply cannot improve our trade balance if we participate in trade agreements that disadvantage us as NAFTA does.**

Stop The Inflow of Illegal Aliens:

[Level 1 Priority] We can build fences and hire Border Guards to stem the tide of illegal aliens or if we actually want to solve the problem we can refuse social services to anyone without a valid visa or proof of citizenship. This means that without proper ID you cannot get a job or a drivers license, cannot get auto insurance or health insurance, cannot enroll in a public school, cannot buy real estate and cannot receive social welfare benefits of any kind. You are effectively locked out of the system and therefore have no reason to cross the border, because you have nothing to gain. Additionally when someone is found to be in the country illegally they will not simply be deported, but as is the case in other countries they will do jail time. End of problem. All that is left is drug smugglers and that requires boots on the ground and tough enforcement.

The border between the U.S. and Mexico is the U.S.'s soft underbelly and if we do not protect it we will regret it. The border is more of a threat to U.S. Security than anything happing in the Middle East. But the bigger issue as relates to the economy is willingness of the Federal Government to curb the inflow of illegal aliens into the U.S., which they have no intention of doing unless forced to do so by the American people. As discussed throughout this book the current administration wants to intentionally bankrupt the U.S. and the economic drain caused by the inflow of illegal aliens from Mexico is conducive to their agenda.

Impose A Value-Added Tax [VAT] and Tariff:

[Level 2 Priority] Caution: Though this is a vitally important issue it cannot be addressed till such time as we get rid of the Federal Reserve and the illegal Income Tax. As it stands now if the government were to impose a [VAT] it would be on top of our current income tax and that would hurt not help the economy. Additionally it would be detrimental unless it was accompanied by a Tariff to curb the inflow of Free Trade Goods from China and other Free Trade countries so a [VAT] must also be accompanied by withdrawal from or renegotiation of NAFTA and the [WTO] World Trade Organization.

According to Auggie Tantillo, Executive Director at the American Manufacturing Trade Action Coalition [AMTAC]: Of 138 major manufacturing nations the U.S. is the only nation that does not take advantage of a "Value-Added Tax" [VAT] in order to protect its manufacturing base and maintain a favorable balance of trade. **By not imposing a Value-Added Tax like other countries the U.S. government has in fact encouraged and enabled U.S. corporations to have their products produced abroad and then imported back into the U.S., resulting in the gutting of the U.S. manufacturing sector and causing the U.S. to have the largest trade deficit in the world.**

Summary: What has been presented to this point is essentially reinstatement of **The American System** which was initially responsible for America's rise to Economic Super Power. This means we rebuild our industrial base by imposing a Value-Added Tax/Tariff, imposing limits on imports where necessary to protect domestic markets, stopping the Super Transportation Corridor, renegotiating NAFTA and other Free Trade Agreements, and have nothing further to do with the SSP or the North American Union. These actions will give us back control of our manufacturing sector but we still will not be able to regain control of the rest of the economy till and unless we get rid of the FED and reform the banking industry. Additionally we need to Reinstate a new Britton Woods fixed currency exchange system and reinstate the legislation that was stripped away in order to allow our economy to be pillaged. Or in other words we go back to our roots and recreate what is proven to work, and that does not include bailing out the banks that got us in this mess, and it does not include continued massive deficit spending on things that do not rebuild our infrastructure and our industry.

3) Election Reform:

[Top Priority] Election reform should be a ****TOP PRIORITY** for the 2010 mid term elections.** Election Reform will not be possible until we have voted out our current **[Carrier Legislators]** and replaced them with a new group of leaders who are not bought and paid for by special interest groups and who come into office agreeing in advance that it is the mandate of the American people to pass election reform including term limits!

We will never regain control of our Government until the special interest groups are neutralized and until term limits are placed on legislators. Election Reform should be considered as a comprehensive single issue. I have just enumerated key issues for clarity's sake.

<u>Establish Term Limits</u>: We hereby resolve that legislators be limited to two consecutive terms.

Our forefathers were clear on the fact that public service was not to be a lifetime office because that leads to power brokering and corruption. Carrier politicians soon become more concerned in securing reelection than serving their constituents and corruption soon follows.

<u>Ban The Lobbyist</u>: Where moneyed interest are allowed to influence and control the government democracy cannot long prevail. We therefore call for the complete abolishment of lobbyist.

When special interest groups pay millions to have lobbyist push legislation favorable to them it results in the undermining of our political system and <u>allows moneyed interest to control the seat of government.</u> Notable examples of this abuse of power can be seen with President Wilson who contrary to campaign promises but loyal to banking interest that contributed heavily to his reelection campaign gave us the corrupt Federal Reserve which has insidiously undermined the U.S. economy and has been the primary cause of America's economic woes. Then there is President G.W. Bush and his support of a bankruptcy bill written by NBNA the largest contributor to his election campaign. And last but certainly not least there is President Obama and the Stimulus

Package written by the scandal ridden ACORN Community Organizing Group of whom he said:

"I've been fighting along side Acorn on issues you care about my entire carrier. Even before I was an elected official when I ran Project Vote voter registration drive in Illinois... Acorn was smack in the middle of it and we appreciate your work."
                                        – Sam Gram-Felsen, Ran Obama's Campaign Blog

Abolish Influence Peddling: We call for a resolution stating that no former politician should be allowed to go to work in any capacity where his political connections might be able to be used to influence political decisions or to unfairly profit those he represents.

This is a particularly serious problem because many politicians when they leave office become lobbyist, influence peddlers, and consultants. What ever you call them they are selling their knowledge and connections to the highest bidder. A notable example of this is the Carlyle Group founded by former Secretary of Defense Frank Carlucci and former President Ronald Reagan to bring together former military and government officials to form a Capital Investment Group that would, use their contacts in order to leverage investments in Defense Industry Projects.

Limit Campaign Contributions: We hereby resolve that campaign contributions be capped at $10,000 per contributor, and in order to prevent wealthy candidates from having unfair advantage, candidates are to be prohibited from spending their own money on their campaign. At the start of the campaign each candidate would be given the same amount of money by the government, and then they would be given more money for each primary based on the number of votes they got. The pool of money for each primary would vary based on the number of registered voters or the number of electoral votes. Candidates would have to get a minimum prescribed percentage of the votes in order to receive funding and in order to continue in subsequent primaries. TV advertisements would be limited and the primary focus of the campaign would be a number of mandatory debates focusing on substantive issues.

As long as lobbyist, special interest groups and corporations are allowed to contribute large sums of money to election campaigns they are able to obligate our politicians. For example as stated a second ago that is how through Wilson we got the Fed and through George Bush we got the current bankruptcy law. Make no mistake the seat of power is for sale. This is the only way to keep moneyed interest from putting their puppets into power.

Outlaw Gerrymandering:

We hereby call for Gerrymandering to be illegal and that Congressional Districts be based on township lines as originally intended.

Congressional Districts were originally based on township lines and they thereby brought people with common issues together so their community could be optimally represented. By artificially redefining districts by age, race, income levels, political affiliations etc. we are committing the worst sort of discrimination which places the election of politicians ahead of the responsibility to serve their constituents. **Additionally President Obama's effort to manipulate the census by asking citizens to complete a profile survey opens the door to Gerrymandering on a national scale.**

4) Energy Reform:

Declare Undeveloped Patents Abandoned:

[Top Priority] We call for legislation stating that: Patents which are deemed to be **[Beneficial or Vital to Society]** which corporations have acquired and failed, after a specified period of time to bring to market shall be **[deemed abandoned and made part of the public domain]** where upon the technology is available for commercialization. Likewise all newly issued patents would be monitored and if the patent holder fails to demonstrate intent to commercially develop the patent it to would likewise be deemed abandoned.

If we are facing the Global Warming Crisis that former Vice President Gore and President Obama say, then they should have no problem giving us access to undeveloped patents which might benefit all of society and maybe even be instrumental in saving the planet. Though Cap and Trade calls for the imposition of onerous tax increases, it does not actually provide technology solutions capable of solving the Global

Warming Crisis! We need solutions not taxes! As a holder of two Patents I know first hand that Patent protection was never intended to be used as a weapon by the Moneyed Elite, to allow them to acquire technology which is vital to society and then withhold that technology for profit reasons.

Precedents exist for this contention. For example one of President Obama's Czars is on record as saying that he felt that under a severe population crisis that forced abortion could be upheld under the Constitution, and there is already a provision for forced vaccinations. The Environment and Healthcare are two of the most critical issues facing the U.S. and the world, so this **[concept of the greater good]** should certainly apply to them.

Additionally in the instance of Real Estate **[a far less critical topic]** the government enforces *EMINENT DOMAIN* in order to force the sale of property deemed to be needed for the public good. Lastly, in order to facilitate the building of the Trans Texas Corridor 35 [TTC-35] **[by private international investors]** G.W. Bush issued EO#12803 which **[allows privatization of U.S. infrastructure]** which in this instance means American Citizens can be forced off their land in order to benefit private corporations. **If the law can be used to benefit private corporations it should be able to be used to benefit society at large and to potentially save the planet!**

DEMAND ACCESS TO TECHNOLOGY

IS NOT THE HEALTH AND WELFARE OF EVERY MAN, WOMAN AND CHILD ON THE PLANET SUFFICIENT REASON TO DECLARE UNDEVELOPED PATENTS ABANDONED AND PLACE THEM IN THE PUBLIC DOMAIN?

Oppose Cap and Trade Legislation As The Farce That It Is:

[Top Priority] We oppose Cap and Trade on the grounds that it will impose the largest tax increase in the history of this country and it gives the government the means to control public access to essential goods and services and given that it contains no viable technology solution capable of actually solving the problem. Lastly, it is nothing more than a means to impose Global Governance, Redistribution of Wealth, Population Control and Forced Limitations on Resource Consumption.

It is imperative that we address climate change, but we need an open exploration of the problem so that we can honestly and objectively identify the cause! And most importantly we need real solutions, solutions that actually solve the problem as opposed to solutions that just line the pockets of the Moneyed Elite.

As discussed a second ago **[on grounds of the greater good]** we need to declare any undeveloped healthcare and energy patents abandoned and part of the public domain. Additionally there appear to be revolutionary technological breakthroughs which the government and corporations are not capitalizing on because to do so would mean cheap, clean, renewable energy would be available to virtually everyone. Unfortunately they appear to be more interested in protecting their existing revenue stream and geopolitical power base than they are in saving the planet. Demand to know the truth. If proven to be commercially viable and if developed these technologies could reduce the world's dependency on fossil fuels and significantly reduce CO_2 emissions which the government claims to be the primary cause of Global Warming. **IMAGINE WE MIGHT JUST SAVE THE PLANET.** What could be more important than that?

VITALLY IMPORTANT: If the U.S. were to support development of these technologies it would [revitalize the economy] and result in an era of prosperity greater than anything ever imagined. Imagine, if the technology were then shared with the rest of the world. The Moneyed Elite would no longer be able to ration scarce resources and an era of global cooperation and peace could be ushered in. Demand commercialization of and access to available technology!

Create A National Energy Development Fund:

[Top Priority] The U.S. should set up an energy development fund to finance development of truly clean, renewable energy solutions and get them to market as soon as possible!

We need to address Global Warming and that is going to require technology solutions. Any solution such as Cap and Trade which does not provide the necessary technology solutions is just a taxing mechanism and nothing more!

Recommended Solution:

Thermal-depolymerzation: Is preferable over conventional Biomass and in particular Ethanol because it requires no crops to be grown and is therefore truly CO2 neutral. It converts garbage and waste products [any carbon based material] into oil, gas and charcoal and in the process significantly solves our waste disposal problems. **It is estimated to be able to produce enough oil to <u>completely eliminate our dependency on foreign oil</u> and that of course has vitally important National Security implications.**

Solar: New solar cell developed in Israel is 1,500 times more efficient than previous technology and makes solar a viable near term alternative to coal and Nuclear power plants.

Compressed Air Engine: French inventor has developed a car the runs on Compressed Air. It can be filled at a service station in about 3 minutes or plugged into an electrical outlet and filled by an onboard compressor in about four hours at a cost of about two dollars. The top speed is 110 Kilometers [68.35miles per hour] and driving distance is 200 kilometers [124.28 miles.] There are also plans for a hybrid that can drive from LA to NY on a single tank of gas Since the car runs on compressed air the only emission is clean air...The car is expected to be on the market in Europe and India in approximately one year. The question is if Obama is so concerned about Global Warming why isn't the car available in the U.S.?

Hydrogen Fuel Cell: Unlike government rhetoric technology appears to exist to convert Water into Hydrogen [the most abundant and efficient fuel on the planet] **on demand**. It is estimated that maintenance free fuel cells can be retrofitted onto internal combustion engines at a cost of approximately $1,500 allowing the cars to run on salt water or fresh water. With cars that run on water our dependency on oil would be dramatically reduced. Demand to know the truth.

Zero Point Magnetic Energy: Represents what physicists say is possibly the most efficient energy source in nature. It is based on the attraction and repulsion force of the positive and negative poles of magnets. Once started by an outside energy source the generator will operate till the magnets are depleted, which is estimated to be approximately 300 hundred years. This technology is apparently capable of replacing the internal combustion engine and it is estimated that a generator could be built at a cost of approximately $5,000 that would supply the entire electrical needs of a home. **Or in other words we could get off the electric grid.** Demand to know the truth.

Other: Wind, Tidal Wave, Surface Wave are all recognized as having varying degrees of potential.

Oppose Development of:

Nuclear: Oppose efforts being made to get nuclear energy categorized as a <u>renewable energy source</u> because it poses unacceptably high long term <u>environmental risks</u> and because if it is categorized as a renewable energy source it will take the focus off of the other truly clean, renewable, inexpensive solutions which are available. **Note:** At one point in my carrier I worked for Atomic Energy of Canada and I have seen first hand just how dangerous radiation contamination can be.

Biomass/Methane: Oppose further development of biomass in general because it is <u>not as claimed CO2 neutral</u>. Specifically, oppose further development of Ethanol because it takes large amounts of agricultural land out of food production resulting in increased food cost and long term it is not a sustainable technology because that land will ultimately be needed for food production.

Creation of Large Scale Global Development Projects:

[Level 3 Priority] As proposed in *[HOBPA]*. Following WWII an international body cooperated to rebuild Europe. Today we need to cooperate in the same fashion to develop clean energy technologies.

5) Healthcare Reform:

[Top Priority] We must support repeal of Obama's National Healthcare Plan before it is put into effect in 2014.

Obama Care will: **1)** Raise taxes [Taxing will commence immediately yet the plan will not go into effect till 2014] **2)** Raise insurance cost **3)** Substantially cut Medicare and **4)** Still leave an estimated 24 million people uninsured. The primary justifications for the plan were to reduce cost and provide coverage to everyone, but it does neither of those things so where is the justification for the plan? I hate to say it, but it would appear that the real reason for the plan is to get access to 1/6 of the GDP and to control our access to life saving medical treatment. **The bill cannot deliver on any of the promised benefits because it adds a layer of government bureaucracy but does not fundamentally change the way healthcare is delivered. It remains a post illness delivery system focused primarily on Pharmaceutical and Surgical Intervention.**

It is estimated that between 50 and 75% of current healthcare costs are consumed by lifestyle and genetic related diseases such as diabetes, cardiovascular pulmonary disease, stroke, heart attacks, cancer and certain heredity/genetic illnesses. What all of these diseases have in common is that they are to varying degrees preventable by lifestyle changes, and cost of care and morbidity can be reduced by early detection. **Given this the only delivery system capable of delivering meaningful cost reductions is one based on <u>Wellness</u>, not post illness intervention.**

One of the shortcomings of Obama Care is a [projected shortage of doctors] which by necessity negatively impacts access, quality of care and morbidity. By contrast a wellness based delivery system would: address this issue by depending less on physicians and more on testing, screenings, follow up and therapy done by technicians and lower paid healthcare professionals such as Nurse Practitioners, Physician Assistants and Physical Therapist etc. leaving the physicians to treat those that are actually sick. Additionally a wellness based system would reduce dependency on expensive drugs, reduce the number of costly surgical procedures, and result in fewer hospital stays all of which would result in lower healthcare cost, plus productivity in the work place would increase due to fewer sick days. Additionally given the reduced cost of healthcare delivery, insurance cost should go down, especially if insurance companies were allowed to [compete nationally] and if [self insured individuals were allowed to form large enough groups to get the type of rates fortune 500 companies get.] The last remaining issue is [Tort Reform], in order to reduce the cost of medical malpractice insurance, reduce the number of frivolous law suits and limit excessive settlements.

NOTE: This is by no means intended to be a comprehensive healthcare program. Its primary purpose is to point the direction we need to be going with healthcare reform. But one thing is for certain and that is that Obama Care is taking us down the wrong road. It can only result in lower quality of care, limited access and unacceptably high costs. A recent survey of doctors indicated that if Obama Care passes <u>45% of them would consider closing their practice or retiring early</u> which would cause a critical shortage that would lead to severe limitations to access. I would note that I am not a doctor, but I worked in the medical field for 22 years and what I have laid out here is based on conversations with doctors, hospital CEO's, CFO's and other healthcare professionals.

6) Reinstatement of Our Civil Liberties:

[Top Priority] The government is dangerously close to being able to impose a police state and we must stop them before it is too late! We need to take a long hard look at the civil liberties which we have allowed to be taken from us in the name of homeland security. It won't make any difference if we straighten out the economy if in the meantime we have lost our freedom to the government. Again, our founding Fathers have warned us if only we will listen.

What follows is a review of the more dangerous pieces of legislation, discussed earlier, that have either been passed or are proposed. Taken by themselves they don't seem too dangerous, but when combined they threaten the very foundation of our Constitution and ultimately threaten the American way of life. We need to take a hard look at all such legislation and take action to regain the civil liberties upon which our Constitution rest. **Our legislators have made a mockery of our Constitution and we must force them to abide by it or we risk losing the freedoms upon which this nation was founded.**

<u>**Patriot Act:**</u> There has never before in the history of America been a document that had the potential to usurp our Civil Liberties the way this document does. President Obama promised during his campaign

that he would not renew The Patriot Act but he went back on his word. We need to put pressure on the government to repeal this legislation.

Executive Order 11921: states that: **"...when a state of emergency is declared by the President, *Congress cannot review the action for six months."*** There are Three Branches of Government. To have all the power in the hands of the Executive Branch undermines the entire concept of Balance of Power and seriously erodes our Civil Liberties not to mention opening the door to a dictatorship. *This basically allows the president to hijack the Government!*

Rex 84 short for "Readiness Exercise": is a plan to test the government's ability to detain large numbers of American citizens in case of civil unrest or national emergency. **[Detain or incarcerate?]**

Operation Garden Plot and Cable Splicer: Are the subprograms which will be implemented once REX 84 is in effect.

Operation Garden Plot: is the program to control the population using United States Army and National Guard units under control of the U.S. Northern Command [NORTHCOM] to provide Federal military support during domestic civil disturbances.

Operation Cable Splicer: is the program to provide for an orderly take over of the state and local governments by the Federal Government.

NOTE: I wasn't too worried about this till I came across a government website advertising for Internment Guards not to assist those displaced by a natural disaster but to guard prisoners. Then I got really, really nervous when I came across this speech made in the U.S. House by Rep. Peter De Fazio [D] Oregon 4th District and broadcast on CPAN. [Google FEMA Rex 84] Title of speech is: Congress Kept Away From Rex 84 FEMA Camp.

*"Most Americans would agree that it would be prudent to have a plan for the continuity of government and the rule of law in case of a devastating terrorist attack or natural disaster, a plan to provide for the coordination and **continued functioning of all three branches of government.** The Bush Administration tells us that there is such a plan. They introduced a little sketchy public version that is clearly*

inadequate and doesn't really tell us what they have in mind, but they said don't worry there is a detailed 'Classified Version' but then they denied the entire Homeland Security Committee of the United States House of Representatives access to their so called detailed plan to provide for continuity of government. They said 'Trust us' ...Trust us the people who brought us warrant-less wire tapping and other excesses eroding our Civil Liberties. Trust us. Maybe the plan just doesn't really exist or maybe there is something there that is outrageous. The American people need their elected representatives to review this plan for the continuity of government."

Military Commission Act: This Act is particularly dangerous because it suspends the ineligible rights of **[Habeas Corpus.]** By definition Habeas Corpus is a legal action, or writ, through which a person can seek relief from the unlawful detention of him or herself, or of another person.

Violent Radicalization & Homegrown Terrorism Prevention Act: The proposed Violent Radicalization and Homegrown Terrorism Prevention Act significantly expands the definition of what a terrorist act is and expands that definition over American Citizens. It has been dubbed the Thought Crime Act because it focuses on ideology rather than actual criminal behavior. Opponents are concerned that the vague terminology in the bill leaves it open to broad interpretation which could be used to seriously restrict the rights of American Citizens to peaceful protest such as written or spoken opposition to government policies, sit ins, protest marches etc. Big Brother looms around the corner.

The Real ID Act: The intent of this proposed legislation is to use a miniature Radio Frequency ID [FRID] chip that would be imbed in drivers licenses and Passports. Anyone without a card [National ID] would not be permitted to board a plane, Amtrak train, open a bank account or enter a Federal building. Don't let this become law. **Just think about it. This would allow the government to literally control our every action.**

Executive Order 10995: And others like it allow the government to take over and control the communication media and opens the door for censorship and loss of freedom of speech.

Summary: The stage is set to impose a <u>Police State</u>. All that is needed is the right National Emergency, real or contrived, and the government can impose Martial Law, lock us down and impose a Dictatorship. Contrary to campaign promises Obama refused to rescind George W. Bush's: **Presidential Directive 51:** This effectively allows the President dictatorial powers. He then turned around and ordered Department of Defense (DOD) to Issue: **Directive 1401.10:** establishing a <u>million man army under his control</u>. **HR 645 National Emergency Centers Act:** Brings local government and police under Federal control. Additionally the Pentagon plans to keep 20,000 troops in U.S. to supposedly bolster Domestic Security.

One has to ask: Are the troops to protect us or contain us? Never in our history have we needed this kind of domestic military. Why Now? Why not rescind Directive 51 with its dictatorial powers? It is as Noah Webster said:

"Before a standing army can rule, the people must be disarmed..."

7) **Education Reform:**

[Level 3 Priority] We resolve to take the public school curriculum out of the hands of the government and revamp it so that our children are taught to respect the Constitution, understand the principles upon which this nation was founded and learn to think critically.

It is important that our children be taught <u>problem solving skills</u> not rote memorization and that they are given the information to allow them to <u>be responsible citizens</u> capable of informed critical thinking. This means that curriculums need to be drastically changed for such subjects as history, government, sociology, business, economics and personal finances and that they must include if not religion at least the moral foundation necessary for living a successful life and being a responsible person.

Additionally I refer you back to Chapter 1 and <u>The Seven Spheres of Influence That Control The Seat of Power</u>. Our government subtlety controls what we think and how we act by controlling **1)** our educational system **2)** the political process **3)** our religious freedom **4)** the news media **5)** the entertainment industry **6)** the financial system and

7) our family values. It is essential that we regain control to all of these spheres in influence if we hope to regain control of our government and our inalienable rights as guaranteed under the Constitution.

Reflect on the following quotes: They sum up the importance of having a morally grounded, politically informed citizenry capable of making decisions based on the greater good.

"If a nation expects to be ignorant and free, in a state of civilization, it expects what never was and never will be."
                                                              –Thomas Jefferson, 1816.

"Democracies have ever been spectacles of turbulence and contention; have ever been found incompatible with personal security or the rights of property; and have, in general, been as short in their lives as they have been violent in their deaths." – James Madison

This is precisely why our founding fathers chose a Republic and not a Democracy as our form of government. As Jefferson knew: *"We cannot long sustain a free civilized society if we don't have an educated public capable of making informed, moral decisions which reflect the inalienable rights of all members of society!"*

Closing Comments

I fully expect this book to be controversial. I expect those I have exposed will come against me and try to discredit and deter me in every possible way. That is a risk I am prepared to take. Once I figured out what was being done to America and its citizens I knew I had to expose it. As Abraham Lincoln said the key is to give the people the truth.

I believe that this nation has a destiny and I don't believe that that destiny is to march like a bunch of blind sheep into financial slavery and fascism. It hasn't been till now that this book could have been written, because it is only now that things have progressed far enough that masses of people are prepared to question what the government is doing to us. Only now are people prepared to consider the possibility that our government has sold us out. Only now have our leaders gotten so bold as to announce to us their intention to establish a One World

Government. Hopefully this book has provided the necessary facts to allow you to recognize how the moneyed interests have systematically taken over our banks, corporations and government, how they have driven us into financial slavery, and how our very existence as a nation teeters on the brink of oblivion. I am not advocating violence but I am advocating that we stand up in mass and demand that sweeping changes be made.

We can no longer afford to stand ideally by and do nothing. We can no longer allow our political apathy to allow us to disengage from the political process. We must stand up and take control of the political process and demand that our voices be heard. There is much for us to do if we want to get back control of our government.

Summary of Key Action Steps

We can make a difference if we stand up as a united group of concerned Americans. Pledge your time, money and energy to support individuals who are running for office and who have pledged to support the issues which you believe are key to **Restoring America** to Greatness! Please don't put this book down and go about your lives as usual. If you do America is done for. The situation is urgent! If we don't unite and stand for freedom we may never get another chance? Communism is at the door.

Action Steps/Key Initiatives:

1) **Banking Reform:**

   - **Support a role call vote on a balanced budget amendment:**

   - **National Usury Law:** To prevent predatory lending rates in the credit card industry.

   - **Two-tier mortgage:** So new mortgages are not required every time a person moves or refinances.

   - **Get rid of the Fed:** To prevent manipulation of monetary and economic system by private banking monopoly.

■ **Repeal illegal federal income tax and reform tax codes:**
So the tax burden on the public can be reduced and so the tax
codes can know longer be used for political leverage.

■ **Establish two-tier credit system:** To facilitate funding for
capital investment to rebuild our infrastructure and manufacturing.

■ **New Bretton Woods System of fixed exchange rates:** To
stop currency speculation.

■ **Repeal current bankruptcy law:** Written by bankers and
implement a new fairer law.

■ **Reinstate dismantled banking and energy regulations:**
Such as The Glass-Steagall Act which are necessary to prevent predatory lending practices.

2) **Trade Reform/Open Borders:**

■ **Support [HRC 40]:** Supports national sovereignty by opposing participation in SSP, North American Union and Free
Trade.

■ **Support [HRC 22]:** Supporting withdrawal from NAFTA.

■ **Stop inflow of illegal aliens:** By requiring proof of citizenship in order to obtain a job, attend school, drive a car, receive
medical treatment or own real estate.

■ **Impose Value-Added Tax [VAT] and Tariff:** In order to
restore U.S. trade balance. **Note:** [VAT] is not to be imposed
on top of existing Income Tax and not unless in conjunction
with a Tariff to limit imports.

3) **Election Reform:** [Top priority for 2010 Midterm Elections] Make
a clean sweep of Washington by voting out all incumbents, both
Republicans and Democrats, [with a couple of notable exceptions
like Ron Paul and Peter De Fazio] and impose a two term limit on
legislators, limit campaign contributions, outlaw gerrymandering
and ban all lobbyist.

4) Energy Reform:

- **Declare undeveloped energy and medical patents abandoned:** If patent holder does not develop technology to benefit society and the planet.

- **Oppose Cap and Trade:** On grounds it is a tax impersonating energy legislation, and it is in fact a means to impose Global Governance, Redistribution of Wealth, Population Control, and Forced Limitations on Resource Consumption.

- **Create a national energy development fund:** To finance development of truly clean renewable energy solutions.

- **Creation of large scale global development projects:** As proposed by [HOBPA] to develop clean energy technology.

5) Healthcare Reform:

- **Support repeal of Obama's healthcare plan:** On the grounds that it will increase cost and reduce quality of care.

- **Support instead a healthcare plan:** Which includes Tort Reform, Nationwide Insurance and a Wellness Based Medical System.

6) Protect Our Civil Liberties:

- **Repeal Patriot Act and <u>Executive Order 51</u>:** On the grounds that they give the President virtual Dictatorial Powers.

- **Repeal EO 11921:** Which states that: "...when a state of emergency is declared by the President, *Congress cannot review the action for six months.*"

- **Repeal Rex 84 & Operation Garden Plot & Cable Splicer:** On the grounds that they allow United States Army and National Guard Units to be used in a manner which could facilitate formation of a Police State.

- **Repeal Directive 1401.1:** On the ground that it establishes a million man standing army reporting to Obama which could be used to impose a Police State.

- **Repeal HR 645 National Emergency Centers Act:** Which brings local government and police under Federal control and also threatens imposition of a Police State.

- **Repeal Military Commission Act:** On the grounds that it suspends the ineligible rights of [*Habeas Corpus*] which protects the public from unlawful detention.

- **Oppose Passage of The Violent Radicalization and Homegrown Terrorism Prevention Act:** On the grounds that it expands the definition of what a terrorist act is over American Citizens and given the vague terminology in the bill it could be used to seriously restrict the rights of American Citizens to peaceful protest such as written or spoken opposition to government policies, sit ins, protest marches etc.

- **Oppose Passage of The Real ID Act:** Which would force acceptance of a National ID Card with a Radio Frequency ID [FRID] chip imbedded in it etc.

7) **Education Reform:** We must take back control of the Public Educational System and stop the rewriting of American History and we must stand up for the Christian principles upon which this nation was founded. We must take control of the Seven Spheres of Influence which control the Seat of Power. See chapter one.

Our Personal Responsibilities!

<u>Stop Being Apathetic and Get Involved</u>: I would remind each and every one of you that we share the responsibility for what we have allowed to happen. We have by in large lost sight of our responsibilities to be an <u>informed citizenry</u> who elects leaders not based on the entitlement programs they promise but based on their commitment to provide responsible leadership. We have become distracted by pursuit of materialism and have chosen not to be involved. I sincerely hope you won't just read this book and then do nothing. Form a group and <u>get politically involved</u>. Take your <u>peaceful protest</u> to the streets of America and demand change. <u>Vote out the incumbents</u> and back candidates that will **"Sign a Pledge to Support the American Restoration Platform"** and then back them with your money and if possible volunteer your time to their campaign.

Stop Being Self-Centered and Take A Moral Stand Based On The Greater Good: If we want to live in a Republic and enjoy the blessings it affords, then we must do as Benjamin Franklin said, *"Keep the Republic"* and the only way to do that is to be involved and to base our decision making not on vested interest but on a moral foundation that insures the inalienable rights of all people of all nations!

Put Aside Your Differences: To save our nation we will have to show a unified resolve. This is not about Liberals/Progressives VS Conservatives or Republicans VS Democrats or the Haves VS the Have-nots. This is about stopping a Global Communist take over by a group of *"Self Appointed Financial Elite"* who view the resources of the world as belonging to them, who have no moral conviction and who plan to forcibly reduce the global population because they view most of humanity as having no value and as just consuming their valuable resources! We need to understand that they mean to enslave us all [Liberals and Conservatives, Republicans and Democrats Rich and Poor]. Under their regime the world will become a **[two class society, the Poor and the Ultra Rich].** There will be no middle class and the poor will be really poor. They intend to lower our standard to living to mere subsistence while they go about the process of purging society of the undesirables till they reduce the population to what they determine to be acceptable levels, [Probably 1 ½ - 2 billion people.]

The wealth of the world is controlled by a few Financial Elite and we will never be anything other than their slaves if we don't take back the key to their power which is their ability to issue currency, thereby allowing them to manipulate the economies of the Sovereign Nations of the world, and the ability to corrupt our Political System and Corporations by putting into power those men who are willing to sell their souls for the allure of wealth and power. Most notably the Office of President has been corrupted, along with most of our self-serving carrier politicians in Washington and many of our Corporate leaders and many top ranking military. *"Power corrupts and absolute power corrupts absolutely."* There are rotten Apples in the barrel and they all have to go to be replaced by honest men and women who are willing to serve the people.

Most Importantly Turn to God and Surrender: Christianity is under attack because these men *"who would be the rulers of us all"*

know that a moral population which is united and determined to prevail cannot be easily defeated, therefore the Christians must go. This
is the time the Bible talks about when it says *"those who prevail to the
end shall see their just reward."* This is the time to test God and see if
we <u>surrender to him and stop worshiping the false God of materialism</u>
if he won't rescue us as he did others so many times in the Bible. This
is the time of purification where God gives us the choice of choosing
righteousness and morality and avoid the worst of what is to come or
to continue in our immoral ways and suffer the consequences of our
sin. This is a time for Global Revival complete with signs, wonders
and miracles and to make that happen we must drop to our knees and
pray as we have never prayed. Victory is with God's people! It is time
to stand up and be counted!

Please don't let the quotes below come true:

*"We shall have a One World Government whether or not we like it.
The only question is whether world government will be achieved by
conquest or consent."*

– Paul Warburg, Council Foreign Relations,
Architect of the Federal Reserve System

*"The super national sovereignty of an intellectual elite and world
bankers is surely preferable to the National Auto-determination
practiced in past centuries."*

– David Rockefeller, Council Foreign Relations

It Is Time To Stand And Be Counted!

I am telling you Obama and his Czars have a Socialist/Communist agenda of *redistribution of wealth* that I do not believe it is shared by the majority of Americans and we better not let them as they would say *"Push and Push"* till they achieve their radical goals. Please remember this is not about Obama. He is just the most recent in a long line of U.S. Presidents committed to imposing a Global Communist Government intent on enslaving us in order to conserve what they see as their natural resources. Their plans hinge on collapsing the U.S. and we have to see to it that, that doesn't happen. The fate of the world literally rest on the shoulders of this generation of Americans. We cannot afford to lose this battle. Please do your part to save America and the world!

May God bless us and our nation and see us through this time of testing!

Sincerely,
Larry Ballard

For other titles
or a free catalog
call 800-729-4131
or visit www.nohoax.com

Visit the author at
www.GeopoliticalAffairs.net
email: larryballard1@yahoo.com

Also by Larry Ballard:

The Economic Tribulation:
How to Survive and Prosper

Printed in the USA
CPSIA information can be obtained
at www.ICGtesting.com
CBHW071022060424
6499CB00015B/1130

9 780984 473311